CIVIL RIGHTS

and

FEDERAL

HIGHER

EDUCATION

EDITED BY

Nicholas Hillman and **Gary Orfield**

HARVARD EDUCATION PRESS
Cambridge, MA

Paperback ISBN 978-1-68253-716-9

Library of Congress Cataloging-in-Publication Data is on file.

Published by Harvard Education Press,
an imprint of the Harvard Education Publishing Group

Harvard Education Press
8 Story Street
Cambridge, MA 02138

Cover Design: Endpaper Studio

The typefaces in this book are Joanna Nova and Adobe Garamond Pro.

CONTENTS

Introduction

The Politics of Education and Educational Inequality

NICHOLAS HILLMAN
AND GARY ORFIELD

SIXTY YEARS AGO, federal policymakers built a framework to promote and protect civil rights for racially and socioeconomically disadvantaged groups through Great Society reforms. Chief among these was the Civil Rights Act of 1964, outlawing segregation of public places and banning employment discrimination. The Economic Opportunity Act of 1964 launched the War on Poverty by proactively investing in low-income individuals and neighborhoods. And in 1965, the Higher Education Act (HEA) built on these reforms by reorienting federal higher education policy to include those groups who had previously been excluded from college opportunities due to racial barriers and lack of money.

These civil rights reforms created a strong and distinctive federal role in higher education policy. Colleges and universities receiving federal funding could no longer discriminate based on race, color, or national origin. And states were required to dismantle dual systems of higher education by desegregating public colleges and universities. As America has become more racially, politically, and economically divided since the 1960s, so too has its higher education systems. These divisions did not happen by chance but, as this book describes, were the result of political action and inaction in several specific federal policy areas: expanding student loan debt; eroding consumer protections; neglecting Minority-Serving Institutions (MSIs); supporting for-profit colleges; questioning affirmative action; and applying market-based accountability without strong federal guidance.

The political victories of the mid 1960s through the early 1970s took considerable political will, coalition building, and negotiation in an effort to promote equal opportunities for people of color and people from low-income backgrounds. But as with any political action, these reforms require constant and proactive attention and advocacy to realize their full potential. Without this ongoing effort, public policymakers can easily move on to other competing priorities and ignore or even obscure the original civil rights goals behind the HEA. There was a strong conservative blowback against the federal role in racial justice, a conservative transformation in the Supreme Court, and a loss of focus on the most disadvantaged students as higher education institutions jockeyed for shares of federal funds and the political pressure grew for more aid to the middle class. This book aims to recenter federal higher education policy debates around the HEA's original focus on promoting civil rights. The need for such a reorientation could not be greater than today, when the nation is reckoning with the long-standing realities of white supremacy and structural racism that negatively affect the lives and well-being of people of color. The Black Lives Matter movement has revitalized—and in many respects reframed—the nation's sense of urgency around racial injustice in all its forms. The COVID-19 pandemic has exposed and worsened racial and economic inequalities that for too long have gone overlooked in policy conversations. The political coalition that emerged in the Biden campaign underlined new multiracial possibilities. And it has been through broad coalitions of community-based organizations, civil rights groups, professional associations, and grassroots activists that a new era of civil rights for federal higher education is coming back into focus.

For example, the Higher Ed Civil Rights Coalition, which includes several organizations such as The Education Trust, Human Rights Campaign, National Urban League, and UnidosUS, recently developed a set of core principles for advancing civil rights in higher education. Their principles, which focus largely on enforcing civil rights laws, implementing strong data and accountability programs, promoting access and success for students of color and low-income students, excluding for-profits from federal aid programs, investing in Minority-Serving Institutions and Historically Black Colleges and Universities (HBCUs), and protecting defrauded students and student loan borrowers, map closely to the topics covered in this book. There is growing consensus that these topics are central to restoring and reimagining the HEA and civil rights enforcement activities to promote fairness and equity in a highly unequal society.

This consensus is growing at a time when federal policymaking in higher education is gridlocked, which presents a serious problem for enacting any meaningful reforms via legislation. The 2020 presidential campaign brought many promises of massive aid on college costs and debt, but the US Congress has become increasingly polarized and, as a result, has largely failed to respond to the coalitions and consensus that are growing around civil rights priorities. This was certainly true during the Trump administration, where the higher education policy agenda centered around deregulation and reversing Obama administration efforts to introduce—in many cases for the first time—needed consumer protections like Gainful Employment and Borrower Defense rules. With Democrats controlling both the House and Senate in the early Biden administration, federal policymakers are poised to make some serious and lasting changes to higher education policy. Of course, those changes will not come in one fell swoop; rather, they will likely occur over time and, possibly, as a result of growing consensus and coalition building.

A central theme of this book is that the *politics of education* and *educational inequality* cannot be separated from the other. However, much of the higher education policy literature does just this by focusing on politics or inequality, but not how politics shape (and is shaped by) inequality. This central theme is carried through each chapter as authors not only focus on the racial and socioeconomic consequences of federal policies but also focus on the politics behind those inequalities. By focusing in this way, this book offers a new way of viewing the civil rights dimensions of the HEA where many of the problems HEA (and Great Society reforms in general) sought to address are still unresolved today. By recentering contemporary debates around those origins, the book offers a renewed way of viewing federal higher education policymaking from a civil rights perspective. Doing so will help researchers and policymakers pinpoint specific federal policy debates that have significant racial and socioeconomic implications (e.g., deregulating for-profit colleges, weakening consumer protections, expanding student loan debt, etc.) to identify promising and evidence-based solutions to these deeply rooted and complex problems.

ORGANIZATION OF THE BOOK

The book begins with two chapters synthesizing key moments and trends in federal higher education policymaking. Gary Orfield (chapter 1) outlines the origins of federal involvement in higher education, where a common theme across several different political eras is that race-blind policies perpetuate racial inequality. The 1890 Morrill Land-Grant Act explicitly addressed race and helped establish several Black colleges, but just six years later *Plessy v. Ferguson* ushered in the "separate but equal" era that would reinforce inequality for the next sixty years. Similarly, the G.I. Bill of 1944 expanded opportunity for veterans regardless of skin color, but the policy did not require colleges to desegregate, so white veterans disproportionately benefited from the program. These stories are repeated throughout federal higher education history, where Orfield argues race-neutral policies benefit white constituents more—and to larger degrees—than people of color. For federal higher education policies to promote civil rights, they must be race conscious.

In chapter 2, Deondra Rose and Suzanne Mettler explain how quickly the civil rights goals of the HEA eroded due to political "decay, drift, and derailment." What began as a landmark law to promote opportunity has become one that policymakers now neglect due in large part to polarization. Rose and Mettler make a clear and compelling case that this policy neglect has taken place at the same time that students of color and low-income students need greater resources to pay for college.

In chapter 3, OiYan Poon and Liliana Garces provide a comprehensive background on affirmative action highlighting not just the outcomes of court cases but the racialized politics behind the lawsuits. This chapter focuses on the racist motivations driving recent anti–affirmative action campaigns that target Asian Americans and aim to create divisions among this key constituency. In an era of widening inequality and political polarization, debates about affirmative action will continue, and this chapter provides the necessary insight and background to understand how those legal and political contests will affect civil rights—particularly for Asian Americans.

Chapter 4 offers a similar synthesis and framing of an urgent political topic, student loan debt, where Jalil B. Mustaffa outlines how failing to maintain HEA while operating race-neutral policies created the Black student debt crisis. In this case, many student debt policy debates are framed around theories of human capital, where investing in a college education "pays off" in the long run. But Mustaffa explains the payoff is not equal for everybody, particularly for Black men and women who often face serious labor market discrimination and intergenerational inequality. To compound this problem, not all students are equally likely to borrow—Black students are far more likely to borrow and to borrow more than white students—and this creates a debt trap for Black borrowers. Mustaffa calls for a new discourse on student debt and outlines strategies for a fairer higher education financing system that addresses rather than ignores racial injustice.

In chapter 5, Erin S. Corbett, Julie Ajinkya, Cody Meixner, and Haruna Suzuki outline just how far away federal policies have drifted from focusing on civil rights. The 1994 Violent Crime Control and Law Enforcement Act prohibited incarcerated individuals from accessing the federal Pell Grant. The precursor to the Pell Grant was created in the 1965 HEA as a way to promote opportunity, yet within just thirty years Congress found a way to close opportunities for people serving sentences—people who disproportionately come from minoritized racial groups and low-income backgrounds. At the time this book was submitted for publication, Congress had passed the Consolidated Appropriations Act of 2021 that effectively will end the ban, though the issues of civil rights and fairness for incarcerated individuals is far from resolved. Another unresolved policy problem deals with federal efforts to hold colleges more accountable for their outcomes, as outlined by Nicholas Hillman in chapter 6. This chapter provides a summary of recent "skin in the game" efforts to penalize "poor performing" colleges for not meeting certain accountability goals. These policy proposals are, like many federal policies both today and in years past, race neutral. By ignoring basic facts about racial inequality, accountability efforts will likely reinforce the very inequality they purport to address. This chapter outlines several promising strategies that would leverage accountability as a way to promote civil rights in an effort to reverse inequalities.

The next three chapters follow a similar line of inquiry, where the authors examine how policies interact with colleges and universities. Andrés Castro Samayoa explores in chapter 7 how Minority-Serving Institutions not only serve the lion's share of students of color in the United States but also how they do so with limited financial resources. MSIs play a key role in promoting educational opportunity and promoting civil rights, and this chapter explains key legislative actions and policy levers to promote greater investment in the colleges poised to make the greatest contributions to promoting opportunity and equity. Chapter 8 examines the opposite end of the opportunity spectrum, where Brian Pusser and

Matt Ericson show how for-profit colleges also serve disproportionate shares of students of color and low-income students, but too often leave them worse off than if they had never attended college in the first place. Both chapters tie directly to the need for ongoing policy maintenance, as Rose and Mettler outlined in chapter 2, where federal policymakers can promote civil rights via investing in under-resourced MSIs while protecting students from predatory for-profit colleges—in both cases, these are where many underrepresented students enroll and policies must treat the different sectors differently in order to address inequalities. Finally, in chapter 9, Gary Orfield revisits a long-standing debate about the role community colleges play in promoting—or foreclosing—opportunities for students of color and low-income students. That many students of color and low-income students are tracked into under-resourced community colleges with poor educational outcomes is a civil rights issue that will not be fixed by "free" community college. Without fundamental changes in degree programs *and* significant investments and improvements to ensure the colleges have adequate resources (i.e., faculty, staffing, aid, and support services) to promote better outcomes for underrepresented students, these schools will only perpetuate long-standing inequalities.

SUMMARY

In 1965 when the HEA was first authorized, the political and demographic profile of America was far different than today. The nation's population was primarily white, racial inequalities were starting to be addressed through civil rights legislation, and income inequality was not nearly as severe as it is today. As colleges and universities have become more accessible to students of color and low-income students, public policymakers have steadily shifted policy attention away from civil rights and toward the interest of middle-class white voters. This pattern of neglect is a symptom of many of the worst features of political polarization and inequality, where the interests of powerful and already-advantaged stakeholders are preserved at the expense of the less powerful and the most disadvantaged. This is precisely how higher education policymaking has unfolded over several generations and in multiple policy areas outlined in this book.

Many of today's federal higher education policies and programs began during the civil rights era; however, as the nation has become more politically polarized, racially segregated, and economically unequal, policymakers have not maintained or strengthened these policies to ensure and promote civil rights. This book shows how public policymakers have lost the political will to engage in comprehensive and ongoing policy maintenance, resulting in sporadic HEA reauthorizations, piecemeal legislation, or budget reconciliation bills to usher new eras of race-neutral policies. The consequences of this underperformance and neglect fall squarely on students of color, low-income students, and the institutions where they enroll. If these issues are left unaddressed, federal higher education policies will continue to drift in this direction and reinforce the very inequalities many policies were designed to address.

Policymakers committed to promoting opportunity and strengthening civil rights must recognize that the current path will perpetuate inequality. This book explains why and it provides a deep examination into how civil rights has become an afterthought—if even thought of at all—in far too many federal higher education policy conversations. As the country becomes more diverse, the costs of this neglect steadily rise. But this book is not simply a critique of what is broken; in fact, each chapter highlights specific ways to improve policies, address inequalities, and promote civil rights through specific action. Our goal is to help inform policy deliberations by providing background context on the civil rights dimensions of specific policies, reporting new data analysis to understand the impacts of policy proposals, and offering new frameworks for understanding the impact of policy changes on students of color and low-income students—both today and long into the future. Higher education can and must become an important part of the solution.

CHAPTER 1

Civil Rights and Federal Higher Education Policy

GARY ORFIELD

ISSUES OF RACE AND CIVIL RIGHTS have been deeply linked to the development of higher education but rarely receive major attention. Standard histories of American higher education focus on key institutions, laws, and leaders of the elite institutions and, as a result, produce a narrative of progress and seldom mention issues of race. The great success stories in higher education focus on the development of major research universities and selective institutions with their ample resources and very well-prepared students. But there is a much darker part of the story. In a diverse and highly unequal society, though colleges see themselves as channels of opportunity, in the aggregate they give the best opportunity to white and well-to-do families and the least to students of color and the poor. That has made colleges a field of struggle for civil rights.

The truth is that opportunity in higher education has always been worse for Black, Latino, and Native students, and usually this inequality has been passively accepted. The civil rights era was the great exception when substantial changes took place. In spite of some significant positive actions, however, profound inequalities remain. Major breakthroughs have been rare and mostly long ago.

Both the civil rights revolution of the 1960s and the reversals in rights and access that followed beginning in the 1980s have profoundly shaped our institutions. Though the early reforms did make a substantial difference, they do not go deep enough or last long, and there was a backlash. Our vast and complex system of higher education has extreme variation. Millions of students of color do not enter at all or quickly leave. Our universities often tend to consider themselves as above the battles over race and ethnicity. They often see themselves as neutrally pursuing truth and merit, inherently committed to fairness and equity; higher education does not often take a critical role of itself.

The widely accepted history of higher education and some of its most important laws are so basic to our national history that students are likely to encounter them even in high school history books. But the official history leaves out important realities about race. For much of our history, policies were developed in a context that tacitly assumed white superiority, not seriously challenged until the mid-twentieth century. Even apparently nonracial policies often produce unequal opportunities and perpetuate racial inequality. Only in times of social movements or enforcement pressure does the normal inattention change markedly.

The United States likes to think of itself as a society of opportunity, mobility, and individualism. This is certainly true of higher education. Faculty and administrators and researchers of higher education are often beneficiaries of real mobility in their lives and have seen it operating in the lives of their students. Though it is widely acknowledged that race was a big problem in the past, often little attention is given to the groups of students who do not enroll or do not succeed.

In the early generations of federal higher education policy, minority education was usually ignored. In terms of the policies of state institutions in the states where Black and Latino students and Native peoples were concentrated, the dominant historic pattern was exclusion and was only seriously challenged by the civil rights revolution of the 1960s and 1970s. There have been negative developments since 1980.

Preparation for college has always been unequal. US public schools have always been largely segregated, except in some areas with few non-whites or places where serious civil rights plans were implemented, for a time, mostly in the South. School segregation declined substantially in the civil rights era but has been significantly increasing for both Blacks and Latinos since 1990, double segregation by race and class.[1] The Supreme Court's decision in Brown v. Board of Education identified segregation as a force that did irreversible harm to children of color.[2] The decision led to a vast effort to dismantle all of the systems of state-imposed segregation in seventeen states with segregation laws. Most of the positive change took place between the 1964 Civil Rights Act and the early 1970s when there was enforcement of civil rights law. Civil rights change in higher education came later and was more limited and briefer.

FEDERAL POLICY BEGINS: LAND-GRANT COLLEGES

Federal higher education initiatives began early. Before the creation of the United States, under the Articles of Confederation, the Northwest Ordinance set the precedent of reserving for education a section of every new township opened for settlement. In 1862, at the height of the Civil War, that idea was extended to higher education, emphasizing colleges offering practical work in agriculture and mechanics. That was the Morrill Act, often called the Land-Grant College Act. Under that act, thirty thousand acres were allocated to each state for each of its Congressmen and senators—much of this land dispossessed from Native tribes and in violation of treaties.[3] It led to the creation of many of what eventually became the nation's flagship public universities. The law was passed in the midst of the Civil War, but it said nothing about the education of Blacks, the great majority of whom were still locked in slavery. When Lincoln was elected in 1860, one-seventh (14.1 percent) of US residents were Black, and 89 percent of them were slaves.[4] All forms of education for slaves were outlawed in many slave states. When the Confederate states rejoined the union, they got grants without any requirement except that Blacks be admitted to the colleges or that colleges be set up for them. The great majority did nothing for students of color.

After the war, the basic agency of Reconstruction, the Freedman's Bureau (1865–72), was very active in education, including aiding Atlanta University and in supporting founding of two important colleges, Fisk and Howard Universities, all three to become leading forces in Black higher education. Many other institutions for Black students were established by religious groups shortly after the Civil War.

When the Second Morrill Act was enacted in 1890, the idea of federal support for colleges was extended beyond the original land grants into something permanent, and race was explicitly recognized. This key educational law demanded separate but more equal education for Black students. (Six years later, in 1896, *Plessy v. Ferguson* made "separate but equal" the law of the land for the next sixty years.) The 1890 law prohibited the distribution of money to states that made distinctions of race in admissions unless at least one land-grant college for African Americans was established. The law brought about the establishment of sixteen public Black colleges.[5]

The civil rights portion of the law provided that "no money shall be paid out under this act . . . for the support and maintenance of a college where a distinction of race or color is made in the admission of students, but the establishment and maintenance of such colleges separately for white and colored students shall be held to be a compliance with the provisions of this act if the funds received . . . be equitably divided. . . ." The law called for "a just and equitable division" of the funds, but "just and equitable" was not defined.[6]

The law required "an annual report . . . regarding the condition and progress of each college."[7] It also required an annual report.[8] Funds could be withheld for noncompliance "and the amount involved shall be kept separate in the Treasury until the close of the next Congress, in order that the State or Territory may, if it should so desire, appeal to Congress. . . ."[9]

This power to oversee the states had been given because of earlier scandals in the sale and misuse of funds. Federal officials investigated South Carolina and determined that the state had clearly failed to establish an appropriate institution for Black students, and the money was withheld. The state appealed to Congress, and Congress voted to give the state the money, anyway, basically ending any effort for actual enforcement.[10] The Black college that was established, which eventually became South Carolina State University, is described by the *South Carolina Encyclopedia* as follows:

> When the first students and faculty arrived in 1896, [six years after the Morrill Act] the campus was a sparse and unattractive place. The main building, Morrill Hall, was still under construction. There were no paved roads, no running water, and no electricity . . . Most students were enrolled in primary and secondary grades. Few students earned college degrees. All students were required to work . . . Many of the early campus buildings were constructed by students under the supervision of faculty.[11]

The campus was not fully accredited until sixty-four years later, in 1960.[12] The failure of the federal government to enforce the "separate but equal" provisions under the Land-Grant College Act led to extreme inequality of funding. A decade after the 1890 act, "expenditures on white land grant colleges exceeded those for Black ones by a ratio of approximately 26:1."[13] The colleges the law had established were not actual colleges offering college-level courses a quarter century after the Second Morrill Act. They were actually functioning as high schools in states that had few high schools for Blacks.[14]

The land-grant college laws and the resulting universities are cele-
brated in the history of American education and were, indeed, key steps
in developing what eventually became a huge system of accessible and
relatively inexpensive universities not for elites and the classics but for
a broader public with a special commitment to development of the land
and businesses of a growing country. The celebrations, however, don't say
much about the racial practices or the failure of the one effort to insist on
equity as the institutions went through their early development. The federal policies simply accepted segregation by law, keeping people of color
out of the strong institutions, and did not equalize resources; vast differences were consolidated.

FEDERAL GRANTS FOR AGRICULTURAL DEVELOPMENT IN A STILL LARGELY RURAL SOCIETY

The next major law that had a lasting impact on American higher education was the creation of the Agricultural Extension Service in the
Smith–Lever Act of 1914. Two important Southern leaders authored this
law, one in the Senate and the other in the House. It came during the
presidency of Woodrow Wilson, the first president raised in the South
to serve after the Civil War and a committed segregationist. It was the
period of Black disenfranchisement and subordination under all the
Southern race laws requiring segregation in every aspect of life, the
period of the national rise of the Ku Klux Klan. In this period, Congress
made an important expansion of the white land-grant colleges by creating what became a powerful systematic connection between the state
universities and farming and rural areas in a society that still had a rural
majority. The basic idea, an idea that became an international model,
was to marry the expertise of research universities and the agricultural
producers and processors.

The federal government passively accepted segregation by law. The new Cooperative Extension Service, in which universities provided research and training to upgrade agriculture across the nation emerged from the 1914 law.[15] The Smith–Lever Act later used the land-grant colleges as the key mechanism in what became a very powerful institution and political force across rural America, the Extension Service. The bill, managed in both houses by powerful Southerners, excluded the Black colleges after Southerners said that they would not support the bill if the funds were shared with the Black colleges. The Black colleges and their supporters were defeated, and the Extension Service developed on an overtly segregated manner particularly in the South.[16] When the New Deal responded to the agricultural depression that was destroying the markets and bankrupting farmers in the Great Depression, this all-white institution working with the county extension agents became an important part of a system that directed the federal funds to the white farmers who received grants for taking land out of production to raise prices, but giving nothing to the largely Black tenant farmers and share croppers whose income disappeared. That became an important cause of the forced migration of desperately poor agricultural workers to the cities.[17]

The experience under these laws showed how, before the civil rights revolution, federal policy had basically accepted the exclusion of Black students and colleges from most of the public higher education opportunities that existed in the states where most lived and reinforced the position of local whites. Until the mid-twentieth century, higher education was mostly for white families with resources, and only a very small minority of adults had college degrees. The idea of mass higher education supported by the government was the great experiment of the postwar US, as the country welcomed back many millions of servicemen and was worried about the ability of the economy to absorb them. The G.I. Bill successfully launched a powerful alternative. The effort was a huge investment with powerful impacts but, sadly, mostly for young white men.

A GREAT EXPERIMENT IN SUPPORTING
MASS WHITE HIGHER EDUCATION

The G.I. Bill was a remarkably far-reaching and effective policy to make higher education possible for many World War II veterans. It was a huge program reaching the majority of young men in a generation and producing a massive increase in college enrollment and completion.[18] The wartime decision by President Franklin D. Roosevelt to create the G.I. Bill launched a first large-scale federal effort to make colleges affordable for veterans of the massive mobilization of sixteen million Americans during wartime. There were large numbers of Blacks and Latinos.[19] In spite of segregation in the armed forces during the war, more than one million Blacks served, overwhelmingly in segregated units. In addition, though they were not formally counted that way, an estimated five-hundred thousand Latinos served, including many Puerto Ricans.[20] The G.I. Bill was a "colorblind" policy, available to former soldiers of any race, but it had very different impacts by race because it was colorblind (or blind to the realities of color) in a world where colleges, particularly in the South, were segregated by law.

The G.I. Bill offered unprecedented opportunities for millions, providing tuition, supplies, and living expenses for students. It considerably increased college going for those eligible for up to four years, depending on their years of service. Even though Blacks were never recruited at the level of whites, there were over a million Black veterans, but they had far less real access. "Data from the Survey of Veterans show more than 28 percent of whites in the 1923–28 birth cohorts enrolled in collegiate level training, while less than 12 percent of returning Black veterans."[21]

One basic reason was the completely unequal public schools that had educated the Black and white soldiers in the totally segregated South and the Latinos in the Southwest. Many of the draftees were unable to meet the very low educational standards required for service. The highest rejections for military service were in the Fourth and Eighth Service Commands, where very large numbers of Blacks and Latinos lived, including ten of the eleven states of the old confederacy.[22] Few nonwhite students completed high school in this period. Many young men drafted were illiterate and not allowed to serve or required first to take literacy training. There were vast differences in training by race, particularly in the South. It was worst in "the former slave-holding states of the confederacy. White children in some of these states like Alabama, Arkansas, Florida, and Georgia were four to five times as likely to attend high school as African-American children."[23] Educational preparation so deeply unequal greatly limited the possibility of college for veterans of color. The country was still strongly committed to racial segregation. A national survey in 1942 reported that less than a third of white Americans approved of integrated education and only one in fifty Southern whites.[24]

The G.I. Bill benefit showed how aid had a major impact on aspirations. A 1944 Army study "showed the remarkable power of the benefits in changing educational aspirations. Prior to the announcement of benefits, only 7 percent of enlisted men indicated that they planned further training or education after the war. After the announcement, 29 percent of white enlisted men and 43 percent of Black enlisted men expressed a definite interest in education after the war."[25] Blacks, by state law, could not attend the white public colleges.

Information was also crucial and unequal. The G.I. Bill provided for "the availability of employment and education counseling services through the Veterans Administration," and the VA operated "regional counseling centers but also contracted with educational colleges to operate an additional 300 sites."[26] One researcher reported that there were, however, "only about a dozen Black counselors for all of Georgia and Alabama and none in Mississippi."[27]

The substantial majority of Blacks lived in the South where Black colleges were the only option for Black veterans, but these schools were too small and had limited offerings. A majority of the veterans applying to twenty-one surveyed Black colleges were turned down for lack of capacity. Almost half of the Black colleges the year the war ended had "fewer than 250 students and 92 percent . . . had enrollment of less than 1000 students."[28] White institutions had the capacity to expand for the new students; Black colleges did not. Although the G.I. Bill had no racial limits, the inequalities and segregation of the higher education system blocked many Black veterans. For those who finished college under the G.I. Bill, it was an unprecedented opportunity for a better life. For those rejected, a severe loss. When you put money, even in a generous program, into segregated systems without strong civil rights policies, you often perpetuate inequality.

The historic experience showed that apparently nonracial policies or supposed guarantees of equity had failed in practice for generations. African American students and the much smaller populations of Latinos and Indians in that period were not prepared for college.[29] The 1940 Census showed that less than 8 percent of Blacks twenty-five years and older had high school diplomas, compared to more than 26 percent of whites.[30]

Colleges Expanding

As the federal role in higher education expanded in World War II with massive research and training responsibilities at universities, which were continued and expanded during the Cold War, military research underwrote the development of powerful research centers and gave generous federal "overhead" funding to the universities. The National Defense Education Act channeled funds into universities to develop needed skills and talents in science, foreign languages, and other areas that helped higher education. The postwar era prosperity brought a vast expansion of the nation's colleges, including a huge growth of community colleges and regional four-year universities. Between 1950 and 1970 the undergrad enrollment zoomed from 2.2 million to 8.6 million.[31] Until the middle 1960s, this was overwhelmingly a state and sometimes local government enterprise in which the federal government was not a central player.

TRANSFORMATION IN THE CIVIL RIGHTS ERA

The moves that made the federal government a major funder of US higher education were direct products of a liberal movement that reached its peak in the 1963–65 period of the most powerful civil rights campaigns. This period changed public opinion and led to enactment of the historic 1964 Civil Rights Act, which fundamentally altered the role of the federal government on race, and the 1965 Voting Rights Act, which enfranchised African Americans in major parts of the South. In that period two laws transformed the federal role: the War on Poverty legislation of 1964 and the Higher Education Act of 1965. The basic impulse was opening up institutions and equalizing opportunity for those who had historically been shut out.

The reforms' unifying goals were inclusion and opportunity. Colleges received a flood of federal funds and came under serious federal pressure on issues of racial equity in admissions and hiring. At the same time campus changes outside the South were stirred by civil rights protests and demands from their own students and faculties, leading to unprecedented initiatives that changed many virtually all-white campuses.

Background of the Civil Rights Era

During the 1948 Democratic National Convention, the Democratic party adopted a civil rights plank in its platform for the first time ever. President Harry S. Truman had created the President's Committee on Civil Rights by executive order in 1946, and it issued a national report on racial inequality calling for federal action. Among its recommendations, it urged conditioning all federal grants and aid on the "absence of discrimination and segregation based on race, color, creed, or national origin."[32] A national team of scholars headed by Gunnar Myrdal completed a massive study documenting the history and present reality of segregation and discrimination, producing the deeply influential book An American Dilemma:

The Negro Problem and Modern Democracy, posing racial reform as the fundamental challenge before US society.[33]

A series of Supreme Court decisions developed legal principles
against racial segregation in higher education finding violations of the
Fourteenth Amendment's guarantee of "equal protection of the laws." The
Court first faced the issues of the inherent inequality of segregation in
decisions about graduate programs in colleges, where the white campus
had opportunities that simply did not exist in the Black programs. In a key
1950 decision about the University of Texas Law School, *Sweatt v. Painter*,
the Court unanimously concluded that the new all-Black law school the
state was developing could not be equal.

> In terms of number of the faculty, variety of courses and opportunity
> for specialization, size of the student body, scope of the library, avail-
> ability of law review and similar activities, the University of Texas
> Law School is superior. What is more important, the University of
> Texas Law School possesses to a far greater degree those qualities
> which are incapable of objective measurement, but which make for
> greatness in a law school. Such qualities, to name but a few, include
> reputation of the faculty, experience of the administration, position
> and influence of the alumni, standing in the community, traditions,
> and prestige. The law school, the proving ground for legal learning
> and practice, cannot be effective in isolation from the individuals
> and institutions with which the law interacts. Few students and no
> one who has practiced law would choose to study in an academic vac-
> uum, removed from the interplay of ideas and the exchange of views
> with which the law is concerned.[34]

The Court noted that exclusion separated students from "most of
the lawyers, witnesses, jurors, judges and other officials. . . ."[35] The justices decided that, under these circumstances, "separate but equal" was an
impossibility.

The 1954 *Brown v. Board of Education* decision went further, concluding that in public schools, "separate is inherently unequal" and caused lasting harm.[36] These decisions undermined the entire constitutional basis of colleges segregated by law and put the federal courts in direct conflict with state authorities. What followed was a decade of intense conflict as most of the Southern states embraced the doctrine of "massive resistance," refused to comply with the constitutional requirements, and virtually brought school desegregation to a halt until civil rights law was radically strengthened.

With the Supreme Court decisions, the segregation laws regulating colleges were rendered invalid, and very small-scale desegregation began. There were dramatic confrontations in Mississippi and Alabama when the federal government overturned the last complete holdouts for absolute segregation.[37] That did not, however, produce significant diversity. The pioneering Black students faced very difficult situations as a token presence in an often-hostile setting. Real change came from the emergence of a historic social movement in the South, changing national attitudes, and the bipartisan commitment of Congress to strengthen civil rights. The social movement in the Black South led to fundamental changes in federal law and policy.

The US Department of Justice (DOJ) had no authority to intervene against Southern defiance. The courts had limited enforcement mechanisms and normally assume that institutions will comply with court orders. The Southern Manifesto, which assailed the Supreme Court's decision and advocated defiance, was signed less than two years later.[38] In the eleven states of the old confederacy, all but three senators signed, as did the entire congressional delegations from seven states and the majority from two others.[39] The document claimed that the *Brown* decision was "a clear abuse of judicial power. It climaxes a trend in the Federal Judiciary undertaking to legislate, in derogation of the authority of Congress, and to encroach upon the reserved rights of the States and the people."[40]

In the face of almost uniform resistance by Southern leaders and the defeat of many Southern moderates after President Dwight D. Eisenhower sent paratroopers into Little Rock, Arkansas, when Governor Orval Faubus called out the National Guard to prevent implementation of a federal court order, something had to be done. Nine years after the Brown decision, when President John F. Kennedy sent his civil rights bill to Congress, 99 percent of Southern Black students were still in all-Black schools, and it seemed that defiance was rendering their rights a dead letter for all but a handful of students.[41]

What changed all this was the civil rights movement, whose origins were closely linked to the Black colleges, which were some of the only institutions actively supporting Black aspirations in segregated states. Jo Ann Robinson, on the faculty of Alabama State College in Montgomery, planned the historic bus boycott well before Dr. Martin Luther King Jr. was chosen as the leader. Robinson could not be the public leader because she worried about her job in the state institution.[42] The president and student leaders from Miles College, outside Birmingham, were very active in initiating the boycott of segregated stores that led to Martin Luther King Jr.'s decisive Birmingham movement that generated national demands for civil rights changes.[43] The group that triggered the Freedom Rides into the South in 1961 was CORE, the Congress of Racial Equality, which had been created mostly by students in the Fellowship of Reconciliation (at the University of Chicago). They were employing "sit-in" strategies from labor battles fighting discrimination in Chicago.[44] CORE sponsored the first "freedom ride" in the outer South in 1947 and later, as the civil rights movement was becoming a national force, led the Freedom Rides into the Deep South in 1961 against violent resistance.

In 1960, four students at North Carolina A&T State University decided to demand service at an all-white dime store lunch counter. Their success in carrying out the peaceful protest stirred growing publicity and brought in many more students.[45] After several days, the idea spread, especially in Black colleges across the South.[46] It spread with the encouragement of

Martin Luther King Jr. A meeting at Shaw University led to the formation of the Student Nonviolent Coordinating Committee (SNCC), which became powerful and produced major civil rights leaders of the next half century, including John Lewis and Julian Bond.[47] The colleges were a critical base for the social revolution that began in the early 1960s. The small colleges that had been created under the Second Morrill Act and by the churches after the Civil War turned out to be a critical resource.[48] Colleges matter.

The legal strategy that led to Brown was largely worked out by a team led by Charles Hamilton Houston at Howard University Law School, in an institution created during Reconstruction by the Freedman's Bureau. Black colleges were a reservoir of support and leadership. Though they got little recognition in the scholarly community, they contributed far out of proportion to the successes that were achieved and to the development of ideas and agendas that changed the country.

The Great Breakthroughs

The protest movement reached a peak in the 1963 Birmingham campaign and won the support of the Democratic party leadership and a substantial block of moderate Republicans as public outrage over the attacks on peaceful marchers spread across the country and made civil rights the nation's most urgent issue. After the assassination of President Kennedy in 1963, President Lyndon B. Johnson's leadership led to enactment of three laws that set the framework for a deep and enduring federal commitment to equity in higher education—the War on Poverty (the Economic Opportunity Act), the 1964 Civil Rights Act and, less than a year later, the 1965 Higher Education Act. These laws set the federal government on a path to be a far larger player in higher education, with a mission centrally defined as equalizing opportunity for poor students and students of color.

The War on Poverty initiative was initially developed within the Kennedy administration partially in response to scholarship, especially a widely read book, Michael Harrington's The Other America: Poverty in the United States, and partially in response to efforts and research, especially that funded by the Ford Foundation.[49] The law embodied a theory of community mobilization. The legislation created the new Office of Economic Opportunity, specified some priorities, and provided discretion to initiate new programs. The ideas of expanding access to college through a variety of support programs and economic assistance were central. In higher education the dominant ideas were that students of color and students in poverty were not going to college because they had neither contact with nor preparation for college and their families couldn't afford it anyway.

The War on Poverty included programs to identify and encourage nontraditional precollege students and was the birthplace of the Upward Bound program that involved colleges taking potential students from poor backgrounds on campus during the summer and the school year to familiarize themselves with college and receive encouragement and support quickly opening on campuses.[50] Later legislation added the other TRIO programs, including the Talent Search and Student Support Services program.[51] The law funded efforts to get teens off the streets and into job and training settings.[52] The new federal Work-Study program enabled students to earn wages for on-campus work in the libraries and kitchens, as research assistants, and so on. The act aimed at helping students "from low income families" who "are in need of the earnings . . . to pursue courses of study" with the federal government paying up to 90 percent of the cost.[53] Public college costs were often still affordable with summer and part-time work. The idea of the law was that there were systemic problems of poverty that demanded a variety of approaches. That sensibility was crucial as the federal government developed the first major ongoing programs of federal aid to public schools and college students the next year.

The year of the civil rights revolution on Capitol Hill, 1964, saw the enactment of the most important civil rights law of the twentieth century, the 1964 Civil Rights Act. The act was possible because of the enormous impact of the struggle led by Martin Luther King Jr. in Birmingham.[54] That struggle showed the country a reactionary angry sheriff, Bull Connor, turning police dogs and fire hoses on peaceful children protesters singing the Christian hymns that were the Sunday morning music of the South. Martin Luther King Jr. was locked up in the city jail, where he wrote the powerful "Letter from a Birmingham Jail" appealing to the country and challenging its religious and civic leaders. Demands for action surged across the country with hundreds of local demonstrations. With the pressure rising in Congress, President Kennedy, who had delayed civil rights changes, decided to make what turned out to be a transformative address to the nation and to put before Congress a far more sweeping bill than he had foreseen. Kennedy asked for decisive federal powers to protect minority rights for the first time in nearly ninety years.[55]

This civil rights struggle had been triggered by generations of battles. The law was closely linked to educational rights though it extended much further to include rights against segregation in restaurants, hotels, and all kinds of public facilities and discrimination in jobs and, of course, voting rights. The bill that Kennedy sent to Capitol Hill included a number of provisions directly linked to the long-term struggle over schools.[56] When the South defied the Brown decision in the 1950s and early 1960s, the DOJ was not authorized by law to file suits to defend students of color even in the most extreme cases. Massive resistance to the decision meant that a few private civil rights lawyers from national civil rights groups were struggling against impossible odds to deal with many strategies to block the courts and the federal courts in the South largely staffed with conservative judges. In Virginia, for instance, Prince Edward County decided to simply close all of its public schools, and all the attorney general could do was to help raise some private funds to provide some schooling for the Black students who had been excluded from the new private white school that received vouchers from the county.

The Civil Rights Act authorized the DOJ to sue in federal court to protect minority rights, sharply changing the equation in these cases. Another part of the act, Title IV, was designed to help find peaceful solutions to local racial conflicts, often about school desegregation efforts, through the new Community Relations Service.

The most important part of the law, Title VI, was initially proposed years earlier by the National Association for the Advancement of Colored People (NAACP) to counter resistance to Brown by creating powerful federal leverage for compliance. The idea was to require civil rights compliance as a condition for receiving any federal aid. Rather than having to sue every individual one of the thousands of Southern school systems in cases that would stretch out over years, this part of the law created a positive duty and a powerful administrative sanction. As the Johnson administration greatly expanded federal aid to schools and colleges, the leverage became much greater. Before the Civil Rights Act, a school district faced only a small risk that a private civil rights group would sue and that, after years, there might be a limited court order. Under the Civil Rights Act, the school districts faced the Department of Justice, not a private lawyer, and all of its needed federal aid would be at risk. The vast majority of Southern school districts, which had done nothing the decade after Brown, soon began to desegregate. Those that did not were sued by the DOJ.

The law was fiercely fought as a vast expansion of federal authority, ending the tradition of passive acceptance of overt racial discrimination. It was only after one of the very longest debates in the history of the US Senate, where filibusters had blocked significant civil rights reforms for generations, was broken that the bill became law on July 2, 1964.[57] For the first time since Reconstruction ended, the federal government had very strong powers to force civil rights change. And there was an administration determined to actually enforce the law.[58]

Historically, the very complex and divisive issues of religion and race had prevented any broad federal action on education. The Catholic Church demanded federal aid for parochial schools if public schools were to get it, dividing the Democratic party. The liberals would demand civil rights protections, and the South, in response, would block proposed education bills to preserve segregation. So nothing got done.

Enactment of the Civil Rights Act settled the race issue; it meant that Brown would be implemented at a much higher level. The status quo could no longer be maintained in the South. So, to get federal aid to education, a primary goal of President Johnson, a one-time teacher of poor Mexican American children, the political problem became how to appeal to a broad national constituency and resolve the religious issue. The solution worked out between the administration and Congress was to make poor children rather than the schools the primary target of educational aid, using the antipoverty framework. With this agreement in place, the basic framework for federal aid to schools, built around poverty levels, was created and has now lasted for almost six decades through administrations of extremely different ideologies. By focusing on schools with concentrated poverty (the number of children with family income below $2,000 at the outset), the federal aid funds disproportionately went to schools serving children and communities of color both in the rural South and in the urban North. So, it was the resolution of the civil rights issue that made it possible to launch an enduring system of federal aid to public schools.[59]

Once the Civil Rights Act and the Elementary and Secondary Education Act (ESEA) were in place, there was the possibility of historic change, and it was a possibility that the Johnson administration seriously pursued and invested great political capital in. In 1965–66 these pieces came together with a force that broke centuries of racial tradition and changed public education in the seventeen states with a history of segregation laws and, in the next decade, began to change it in public schools outside the South and colleges and universities, especially in the nineteen states with racially separate public colleges.

The same spirit focused on access, poverty, and race shaped the engagement of the federal government as a basic funding source for higher education—not in direct aid to colleges but through aiding students from low-income families go to college. Much of this money reached the colleges, of course, in the form of tuition, fees, and room-and-board payments. Expanding the market of students able to pay for college helped colleges expand their size and reach. The goal was to make college possible for millions of students who would not likely have gone. This and the TRIO programs, which also have survived to the present, had a very clear goal, but it would come unfocused over time as the political context changed. By 1972, when the college aid program of the 1965 law evolved into the Basic Educational Opportunity Grant (later named Pell Grant) for low-income students, the basic framework of the federal higher education program was coming into focus in a policy that would remain a central element for the next half century.

Reconstructing the Racial Patterns of Southern Higher Education

After Brown and the 1964 Civil Rights Act, the traditional segregation of public higher education in the South was in clear tension with the law. The dramatic impact on higher education came after federal courts found the Nixon administration guilty of failing to enforce the 1964 Civil Rights Act and ordered the federal authorities to require plans to desegregate the campuses. This effort brought a substantial increase in Black student access to historically white schools and a temporary surge of state funds to help equalize the notoriously less-funded Black campuses. Without the gains from that period and an overwhelming reliance on the Pell Grants and other federal funds, the Historically Black Colleges and Universities (HBCUs) in many cases, they could not have improved and certainly would not have been able to implement important new programs.

Outside the nineteen states with a history of racially separate public colleges, civil rights law and the civil rights movement had major impacts as well. The largest impact was the creation of affirmative action on almost all of the nation's highly selective universities, through voluntary action by universities but, often, under strong pressure from students affected by the civil rights movement. Almost all universities are federal contractors, and the federal agencies required them to develop affirmative action plans to diversify their hiring and report results. There were no quotas and virtually no sanctions, but the government did have the power to cancel contracts and, if discrimination was found, to cut off federal aid. These policies had tangible impacts on most campuses, and affirmative action has persisted though it is banned in public campuses in nine states.

The particular form the suddenly expanded federal role took was a product of the era of civil rights and social reform, but the decisions taken then are still important influences. The civil rights issues changed many of the leading colleges of the South and the Southwest, which historically had no significant nonwhite enrollment. In intellectual terms the job discrimination provisions helped create faculty diversity, which affected research and teaching. Both the student and faculty diversity created different intellectual developments and socialized millions of young Americans in more diverse settings.

The civil rights revolution and the model of the 1964 Civil Rights Act spread to other arenas with lasting impact on higher education, setting the stage for legal mandates to provide higher education for the handicapped and to end sex discrimination in all major operations of higher education. The Rehabilitation Act of 1973 opened the door, and colleges were required to provide appropriate services under Title II of the Americans with Disabilities Act and Section 504 of the Rehabilitation Act of 1973. In terms of gender equity and sexual discrimination, the key law was Title IX of the Education Amendments of 1972.[60] Major structural features of today's higher education were shaped by these laws, which were modeled on earlier civil rights laws. The central theme of the expanding federal role in education still was bringing down barriers and widening opportunity and embodying a more expansive vision of civil rights, arming the government and students with both incentives and powerful sanctions.

When the Basic Educational Opportunity Grant was enacted in 1972, it expanded the commitment to grants for low-income students and set the stage for a program that has persisted through generations. The goal was to make it possible for many low-income students to go to college. In 1980 this program covered more than three-fourths of the price tag of attending a public four-year campus.

The 1970s brought a great increase in college diversity. In an extraordinary development, the likelihood that Black and Latino high school graduates would go to college was briefly as high as the white levels (though the graduation levels never equalized). The conditions of the 1970s were ideal in several respects. States were rapidly expanding colleges. Tuition rose very little in the decade, and aid was sufficient to make college possible because affirmative action efforts were widespread. Colleges embraced race-conscious policies that changed outcomes. That involved changing methods and standards and recruitment. Students who would not have been admitted previously were admitted and given support, and the great majority succeeded. Recruitment networks were expanded to include neighborhoods and schools of color. Since many students were lacking needed skills, special summer transition programs were often begun. In the space of a few years, America's most prestigious colleges went from virtually all-white to some significant diversity.

The late 1970s, however, also brought signs of a conservative turn. Affirmative action was under attack by opponents in the federal courts, especially in the first major Supreme Court consideration of the conservative theory that it was discrimination against whites. In the *Bakke* decision, the Court by a single vote supported very limited use of race as a "plus factor" because diverse classes were more intellectually stimulating than segregated white ones.[61] The Court rejected the university's plan for actually setting aside a modest share of the medical school seats for students of color in a school with a very segregated white history. Limited affirmative action survived, but anything that looked like a "quota" was forbidden.[62] This battle has been going on ever since with major decisions in 2003 and 2016. The Trump administration fought affirmative action, and new challenges are passing through the lower courts though one of the first actions of the Biden administration was to drop a suit against Yale University's plan.

The same year *Bakke* was decided the state of California adopted Proposition 13, a constitutional change sharply limiting taxes, helping set off sweeping tax cuts across the country and in Washington when California's Ronald Reagan became president in 1981.[63] Those changes together with a severe recession and major inflation led to cuts in state funds for colleges and cuts in the Pell Grant. Lacking funds, state and higher education officials decided to shift much more of the burden of rapidly rising costs to students and parents at the same time as the buying power of the Pell Grants fell. Although there were significant fluctuations, this has been the basic pattern ever since, four decades of rising costs and declining value of Pell Grants. As civil rights advocates have often pointed out, if you get a door open and cannot afford to take advantage of it, you have a right in name only.

The reaction against civil rights in a period of strong conservative power and control of the federal government for long periods remade the basic framework of policy over the period following 1980. The 1980 election was also a turning point for civil rights enforcement and civil rights law. The legal requirements for changes in the Southern universities had intensified in the 1970s under court orders. By 1990 they were largely shut down.

After Brown, mandatory segregation of public colleges in seventeen states was illegal, but little changed. Whites did not enroll in the historic Black colleges, and Blacks were a token presence and faculty of color were virtually nonexistent in public universities. Federal authorities concentrated on the vast job of desegregating school districts. The Nixon administration, elected in a campaign that promised to restrict civil rights enforcement, did almost nothing. Eventually, a federal court found it guilty of intentional failure to enforce the Civil Rights Act and ordered the preparation of state plans for the desegregation of their higher education systems.[64] All states submitted plans that were found to be inadequate, and the courts ordered federal authorities to take additional steps. Finally, under the Carter administration in the late 1970s, states submitted revised plans. The emphasis was on creating very attractive programs on the historically Black campuses to attract potential local white students as

well as serve local Blacks. In some cases, shocking inequalities were reme-
died. On the white campuses, affirmative action efforts like those used in
the North were often implemented, and there were special scholarships
and outreach programs.[65]

Under President Reagan, the effort was quickly rolled back. The
administration quickly shut down a major confrontation with the University of North Carolina, one of the South's preeminent institutions,
sending a strong signal that the sanctions in the Civil Rights Act would
not be used.[66] The Reagan administration changed the focus from actual
results in terms of enrollments to compliance with agreed improvements,
for example, providing a new program or a new building to a particular
campus. If those things were done, they decided, that was enough, and
the state could be considered in full compliance even though there had
been little or no progress in the actual integration. As the Supreme Court
became more conservative, the rules changed and the lower federal courts
dropped the effort to force the executive branch to enforce the law in
1990.[67] There was a significant higher education decision in a Mississippi
case, United States v. Fordice, a 1992 case in which the Supreme Court ruled
that states with a history of de jure segregation were required to take affirmative measures, including racial preferences, to remedy the vestige. It
was never seriously enforced.

After the Supreme Court was deeply changed by four Nixon appointments, the Court sent ominous civil rights signals in its response to efforts
to equalize and integrate public schools. In the 1973 Rodriguez decision, a
five-to-four majority concluded that there was no right to equal educational resources in the US Constitution.[68] In an extremely important decision, Milliken v. Bradley, the Court ruled that even if there was proof that
central city students had been intentionally segregated by state policy,
the suburbs could not be included in a desegregation plan—making real
integration impossible in many cities in our metropolitan society.[69] The
two decisions together meant that the students of color had no real rights
to either integrated or equal schooling as separation and stratification

intensified. That meant, of course, that students of color would be less prepared for college in their inferior schools.

The deep and lasting changes came with the Reagan administration, which substantially cut college aid for poor students, opposed integration efforts in schools and colleges, appointed active opponents of civil rights to run civil rights agencies, and attacked the whole civil rights effort as a distraction from the serious work of raising educational standards. Reagan had been an active opponent of the 1964 Civil Rights Act and did very little to enforce it. Racial gaps widened. President Reagan named a consistent opponent of civil rights, Justice William Rehnquist, as Chief Justice. What followed was a long period of conservative decisions. The real force of civil rights on major moves toward racial equity had lasted only a few years. The federal courts had kept it going through the 1970s. Reaction and reversal or abandonment of serious efforts was operating in full force by the 1980s.

The other historic change came with a continuing reduction in state funding of higher education as many states enacted tax cuts and had to cope with growing health care and incarceration costs arising from the "war on drugs." The Reagan administration cut student aid, and the Pell Grant covered increasingly smaller parts of total college costs, not sufficient to make college feasible for truly low-income students. The ending of serious enforcement of the Civil Rights Act and the dramatic increase in costs raised barriers higher while weakening the tools to overcome them.

The 1990s brought basic challenges to what remained of civil rights policy. In 1991 the Supreme Court authorized the termination of school desegregation plans, sending back many students of color to segregated neighborhood schools.[70] A 1996 Court of Appeals decision abolished affirmative action in Texas.[71] In California, a referendum battle resulted in the nation's largest state outlawing affirmative action in the state's public colleges and universities in both admissions and employment with the passage of Proposition 209 in 1996.[72]

Federal financial aid was increasingly shifted from a poor, more heavily nonwhite group of recipients to a higher-income, whiter group, often through tax subsidies. Higher education became highly stratified by income as tuitions increased many times faster than family income, and US family incomes became the most unequal in a century. Beginning with the Middle Income Student Assistance Act of 1978 and the 1996 Hope Scholarship legislation, there was a major expansion of subsidies for higher-income families that were entitlements rather than annual appropriations and grew much faster than the Pell Grant for low-income students. By 2017, the tax subsidies were far above the Pell Grant dollars.[73] The Pell Grant had declined radically in terms of its ability to pay costs for low-income students. As late as 1988, 91 percent of federal aid was awarded on the basis of student need. By 2018, it had plummeted to 33 percent.[74] As financial barriers grew, the shift from the poor and nonwhite to the middle class changed the balance and widened the gap.

Except for the ongoing struggle to protect affirmative action, which is now deeply rooted in selective colleges, there hasn't been any substantial focus on civil rights policy in higher education for a long time. The 1990s brought open war on affirmative action, the end of federal court requirements that the Office for Civil Rights (OCR) enforce the Civil Rights Act, general weakening of civil rights laws, and a continuing failure to address increases in the cost of college.[75] The 1996 California affirmative action ban was a devastating blow to college opportunity in a state that was uniquely important for Latinos, more than 30 percent of the national total. The effort soon spread to several more states.

The loss of affirmative action in the two largest states in 1996 set off a nationwide battle and a mobilization of the academic world, with four major Supreme Court cases. Affirmative action was preserved by a single vote in the 2003 *Grutter* decision, but only in a form that required much more complex and costly holistic admission processes.[76] That seemed to settle the issue for the time, but three more cases would be decided by the Supreme Court in the next two decades and new cases arising during the Trump administration as three appointments of far-right justices changed the legal future. The Court upheld a challenged Michigan referendum banning affirmative action.[77]

None of the basic civil rights laws have been repealed, but most of the time they have been applied by GOP administrations opposed to civil rights, elected by virtually all-white electorates or by cautious moderate Democratic administrations that did not give the issues priority. There has not been a majority of Democratic appointees on the Supreme Court since 1972, and since the Reagan administration, there has been a systemic selection of young highly conservative judicial appointees, usually identified through the mechanism of the conservative Federalist Society. With occasional exceptions on individual cases, they have been civil rights opponents.[78]

Most of the explicitly racially targeted financial aid has been eliminated. Under the George W. Bush administration, the federal government pressed against race-conscious programs, and colleges received letters suggesting possible legal risks if they continued them. The Obama administration took a positive view, but the Trump administration was actively opposed. The Biden administration promised to renew federal commitments to civil rights reforms that have long been contested or largely neglected but faced a profoundly conservative Court.

The gaps did not close. The extremely high desire for college education led far more high school graduates to start college in recent decades, but students of color, especially in community colleges and for-profit schools, have enormous attrition levels. Enrolling means nothing if you leave with no credential, gave up earnings, and end up with a debt that cannot be forgiven even in bankruptcy. That happens often. The racial gap in access to the selective colleges has actually widened. Many students of color do not make it into the second term or the second year.

While civil rights agencies still have significant power, there is little enforcement, and broader issues with clear civil rights consequences are largely ignored. The Supreme Court increasingly limited the ability of plaintiffs and civil rights groups to bring private lawsuits. Long-term patterns of policy and practice that produce strong racially disparate results go unchallenged. There is a much higher standard of proof now to get any civil rights remedy.

The shift of federal support for college access from direct grants to tax-based subsidies and from grants to loans has harmed minority access by shifting resources from groups with more students of color and students in poverty to higher-income families. This pattern raises serious civil rights concerns, especially since the level of grants became so low that they decisively limit choice and access for students of color with limited family income and wealth.

The various colorblind higher education policies of the Obama administration illustrate the need for a civil rights perspective in designing policy if the massive gaps are to be closed. The administration was positive about civil rights, but there was no overall strategy. The policies for the recovery from the Great Recession included a substantial temporary increase in the Pell Grant but also a permanent increase in tax subsidies and benefits for student debt, the first going to many low-income students of color; the second going mostly to whites already in college or graduated. The administration took a strong stand against predatory practices of for-profit colleges, which often exploited and indebted students of color, but it also pushed for outcome accountability that, without adjustments for differences in student preparation, tended to harm campuses committed to serving students of color.[79] The administration strongly encouraged and defended affirmative action but proposed no systemic solutions. The Trump administration took a very different turn, fostering for-profit colleges and actively advocating the elimination of affirmative action.

If the federal government is to be fair to students of color, policy requires deeper understanding of the realities of their communities and families and to the actual effects of policies on students' opportunities. There is increasing evidence that race-conscious policy is the only way to achieve major gains toward racial equality in higher education, but it has been seriously limited. If the policies widen racial gaps, it is a civil rights crisis, but the federal role in racial equity has shrunk dramatically.

By the later 1980s, the courts as a possible avenue for civil rights gains in addressing systemic issues in major institutions had been foreclosed because the courts became far more conservative. There is still, however, substantial power in Congress, in the president, and in the civil rights agencies, particularly the Office for Civil Rights of the Education Department and the Civil Rights Division of the Department of Justice. These powers could be activated if the country's politics moved in a substantially more progressive direction.

CONCLUSION

The evolution of higher education policy has been deeply intertwined questions of racial inequality and civil rights. Until the 1960s, federal policy largely accepted the status quo of official segregation in the states where most people of color lived and inequality everywhere.

A major social movement and political changes in the 1960s and 1970s, accompanied by major reforms in student aid, made it possible for students from many low-income and nonwhite families to go to college. That period shaped many basic instruments and policies that have lasted, and the impetus of expanding rights scurried well beyond the issue of race. But the gains in college access were gravely limited by rapidly rising financial barriers and inadequate support.

The Nixon administration reversed course on civil rights and began to transform the courts. The courts changed and civil rights remedies were limited. The Reagan administration sharply weakened civil rights enforcement and reduced aid; tuition soared. Aid grew for the middle class, and access was more closely linked to family resources. Affirmative action, which made significant diversity in higher education possible in elite colleges, was not a government policy but has been a continuing point of serious contention since the 1970s, surviving a series of Supreme Court challenges so far by a single vote and facing another.

The history of federal higher education policy shows that when race and civil rights are ignored in spite of severe racial inequalities, programs perpetuate inequality. When there is a serious focus on race and on related financial barriers, major changes can happen. There has been no consensus in recent decades about policies. Since 1980, civil rights policy has had little impact as the system has become increasingly unequal.

Race and class issues about higher education have not gone away. There is an extremely high demand for higher education from all groups and deeply unequal success. Step by step, nonwhites and the poor have been limited to the less-resourced, less-effective institutions, and all groups of students have had to cope with historically large debts that stay with them whether or not they finish college, get degrees, and find jobs. Middle-class demands for aid have pushed aside the priority for the poor fundamental to the modern federal role. There has been a historic reversal of the policies set in motion a half century ago as the federal government became a major force in higher education.

The major changes expanding higher education linked to civil rights came at a time of a large social movement and had long-lasting impacts but were gravely weakened in a conservative era. The year 2020 brought another social movement over race and a move to the left by the Democratic party, with sweeping promises of college aid. As the demography of the country continues to change and white young people are now the minority in both the South and the West, this may be another period in which the link between civil rights and policy for higher education once again become visible and formative. It is long overdue.

CHAPTER 2

The Polarization of Higher
Education Policy

DEONDRA ROSE AND SUZANNE METTLER

*Our society will not be great until every young mind is set free
to scan the farthest reaches of thought and imagination.*
—President Lyndon B. Johnson, 1964

WHEN PRESIDENT LYNDON B. JOHNSON delivered the commencement address at the University of Michigan in 1964, at the height of the civil rights movement, he laid out his Great Society and War on Poverty initiatives and invited the graduates and their entire generation to help realize the ambitious agenda for eradicating poverty in the United States. Johnson—a former schoolteacher—signaled his conviction that higher educational opportunity represented a necessary pillar in any assault on poverty. Echoing civil rights leaders who worked to shed light on the economic plight of the nation's most marginalized citizens, Johnson asked the graduates: "Will you join in the battle to give every citizen the full equality which God enjoins and the law requires, whatever his belief, or race, or the color of his skin? Will you join in the battle to give every citizen an escape from the crushing weight of poverty?"[1] His initiative would lead the nation in a pivotal turn toward expanding access to college to less advantaged Americans.

Higher education figured prominently in Johnson's vision for social reform, particularly as it related to achieving greater equality for low-income citizens and racial and ethnic minorities. He pushed lawmakers to create innovative new policies that succeeded for several decades in extending opportunity. The United States gained the distinction of having more young people with college degrees than any other nation in the world. More recently, however, progress slowed as policies ceased performing as effectively as in the past, and lawmakers failed to update them to adapt to changing circumstances.

The problem is not that the American public has lost faith in education policy. Americans consistently list education as a top issue priority; in 2020, 67 percent of Americans identified it as such, just behind fighting terrorism (74 percent), and on par with strengthening the economy and reducing health-care costs.[2] Rather, political changes have imperiled policy innovation and updating. Partisan polarization looms large, both among elected officials and the public. Lawmakers have found themselves increasingly at odds about how to reform policies. Among citizens, Democrats and Republicans diverge by twenty-eight points in the extent to which they prioritize education generally, and in recent years Republicans have become more skeptical about higher education.[3] Plutocracy, too, undermines policy reform as lawmakers, in an era of soaring economic inequality, cater more to the priorities of the affluent and vested interests than those of students and ordinary citizens. These developments are most detrimental to the very students whose needs were the top priority when our landmark higher education policies were created: those from less advantaged, lower-income backgrounds and racial and ethnic minorities.

PROMOTING EQUALITY THROUGH THE HIGHER EDUCATION ACT OF 1965

The nation's reckoning with the civil rights movement brought the issue of poverty and unequal opportunity to the fore. In 1959, more than one in five Americans lived in poverty (22.4 percent), and the problem was especially prominent among the nation's Black population: while 18.1 percent of white Americans lived in poverty that year, a stunning 55.1 percent of Black Americans did.[4] As Gladieux and Wolanin note, "The civil rights movement had dramatized the shameful plight of Blacks in America and the 'rediscovery' of poverty amidst unprecedented affluence sparked the national conscience."[5]

The Johnson administration turned to the task of addressing the challenge of poverty using a fusillade of social policy programs including Medicare, Medicaid, work training, urban renewal projects, and programs promoting education at all levels. Johnson's landslide victory against Barry Goldwater and Democrats' solid majorities in the House and the Senate created a political context that was hospitable to the creation of such bold innovations in social policy.[6] Recognizing the opportunity this propitious political context provided, President Johnson threw the full weight of his office behind path-breaking education programs like Head Start and the Elementary and Secondary Education Act (ESEA), which provided unprecedented support for the nation's elementary, junior high, and high schools. But Johnson wanted to promote opportunity beyond the high school level as well; as Gladieux and Wolanin note, "[a] greater responsibility was laid at the doorstep of higher education to reduce barriers of income and race."[7]

And so, in 1964, the Johnson administration presented the Higher Education Act (HEA) to Congress. Building on policy precedents that had offered financial assistance to both higher educational institutions and to individual students, the HEA offered additional loans to students, work-study funding, and the nation's first need-based grants for college students.[8] The policy benefited from forceful presidential advocacy and bipartisan support that facilitated rapid passage.[9]

The HEA was pathbreaking in that it offered substantial support for higher educational institutions themselves—particularly those offering crucial support for traditionally marginalized groups of students, such as racial and ethnic minorities. The law began, in Title I, with grants provided to colleges and universities to support urban extension programs that offered valuable services to needy communities. Next came funds for colleges to purchase library materials and, in Title II, to support training in library sciences and research. A national teacher's corps was embodied by Title V, which was sponsored by Senator Ted Kennedy (D-MA). Perhaps the most controversial aspect of the proposed legislation, it sought to generate a cadre of educators who could serve in the nation's most impoverished schools. Colleges and universities were promised grants to support classroom infrastructure in Title VI.[10]

In addition, the HEA enhanced the federal government's commitment to supporting individual college students. Title IV of the HEA, its best-known component, sustained and expanded the student financial aid that had been established under Depression-era work-study programs and the 1958 National Defense Education Act. It established the guaranteed student loan program, which permitted students to seek school loans from commercial banks with the promise that the federal government would subsidize interest during enrollment and insure against default.[11] Title IV broke new ground in offering Educational Opportunity Grants, which provided the first need-based federal grants for college students. To participate in the program, colleges and universities applied for funding, which they would allocate to students who could demonstrate substantial financial need.[12] The commitment to providing need-based financial aid to civilian students represented a significant departure from earlier programs like the G.I. Bill, which had allocated benefits on the basis of military service.[13] Moreover, the creation of the HEA appeared to resolve the long-standing debate over the propriety of providing student aid without regard to merit.[14] In line with the president's objective of expanding educational opportunity to the most marginalized citizens, this deemphasis on merit signaled lawmakers' commitment to democratizing higher educational access.

Title III of the Higher Education Act served as a testament to lawmakers' focus on promoting civil rights through higher education. Central to their strategy for doing so was providing support to higher educational institutions that had traditionally supported low-income and minority students: Historically Black Colleges and Universities (HBCUs) and community colleges.[15] HBCUs, which emerged as a result of segregation in US educational institutions dating back to the early nineteenth century, struggled under the weight of bearing the primary responsibility for educating Black Americans while being denied adequate support from federal and state governments. Community colleges had seen dramatic growth in enrollments during the postwar era, and by the end of the 1960s, they educated nearly a third of American undergraduate students.[16]

Originally intended to target support to HBCUs, Title III provided $30 million to support "developing institutions."[17] The struggles of predominantly Black colleges had emerged during Rep. Edith Green's 1964 subcommittee hearings on education, and she encouraged US Commissioner of Education, Francis Keppel, to provide them with assistance. Members of the 1964 Legislative Task Force on Education—which included Keppel—invoked the term *developing institutions* as "a euphemism for weak black colleges."[18] Lawmakers adopted this broader terminology, which allowed them to also provide support under this funding mechanism for small colleges that faced chronic financial struggles. Title III's capacity to target support to HBCUs was weakened, however, by the legislation's broad language, which expanded the number of institutions that would qualify for the title's funding.[19]

Nonetheless, the Higher Education Act's statutory construction signaled federal lawmakers' commitment to mitigating inequality and promoting civil rights by providing access to postsecondary education.

A year after its passage, the federal government spent a full $3.5 billion on higher education, compared to only $655 million ten years earlier.[20] By 1970, the HEA provided millions of grants, loans, and interest subsidies that reached a full quarter of the nation's postsecondary students.[21] This substantial federal support for college students contributed to a precipitous increase in the number of students enrolled in American colleges and universities. By 1974, 8.8 million students were attending these institutions, up from 2.5 million in 1955. This increase was particularly pronounced among African Americans, whose enrollment soared from 95,000 in 1955 to 814,000 in 1974.[22]

The HEA quickly became recognized as a landmark law, remaining ever since the foundation of federal efforts to influence higher education. Notably, it had been enacted in an era when a Democratic president sat in the White House, large Democratic majorities dominated both chambers of Congress, and members of both parties supported expanding opportunity through higher education. In the House, it was enacted by a vote of 313 in favor to 63 opposed, with only 41 out of 75 Republicans opposed and 22 out of 238 Democrats opposed.[23] As we will see, the contemporary period features very different politics, and the impact on policy has been vast.

DECAY, DRIFT, AND DERAILMENT

The Higher Education Act was established with the assumption that it would be maintained and updated regularly, and accordingly, for the first three decades of its existence, lawmakers reauthorized it every four to six years. These occasions gave lawmakers the opportunity to consider the program's performance in light of its original objective of mitigating inequality by expanding access to higher education, and to make modifications and adjustments so that it could continue to achieve its goals amidst changing circumstances.[24]

Some reauthorizations featured major amendments that dramatically modified the legislation, and that was the case for the HEA in 1972. The milestone reauthorization that year saw the continuation of the programs that were included in the 1965 legislation, as well as the momentous addition of the new Basic Educational Opportunity Grants, which were renamed Pell Grants in 1980 for Senator Claiborne Pell, who initiated the idea for them. This program ensured grants to low-income students, and they quickly became the primary vehicle for opportunity in higher education. Lawmakers gave responsibility for administering the grants to the federal government, rather than campus aid administrators. The reauthorized legislation also included the State Student Incentive Grant Program, which provided states with federal funding to support their efforts to provide their own student aid programs. The 1972 reauthorization also saw the creation of the Student Loan Marketing Association (also known as Sallie Mae), a government-sponsored private corporation to administer federal student loans;[25] this plan provided an alternative to the Republican-supported tuition tax credits, and it managed to win bipartisan support. The *Washington Post* heralded the 1972 amendments as a "true breakthrough" that "would go a long ways toward equalizing opportunity."[26] Indeed, on final passage, there was no difference in the degree of Democratic and Republican support for the amendments.

Today the HEA remains in place, but increases in college graduation rates in the United States have slowed, particularly for Americans in the bottom three-quarters of the income distribution. Most reauthorizations since 1972 have involved more modest changes, but nonetheless such routine updating continued on a regular basis until 1998, after which higher education policymaking grew considerably more fraught. Only one reauthorization has occurred since then, in 2008, and another has been overdue since 2013.

On occasion, lawmakers update parts of laws outside of reauthorizations, as occurred in 2010 when Congress enacted a student aid bill that reformed Title IV of the HEA and was signed into law by President Barack Obama. The 111th Congress, with the exception of 1993–95, the only time with Democratic majorities in both chambers and a Democratic president in the White House since the Carter administration, was well poised to reform student aid. The student aid bill achieved major goals that reformers had pursued for years. First, it terminated bank-based student loans, cutting out the "middle man" that had been driving the policy for years and was profiting at the expense of students and taxpayers, and replacing it with direct student loans. Second, the bill updated Pell Grants, increasing rates. Unfortunately, the American Graduation Initiative—which would have devoted considerable funds to community colleges—was axed at the eleventh hour, as was a plan to make Pell Grants an entitlement. While the changes in the 2010 bill nonetheless helped a great deal, more is needed for the HEA to continue to achieve the major purpose for which it was established, to mitigate inequality and provide opportunity.

Contemporary reformers like to envision bold new plans, rooted in slogans like "free college," but in fact any changes must reckon with what already exists. Today, the HEA can be considered part of the "policyscape," the vast network of existing policies in numerous areas that were created earlier, typically in the mid-twentieth century, and which persist and continue to shape American social, political, and economic life. The HEA, like other such policies, involves major commitments of government resources, and it influences the behavior of both institutions (in this case colleges and universities) and ordinary Americans (as demonstrated by Americans' FAFSA applications, for example).

Yet in the absence of more regular and comprehensive maintenance and updating, such policies can fail to function as intended and cease to yield the outcomes they once did, and the Higher Education Act has fallen subject to such decay and derailment. This pattern is not particular to the higher education domain; rather, it has become a regular feature of numerous areas ranging from elementary and secondary education to the environment, immigration, social policy for the poor, and numerous others. Only a few policy domains—such as military and antiterrorism policy—continue to be reauthorized or somehow updated regularly.[27]

Public policies, if left unattended or insufficiently maintained, can cease to generate the outcomes for which they were intended, a circumstance known as policy "drift."[28] This can occur because the policies themselves fall into disrepair or because circumstances change around them, affecting their ability to function well. Three types of problems generated by poorly maintained policies have affected the HEA.

First, *policy design effects* can make policies vulnerable to falling into disrepair. Pell Grants have been subject to such deterioration because, unlike Social Security, they lack automatic cost-of-living adjustments, and they are not indexed to inflation, not to mention to the cost of tuition, which has increased far more quickly. This means that Pell Grants necessarily diminish in their real value or purchasing power unless lawmakers update them on an annual basis, and that requires considerable political effort and cooperation through multiple stages of the budget process. Since such updates have been rare, Pell Grants have fallen in value from covering 80 percent of the cost of tuition, room and board, and fees at a public four-year college in the 1970s to 28 percent in 2019–20.[29] Because Pell Grants cover so much less, students have turned to borrowing more; the amount of debt the average student has taken on to graduate from a four-year public university has grown from $11,800 in 2002–03 to $15,400 in 2017–18, in 2018 dollars.[30]

Second, policies can become subject to *unintended consequences*, as vested interests take advantage of the resources policies provide and transform them into business opportunities for themselves more than the intended beneficiaries. For decades, banks benefited from student loan policies until the 2010 reforms terminated bank-based lending. An enduring problem, however, emanates from for-profit colleges, which enroll only 7 percent of undergraduate students but use a disproportionate share of student aid dollars (e.g., 13 percent of all Pell Grant funds and 14 percent of unsubsidized federal loans). Students who attend these schools have the most difficult time later on repaying what they borrowed to attend:

among borrowers who graduated, only 52 percent had entered repayment in 2011–12, and among noncompleters, only 34 percent had done so (compared to 74 percent and 46 percent, respectively, of students at public two-year colleges).[31] Students at for-profits took on much more debt, furthermore: 32 percent of those who graduated in 2015–16 with bachelor's degrees had $50,000 or more in debt compared to just 7 percent of such students at public four-year colleges and 12 percent at four-year private nonprofit colleges.[32] The for-profit schools target especially low-income students, first-generation students, and students of color—the very students whom Johnson particularly had in mind in promoting the Higher Education Act: Black and Latino students make up less than one-third of all college students, but more than half of all enrolled in for-profit colleges. Unfortunately, they are often left worse off after attending such schools than if they had never aspired to attend advanced education, dropping out at particularly high rates and more likely to take on debt that they are unable to pay off.[33] Meanwhile, the shareholders of these colleges, the largest of which are publicly traded on Wall Street, make handsome profits.

During the Obama administration, the Department of Education (ED) engaged in rulemaking aimed at regulating these schools, making it more difficult for the worst actors among them to stay in business. During the Trump administration, by contrast, the ED repealed these rules, known as "Gainful Employment," once again giving free rein to these schools that often yield disastrous consequences for the most disadvantaged students.[34]

Third, *lateral effects* occur when policy developments in other areas make another policy function differently than intended, and that has occurred to the HEA as state governments have pulled back on their support for public universities and colleges, causing tuition to increase. Spending on higher education represents the largest discretionary item in most state budgets. States have faced rising costs since the 1990s in K–12 education spending, incarceration, and Medicaid. They have made up the difference by relying on students themselves and their families to pay a larger share of the costs of higher education, as well as saving costs through measures that adversely affect quality, such as increasing class sizes and relying on more online education. The cost of tuition, fees, and room and board at the average four-year public university has increased from $12,440 in 1999–2000 to $21,950 in 2019–20, in 2019 dollars.[35] These changes, in combination, hurt less-advantaged students the most, reducing their chances of graduating.

HOW POLITICS AFFECTS HIGHER EDUCATION POLICY

In higher education policy, just like in many other domestic policy areas, new policy innovation has become very rare, and policy maintenance has grown increasingly difficult and infrequent as well. Broad developments in American politics over the past thirty years explain these changes, and two major trends figure prominently: polarization and plutocracy.

Polarization in the United States has grown as the two political parties have become transformed over time. Both parties in Congress have become more homogenous ideologically, as party-line voting has become more common and crossing party lines rarer. In addition, partisans now exercise greater "teamsmanship," reflecting the fact that the two parties have grown more competitive, each standing a chance to win control of each chamber in most elections, and fighting tooth and nail to do so.[36] In the mid-twentieth century, Democrats dominated Congress most of the time. Further, both parties contained some liberals and some conservatives: the Republican Party combined business-minded fiscal conservatives and social liberals, while the Democratic Party included both urban, ethnic voters in the North and southern Democrats, who opposed civil rights. After the enactment of civil rights legislation, conservatives gradually left the Democrats and moved to the Republican Party. By the 1970s, the Republican Party embraced social conservatism, and social liberals shifted away from it.

In Congress, polarization not only stymies the development of new legislation; it also thwarts the updating of existing laws, owing to several related developments. Party leaders have altered institutional arrangements in ways that deter policymaking and promote public relations instead. They seek to accentuate differences in party positions on issues rather than to promote the bipartisanship, negotiation, and compromise required for laws to be enacted.[37] These patterns emerged beginning in the late 1970s, promoted by House freshman Newt Gingrich, and they have been on the rise particularly since he became Speaker in 1994, pushing the GOP to focus more on distinguishing itself from Democrats than engaging in policymaking. After the election of President Barack Obama in 2008, conservatives mobilized through the Tea Party and won back Congress in the 2010 election, with several of the few remaining moderate Republicans ousted by hard-liners. Leaders of the Freedom Caucus subsequently encouraged members to be uncompromising.[38]

Although during the 1980s and 1990s the higher education committees still exhibited more bipartisanship than several other committees, since then they have grown more fractious as well. The major landmark higher education laws were each created during the low-polarization years of the mid-twentieth century, from the G.I. Bill in 1944 to the National Defense Education Act in 1958, the Higher Education Act, and the establishment of Pell Grants in 1972, and each received wide bipartisan support on final passage. More recent reauthorizations of the HEA and the passage of other student aid bills, by contrast, have occurred mostly along party lines, to the extent they have happened at all. Even amendments to higher education laws now exhibit much greater partisan gaps since 1995, in both chambers, than they did previously.[39]

The other major trend in American politics that has deterred policy maintenance to restore the original goals of the HEA can be termed plutocracy. As economic inequality has grown—and political competition has increased—the cost of congressional campaigns has increased dramatically, and spending on lobbying has soared as well.[40] Industries seeking to influence policies are among the big spenders, and as lawmakers seek to be responsive to them, this can harm responsiveness to the general public as well. Such dynamics explain why, in some instances, even in an era of high polarization, lawmakers do share unity across party lines on issues that matter to vested interests. In the case of the for-profit colleges, although the Senate has grown increasingly polarized on the issue over time, House Democrats and Republicans have both worked to protect the industry.

CONCLUSION

The Higher Education Act of 1965 represents one of the most consequential legislative accomplishments of the civil rights era. Passed with the purpose of promoting equal opportunity by expanding access to higher education, the landmark policy offered valuable support to colleges and universities and to individual students. In doing so, it enhanced the federal government's commitment to higher education and paved the way for millions of students—including racial and ethnic minorities who have been traditionally underrepresented in the nation's colleges and universities— to pursue college degrees and the socioeconomic benefits that typically accompany them.

While the HEA successfully expanded support for college students and higher educational institutions, the policy no longer represents the powerful driver of educational opportunity and socioeconomic mobility that it once did. Without adjustments for cost-of-living increases, tuition increases, or inflation, the HEA's power to help beneficiaries meet the cost of college is significantly weakened. For-profit colleges have seized the opportunities provided by the law to maximize profits, while the federal government has lacked a strong and consistent response to ensure that students can access quality education that leads to gainful employment, enabling them to repay what they borrow to attend college. Moreover, the HEA's capacity to mitigate inequality by expanding higher educational opportunity is also limited by political factors. The decline of state funding for public colleges and universities has made more students reliant on securing financial aid from student loans. Increasing polarization in Congress and the resulting gridlock have precluded reauthorization, which would give lawmakers an opportunity to perform maintenance on the HEA. Finally, the decay, drift, and derailment of the HEA also reflect the political clout of monied industries that have a stake in maintaining the status quo and that actively lobby lawmakers to preserve it.

These forces have contributed to the delay in the HEA's reauthorization since 2013. Until enough support exists in Congress to strengthen the Higher Education Act, lawmakers will likely delay creating a comprehensive reauthorization, opting instead to engage in piecemeal efforts to satisfy some of its functions, such as by providing resources to Historically Black Colleges and Universities and community colleges. In the meantime, the policy will continue to underperform in its mission of aiding the low-income and minority student populations that it was created to help.

CHAPTER 3

Asian Americans and Race-Conscious Admissions

Understanding the Conservative Opposition's Strategy of Misinformation, Intimidation, and Racial Division

OIYAN POON AND LILIANA M. GARCES[1]

AS OUR NATION becomes more politically polarized, colleges and universities find themselves in the middle of increasingly tenuous debates about affirmative action in college admissions. Between 2010 and 2020 alone, while the US Supreme Court was considering the constitutionality of race-conscious policies in postsecondary admissions, a new wave of attacks in the conservative agenda to dismantle affirmative action emerged.[2] First, in 2014, a long-time opponent of affirmative action, Edward Blum, created the organization Students for Fair Admissions (SFFA) to recruit plaintiffs, particularly Chinese American students, to initiate new lawsuits that are currently making their way through the lower federal courts. Second, the Office for Civil Rights division of the Trump administration's US Department of Justice (DOJ) redirected agency resources to investigate claims of discrimination at institutions employing race-conscious admissions policies.[3] In one case, the DOJ reopened the investigation of a complaint filed by a Chinese American student against Harvard University, which the US Department of Education (ED) had previously evaluated and dismissed in 2015 under the Obama administration. In 2018, the Departments of Justice and Education rescinded prior guidance on race-conscious admissions that had been issued during the Obama administration.[4] These changes by the Trump administration discourage the use of constitutionally permissible race-conscious policies in postsecondary admissions and seek to intimidate or threaten colleges and universities (that remain committed to using them) with the possibility of DOJ investigations.

In many respects, these attacks on race-conscious policies are not new. They build on a history of challenges against affirmative action that have played out in legal and policy arenas for over half a century. In the federal court system, for example, past challenges have culminated in five separate US Supreme Court decisions: Regents of the University of California v. Bakke (1978), Grutter v. Bollinger (2003), Gratz v. Bollinger (2003), Fisher v. University of Texas I (2013), and Fisher v. University of Texas II (2016). In each case, the US Supreme Court has preserved the constitutionality of the policy. However, starting with the 1978 Bakke case, each ruling has also severely limited its practice. When not successful in the courts, opponents have turned to the court of public opinion and the political arena, funding campaigns to ban the policy at public postsecondary institutions via statewide ballot initiatives and other laws or measures. These laws are now in place in eight states, including California (1996), Washington (1998), Florida (1999), Michigan (2006), Nebraska (2008), Arizona (2010), New Hampshire (2011), and Oklahoma (2012).[5] Challenges have also involved the Department of Justice and Department of Education, which investigate complaints of discrimination from individuals against institutions.

What is different about the most recent wave of coordinated attacks is that affirmative action opponents are exploiting a new generation of conservative racial political activism among Chinese American immigrants who oppose the policy, as well as changes to sectors of the political system under the Trump administration, such as the Departments of Justice and Education, and the US Supreme Court. Continuing a prior line of attack that began in the 1980s, affirmative action opponents are manipulatively using the argument of discrimination against Asian Americans to condemn the policy, seeking to split cross-racial coalitions that support the policy.[6] This time they are capitalizing on a unique and recent rise of Chinese American immigrant opposition to affirmative action, which can be explained by a culture shift connected to changes in US immigration policies that privilege highly educated and professional class immigrants, limited social interactions with other people of color including other Asian Americans across class and ethnic differences, and misinformation on affirmative action circulated via the social media platform WeChat. The positioning of Chinese Americans, an ethnic minority group, as plaintiffs against race-conscious admissions in new legal cases is part of a broader and strategic political effort. In a 2015 speech, Edward Blum stated that he "needed Asian plaintiffs" to continue his legal campaign against affirmative action.[7] In this way, anti–affirmative action activists, funded by conservative political donors, are leveraging federal and state courts and other parts of government, such as the Department of Justice, that are hostile toward affirmative action policies under the Trump administration.

Although most media accounts characterize the Asian American plaintiffs involved in the lawsuit and the Office for Civil Rights complaint against Harvard as representative of Asian Americans in general, the best evidence shows that the majority of Asian Americans support affirmative action.[8] For these reasons, the public should not be distracted by a highly misleading characterization of the "Asian American position" regarding race-conscious admissions.[9] There is no singular Asian American position.[10]

Most Asian Americans across ethnicity have long supported affirmative action policies, as demonstrated by survey research on law students' opinions of the policy; *amicus curiae* ("friend of the court") briefs submitted in favor of the policy in the *Bakke*, *Grutter* and *Gratz*, and *Fisher* cases; voting data; college student views; and analysis of opinion polling data.[11] At the same time, others suggest a more divided Asian American opinion on the matter.[12] And while some Chinese Americans have opposed affirmative action in *amicus* briefs starting with the 2003 *Grutter* and *Gratz* cases, Chinese American opposition remains a relatively small minority voice among the larger Asian American population.[13] However, anti–affirmative action activism led by Chinese Americans, a vocal and well-resourced segment of the population, can create a public spectacle garnering mainstream media attention, and a dangerously outsized influence on public debates over affirmative action.

In this chapter, we summarize the battle over affirmative action in the legal and policy arenas from the 1960s to the present. We draw from research addressing the relationship between Asian Americans and race-conscious admissions policies to present evidence of sustained overall Asian American support for the policy despite increased Chinese American opposition. We conclude by looking ahead, considering strategies within and outside the legal arena to address this renewed wave of attacks on affirmative action, or race-conscious admissions in postsecondary education, more specifically.

BATTLE OVER AFFIRMATIVE ACTION IN THE LEGAL AND PUBLIC POLICY ARENAS

1960s: Early Stages of Affirmative Action

The first time the term *affirmative action* explicitly appeared in public policy is traced back to President John F. Kennedy's 1961 executive order requiring that federally funded programs take "affirmative action" to ensure hiring and employment practices free of racial bias (Exec. Order 1961).[14] The efforts of the civil rights movement culminated in the Civil Rights Act of 1964 and various executive orders for affirmative action. The explicit articulation of affirmative action during this time started from a perspective of nondiscrimination (i.e., the obligation to avoid discrimination) that then developed within the employment context, starting in early 1970s, into an *affirmative* duty to rectify past discrimination (i.e., compensatory treatment).[15] These early affirmative action efforts were grounded in the need to address racial inequities created by racial segregation policies and other exclusionary laws. By the late 1960s and early 1970s, federal courts were authorized to enforce comprehensive desegregation plans across the country, essentially ordering that race be considered in educational policies and practices to remedy the effects of racial segregation.[16] Under Title VI, the federal government required nineteen states, which had enforced segregation by law, to submit desegregation plans.

When not required to adopt such plans by legal mandate, *voluntary* race-based affirmative action policies in postsecondary education emerged among some colleges and universities acting on a moral imperative to address centuries of racial oppression.[17] At the most selective institutions, these *voluntarily adopted* policies started in the early 1960s, inspired by the civil rights movement. Others joined years later, in response to direct action campaigns by Black college students and their allies.[18] The resulting policies and practices included aggressive outreach to and recruitment of Black students and the consideration of their race as a favorable and "matter of fact" factor in admissions; Asian Americans and other people of color were also included in these affirmative action programs.[19]

1970s: Regents of University of California v. Bakke

Soon after voluntary affirmative action policies were established, opponents launched legal challenges. Litigation in this area culminated in 1978 with the *Regents of the University of California v. Bakke* decision. This ruling changed affirmative action policy from one that could address ongoing consequences of decades of racial oppression to a policy that allows admissions offices to consider all aspects of an individual's identity, including their racial or ethnic background, for the purpose of furthering the educational benefits of diversity.[20] The case involved a challenge to the University of California–Davis, School of Medicine's consideration of race in its admissions decisions. The school reserved sixteen of one hundred places for qualified disadvantaged minority ("Black," "Asian," "Indian," or "Chicanos") students. In contrast to other institutions with a history of legally enforced segregation, this medical school had adopted its set-aside policy to remedy inequities and address the effects of societal discrimination.

Allan Bakke, a white applicant who had been denied admission to the medical school twice and turned down by all twelve medical schools to which he applied, challenged the policy on the grounds that it violated the Equal Protection Clause of the Fourteenth Amendment. The school defended the policy on the grounds that it was needed to (1) address the effects of past discriminatory practices and existing racial and ethnic inequities in higher education; (2) improve the delivery of health-care services by increasing the number of physicians who would practice in underserved communities; (3) reduce the dearth of traditionally disfavored minorities in medical school and in the medical profession; and (4) obtain the educational benefits that flow from having an ethnically diverse student body.

In six separate opinions with no clear majority and a controlling opinion by Justice Lewis F. Powell Jr., the Court applied *strict scrutiny*, a legal test that had not previously been applied to affirmative action policies in higher education.[21] This test requires that an institution have a compelling interest in the policy and that the policy be implemented in a way that is "narrowly tailored" to that interest.[22] By applying the strict scrutiny test, the Court ultimately equated efforts to promote access to education for racial minorities with discriminatory practices against whites, marking an important shift in judicial decision-making bearing consequences for admissions practices and the framing of affirmative action policies in the public arena that persist today.[23] The decision also rejected all but the last (i.e., the educational benefits of diversity) of the university's justifications for a compelling interest. No longer allowed to expressly consider the effects of societal discrimination or racial inequities to justify voluntarily adopted race-conscious policies, institutions that sought to expand access for underrepresented populations had to focus their efforts on a broader notion of diversity for educational benefits, of which race could be only one of many factors considered.

1980s–1990s: Asian Americans, Claims of Discrimination, and Bans on Affirmative Action

Following the *Bakke* decision, a complicated connection between affirmative action and Asian Americans began to develop in the 1980s. Between 1983 and 1986, Asian American students accused high-profile selective institutions, including Brown, Harvard, Princeton, Stanford, Yale, the University of California–Berkeley (UC Berkeley), and the University of California–Los Angeles (UCLA), of discriminating against them in favor of white applicants.[24] At the federal level, the DOJ and ED conducted investigations of these claims of discrimination against Asian Americans at Harvard, UC Berkeley, and UCLA.[25] In 1990, after two years of investigation, Harvard was exonerated because discrepancies in admission rates could be attributed to differences in legacy and other special admissions considerations. UCLA was ordered to admit certain mathematics graduate students who had previously been denied admission. UC Berkeley voluntarily apologized for restricting the admission of Asian Americans in favor of white applicants.[26] These claims of discrimination against Asian Americans were based on allegations that universities maintained "ceilings" or "quotas" against Asian Americans—a practice that is different from affirmative action. As Kang explained, they involved "negative action," a phenomenon where Asian American applicants are unfavorably treated in the admissions process in comparison to white applicants who are equally qualified.[27] In other words, negative action happens when an Asian American applicant would have been admitted had the individual been a white applicant.

However, conservative and neoconservative groups misleadingly framed "negative action" against Asian Americans to be the same as

"affirmative action" and as the "logical and inevitable outcome of preferences for 'other' minorities."[28] In this way, white conservative politicians and pundits, like Congressman Dana Rohrabacher and George Will,
manipulated the discourse, characterizing Asian Americans as harmed by
"unfair racial preferences" for Black and Latinx students.[29] This deceptive
discourse co-opted Asian American grievances over exclusionary admissions practices, and aligned them with the politics of white resentment
shown to underlie white conservative attacks on affirmative action.[30]
This conservative attack essentially views affirmative action policies as a
"theft"—by Black and Latinx students—of opportunities that belong to
whites.[31] By using Asian Americans to challenge affirmative action (i.e.,
SFFA v. Harvard; OCR investigation), opponents cast Asian Americans as
a racial minority in opposition to these policies, while simultaneously
obscuring white interests to maintain a white monopoly on access to
opportunities.[32] Contrary to how anti–affirmative action interests framed
their complaints, Asian Americans in this case were not claiming that
affirmative action was anti-Asian.

Relatedly, the mainstream media at the time (and today, as we discuss later) perpetuated misinformation about affirmative action and Asian
Americans by reporting on false claims of affirmative action as anti-Asian.
Such reporting, disconnected from research, evidence, and historical context, racially positions Asian Americans in dangerous opposition to other
people of color, using racial stereotypes of high achievement among Asian
Americans, a racial minority, to dismiss protests against racism, a problem
that Asian Americans also experience.[33] This approach allows predominantly white-led anti–affirmative action campaigns to deflect accusations
of their campaigns as racist by claiming concern for Asian Americans, a
racialized minority group.[34] Although anti-Asian American discrimination is a legitimate concern given long historical evidence[35] and findings
of investigations in the 1980s, such racist practices are distinctly different
from affirmative action policies that advance racial equity.[36] In effect, false
assertions of affirmative action as harmful to Asian Americans cynically

use a racialized argument to further roll back affirmative action, a policy that advances racial equity and recognizes diverse student talents.[37]

Around the same time, in the early to mid-1990s, Ward Connerly and like-minded conservative activists and groups organized and funded a number of statewide initiatives to ban affirmative action. The first successful initiative passed in California (Proposition 209) in 1996, with Washington (Initiative 200) following in 1998. Currently, eight states have passed laws that prohibit affirmative action at public institutions. Of these, six (Arizona, California, Michigan, Nebraska, Oklahoma, and Washington) implemented the bans through voter-approved initiatives or referenda, and two banned the practice by executive decision (Florida) and legislative vote (New Hampshire).[38] The language of these ballot measures is nearly identical, asserting a general prohibition of discriminatory or "preferential" treatment by the state on the basis of race, sex, color, ethnicity, or national origin in the operation of public employment, public education, and public contracting.[39] Public institutions affected by the proposal include state and local governments, public colleges and universities, community colleges, and school districts. Both bans in California (Proposition 209) and Michigan (Proposal 2) were challenged in federal court as unconstitutional. The challenge to the ban in Michigan ultimately reached the Supreme Court, which reversed the sixth circuit to uphold its constitutionality.[40] The bans on affirmative action have led to substantial drops in the racial diversity of student bodies at public selective undergraduate institutions, in graduate fields of study, and in law and medical schools.[41] The negative consequences also extend beyond admissions, undermining efforts necessary to support the educational experiences of students already enrolled.[42]

In 2020, as the Black Lives Matter movement gained momentum with the tragic police murders of George Floyd and Breonna Taylor, among many other Black people, civil rights organizations launched a campaign to repeal California's ban on affirmative action. The ballot measure—Proposition 16—was rejected by voters during the November 2020 election, with 56 percent of voters electing to maintain the state ban. Some political analysts attribute California's failure to overturn the affirmative action ban to the confusion of Proposition 16's language and the original language of Proposition 209, which framed policies for racial and gender equity as discriminatory.[43]

Late 1990s–2016: Grutter, Gratz, and Fisher Cases

Other well-financed and strategic efforts by conservative groups to end affirmative action via the courts in the mid-1990s ultimately culminated in two separate US Supreme Court decisions in 2003, Grutter v. Bollinger and Gratz v. Bollinger.[44] The Center for Individual Rights initiated and recruited plaintiffs for both cases.[45] In 1997, Barbara Grutter sued the University of Michigan Law School and claimed that the school's race-conscious admissions policy was unconstitutional.[46] A white woman, Grutter argued that the race-conscious admissions policy—which had been modeled after the type Justice Powell had endorsed in Bakke—violated the Equal Protection Clause of the Fourteenth Amendment because a higher percentage of minority applicants were admitted than white applicants with similar test scores. The law school argued that the policy was needed to further a compelling interest in student diversity, which required the enrollment of a "critical mass" of students of color (i.e., more than a token number) to help diminish the impact of stereotypes and racial marginalization. Further, the school argued the admissions process met the narrow tailoring requirements of strict scrutiny because it was based on individualized consideration of every applicant.

The Gratz case involved another white woman, Jennifer Gratz, who had been denied admission to the University of Michigan's undergraduate College of Literature, Science, and the Arts. With support from the Center for Individual Rights, she filed a separate lawsuit in 1997 to challenge the undergraduate admissions policy, which awarded extra points to some candidates on the basis of their race. In a five-to-four majority opinion authored by Justice Sandra Day O'Connor, the Court in Grutter upheld the law school's policy as constitutional, concluding that the law school had a compelling interest in student diversity and that the policy satisfied each of the requirements of "narrow tailoring." The Court issued a separate decision in *Gratz*, striking down the undergraduate admissions policy on the grounds that the policy's point system was not flexible enough to comply with the individualized consideration outlined in *Bakke*.

Having lost *Grutter*, the conservative attack on the policy continued in the legal arena, this time in a case orchestrated by Edward Blum, who recruited Abigail Fisher to initiate a lawsuit against the University of Texas at Austin (UT Austin) in 2008.[47] At the time, the composition of the Court had become favorable to a conservative attack on affirmative action, as Justice Samuel Alito had replaced Justice O'Connor since the *Grutter* case.[48] Fisher challenged the university's race-conscious policy and claimed that it did not follow the parameters set forth by *Grutter*. In 2005, the university had revised its holistic admissions policy to consider race as one among many factors in admissions, after *Grutter* overruled *Hopwood*, a 1996 Fifth Circuit decision that had prevented the university from considering race.[49] Fisher argued that the university had reached an adequate level of racial and ethnic diversity through the Texas Top Ten Percent Plan (which Texas passed after *Hopwood*), so that the consideration of race as a factor in admissions decisions was not necessary and thereby unconstitutional. The university argued that it needed the race-conscious policy so that it could attain a more racially and ethnically diverse student body than it had been able to achieve under the Top Ten Percent Plan.

In its review of the case, which it heard twice, the Court issued two separate decisions, one in 2013 (Fisher I) and another in 2016 (Fisher II).[50] In its 2013 decision, the Court sent the case back to the Fifth Circuit for further review, leaving in place the core principles that allowed for race-conscious policies. Few observers expected the seven-to-one ruling given the composition of the Court at the time. In its 2013 ruling, the Court clarified that the lower court had to conduct its independent determination of whether the race-conscious policy was narrowly tailored to obtain the educational benefits of a diverse student body. The Court's decision also clarified the importance of considering workable "race-neutral" alternatives, stating that if a nonracial approach could promote diversity "about as well and at tolerable administrative expense," then the university could not consider race directly.[51] After reconsidering the case based on the Court's request, the Fifth Circuit in July 2014 concluded that the university's admissions policy met the Court's requirements, as clarified in *Grutter*.

Fisher then appealed, arguing that the Fifth Circuit still had not applied the Court's requirements in past cases correctly. In 2015, the Court agreed to hear the case for a second time, a rare move reflecting the changed composition of the Court, with the four votes required to grant the petition to hear the case (i.e., petition for *certiorari*). Part of the determination concerned whether the university would be allowed to complement the percent plan with a race-conscious holistic review process or whether the percent plan was deemed sufficient. In yet another victory for the university in 2016, the Court's four-to-three opinion authored by Justice Anthony Kennedy affirmed the Fifth Circuit's ruling, upholding the constitutionality of the university's race-conscious admissions policy.[52]

CURRENT CHALLENGES, NEW PLAINTIFFS

In July 2014, when the Fifth Circuit ruled for a second time (after a remand from the Supreme Court) that the UT Austin's race-conscious admissions policy was constitutional, Edward Blum created an organization called Students for Fair Admissions (SFFA) and began intentionally recruiting Asian Americans to serve as plaintiffs in future legal challenges. As he shared in public remarks at a Chinese American community event in Houston in 2015, he "needed Asian plaintiffs" to continue his legal attacks on affirmative action.[53]

In November 2014, while the Supreme Court was considering whether to hear the *Fisher* case a second time, SFFA filed lawsuits against

Harvard University and the University of North Carolina–Chapel Hill.[54] SFFA had successfully recruited plaintiffs via their websites.[55] Unlike prior challenges that have involved public colleges or universities and the Equal Protection Clause (EPC) of the Fourteenth Amendment to the US Constitution, these lawsuits are based on Title VI of the Civil Rights Act of 1964.[56]

In the complaint against Harvard, SFFA lists anonymous Asian Americans as plaintiffs and advances many of the same arguments asserted in prior cases. They claimed that the university intentionally discriminates against Asian Americans and that its race-conscious policies constitute racial quotas. The basic thrust of the challenges against both institutions is that the race-conscious admissions policies do not satisfy strict scrutiny and, as argued in past cases like *Grutter* and *Fisher*, that *Bakke* should be overruled. Underlying the arguments in the cases is an overall assumption that standardized test scores and metrics should be privileged in admissions above all other characteristics, an approach that the Court has rejected since *Bakke*.[57] Indeed, as Justice Kennedy stated in *Fisher II* (2016), in the context of discussing class rank under the Top Ten Percent Plan, "privileging one characteristic over another does not lead to a diverse student body."[58] In September 2019, the trial court in the Harvard case rejected SFFA's allegations of discrimination against Asian Americans, finding that Harvard's race-conscious admissions policy met constitutional requirements. SFFA thereafter appealed. In November 2020, the US Court of Appeals for the First Circuit upheld the legality of Harvard's race-conscious holistic admissions policy, affirming the lower court's ruling that there was a lack of evidence to support SFFA's claims of anti-Asian discrimination.[59] Court observers anticipate SFFA will petition the US Supreme Court for review. Since the Court issued its decision in *Fisher* in 2016, the ideological balance on the Court has increased its conservative representation with two justices appointed by President Donald Trump: Justice Brett Kavanaugh, who replaced Justice Kennedy following his retirement, and Justice Amy Coney Barrett, who replaced Justice Ruth Bader Ginsburg after her passing. If the Court agrees to hear the case, which requires only four votes from the nine Supreme Court Justices, it could signal that the Court, with its changed composition, may want to overrule decades of established precedent, with a host of negative consequences for established practice.

In a parallel effort to these lawsuits, in May 2015, the Asian American Coalition for Education (AACE), an organization founded by Yukong Zhao in 2015, lodged a complaint against Harvard University with the Department of Education and the Department of Justice. AACE's complaint against Harvard was submitted on behalf of Zhao's son Hubert, and includes allegations of discrimination against him and other Asian American students.[60] In summer 2015, the Department of Education evaluated and dismissed the complaint.[61] To date, the ED complaint remains closed. However, in late 2017, the Department of Justice under President Trump reopened the investigation against Harvard. AACE's website attributes this outcome to its advocacy efforts.[62]

Moreover, in July 2018, the Departments of Justice and Education rescinded Obama era guidance documents on race-conscious admissions, which clarified the implications of Supreme Court cases like *Grutter* and *Fisher* for higher education practitioners and administrators, outlining the legal framework and actions institutions could take to achieve diversity and advance their educational mission.[63] This recission does not change the law under *Fisher* and other Supreme Court precedent, which uphold the constitutionality of considering race as one factor in admissions. However, it did discourage its use by replacing the guidance with a former version, issued during the George W. Bush administration, encouraging the implementation of so-called race-neutral approaches for achieving diversity. Additionally, the Trump administration directed resources to investigate claims of discrimination at institutions that employ race-conscious admissions policies.[64] In September 2018, the DOJ announced that it was reopening an investigation of Yale's admissions practices.[65] In 2020, after his unsuccessful attempt to challenge the constitutionality of UT Austin's race-conscious admission policy in *Fisher*, Ed Blum and SFFA filed two new lawsuits against the university, first in state court and then again in federal court.[66]

The pending cases in federal court—combined with resources and actions from the DOJ under President Trump to reopen complaints against Harvard and Yale and rescind guidance on race-conscious admission— comprise a coordinated campaign of legal intimidation that can have a chilling effect on institutions. While these private universities, and other public institutions, like UNC–Chapel Hill and UT Austin, have some of the largest endowments in the country positioning them to defend themselves against lawsuits, it is possible that institutions lacking the financial resources to defend against lawsuits may change admissions policies and practices in order to avoid potential legal threats. For example, the College of Charleston ended its practices of race-conscious affirmative action in 2018 without publicly reporting this policy change.[67] A 2014 survey of 338 institutions that collectively enrolled 2.7 million students showed that 27 percent and 34 percent of public and private participating institutions, respectively, considered race as one among many factors in admission.[68] Of the institutions that participated in the survey and accepted 40 percent or less of applicants, 60 percent reported considering race as one among various factors in admissions. However, another recent study found that over the last twenty years, a public commitment to race-conscious admissions has become far less common, particularly among institutions that are relatively lower in the status hierarchy.[69] That study found that it is the "most competitive" universities that have continued their public commitment to race-conscious admissions practices. While the reasons for this trend have not been studied directly, it is worth noting that the "most competitive" institutions are also those with more financial resources to defend against potential legal action.

Despite white affirmative action opponents' efforts to assert their agenda as one for Asian American rights, Asian Americans have long supported affirmative action, as evidenced by voting data, research, and advocacy led by long-established Asian American civil rights organizations.

Where available, voting data in state ballot initiatives indicate that the majority of Asian American voters rejected bans on affirmative action. Although voting data from the 2020 California election in Proposition 16 were not available for analysis at the time of writing this chapter, 61 percent of Asian American voters rejected Proposition 209 in 1996.[70] In Michigan, 75 percent of Asian American voters rejected Proposition 2 in 2006.[71] Among Asian American undergraduates enrolled at four-year colleges and universities across the US, 62.6 percent disagree with efforts to abolish the policy.[72] Moreover, Asian American law students have also demonstrated strong support for affirmative action.[73]

These data are consistent with results from nationwide multilingual opinion polls conducted since 2012, which have shown that an overwhelming majority (68 percent) of Asian Americans support race-conscious admissions.[74] Even when asked about affirmative action as specifically applied to higher education, 69 percent of Asian Americans polled expressed support for the policy.[75] Although support for affirmative action among Chinese Americans, who represent 23 percent of the Asian American population, has drastically declined from 78 percent in 2012 to 41 percent in 2016, the majority of all other Asian American ethnic groups and Asian Americans on the whole remain supportive of the policy.[76]

Given overall Asian American support for affirmative action according to research, opinion polls, and voting data, advocacy for the policy by long-standing Asian American civil rights organizations has been consistent with community interests. Emerging from the civil rights movement, many of these organizations were founded in the 1970s to represent Asian American interests in advocating for racial equity.[77] Collectively and independently, these Asian American and Pacific Islander organizations across the country have submitted amicus briefs to federal courts in favor of affirmative action.

In opposition to these efforts, newer Asian American–identified organizations, which are predominantly led by Chinese Americans, started to submit anti–affirmative action amici with the Grutter and Gratz cases.[78]

Some of the briefs opposing race-conscious admissions, submitted in the *Fisher* cases, were coauthored in partnership with the Louis D. Brandeis Center for Human Rights Under Law and the Judicial Education Project, demonstrating a political alignment between these Asian American *amici* and conservative white organizations.[79]

Ideologically, anti–affirmative action briefs presented what Moses labeled a racial libertarian view, which defines the notion of racial equality as "sameness of treatment, regardless of history, context, or social structures."[80] From this perspective, the state and other social institutions like colleges and universities should not be allowed to intervene in systems that are presumed fair and racially neutral. Correspondingly, many arguments across the anti–affirmative action briefs framed affirmative action as "racial preferences" for non-Asian American applicants with lower grade point averages and test scores. Importantly, this perspective also assumes such measures to be racially neutral metrics of academic potential and merit, leading them to rely heavily on a misinterpretation of statistical analysis from Espenshade and Radford's study of admissions processes at selective institutions.[81] In their study, the authors found that, on average, admitted Asian Americans had SAT scores that were about 140 points higher than those of white students.[82] Their study did not model or account for contemporary holistic review procedures, by only including a limited number of factors and experiences that admissions officers consider.[83] However, references to this study fail to mention the study's limitations. One of the authors, Espenshade, has acknowledged that his work does not present conclusive evidence of discrimination against Asian Americans.[84] Importantly, affirmative action opponents also overlooked the study's finding that race-conscious admissions at selective colleges and universities increased the admission chances of low-income Asian Americans.[85] This finding challenges the proposition that race-conscious admissions policies disadvantage Asian Americans.

Interestingly, these anti–affirmative action briefs also maintained a narrative of Asian Americans as a racially marginalized population,

positioning affirmative action as a policy akin to racist anti-Asian policies like the Chinese Exclusion Act and Japanese American internment
in World War II. These briefs also depict affirmative action as similar to
anti-Jewish quotas practiced by Ivy League institutions in the early twentieth century. They argued a false equivalency between race-conscious
policies for racial equity and reprehensible anti-Semitic discrimination.[86]
AACE and other newer Asian American–identified organizations submit-
ting amicus briefs against race-conscious admissions do not represent the
perspectives of the majority of Asian Americans.

Although research, data, and opinion polls consistently continue
to find that the majority of Asian Americans strongly support affirmative action, a 2017 opinion poll shows that support for affirmative action
among Chinese Americans (who represent 23 percent of the Asian American population) declined from 78 percent in 2012 to 41 percent in 2016.[87]
Changes in Chinese American opinion can be explained by shifts in US
immigration policies, social segregation among Chinese American immigrants, and the spread of misinformation on WeChat, as documented by
research.[88]

LOOKING AHEAD

Strategies within and outside the legal arena are needed to address the
current wave of attacks on race-conscious admissions. In addition to capitalizing on opposition to affirmative action by some Chinese American
immigrants, long-time conservative actors and organizations are benefit-
ing from changes by the Trump administration, including the rollback of
Obama era guidance on race-conscious admissions and the redirection of
DOJ resources to investigate claims of discrimination at institutions that
employ race-conscious admissions. These changes not only discourage
the use of constitutionally permissible policies but also seek to threaten
universities that remain committed to using them with the possibility
of DOJ investigations. There is much anticipation that the Biden-Harris

administration will reinstate guidance on race-conscious admissions and redirect the DOJ and other federal resources away from investigating frivolous claims that race-conscious admissions is a discriminatory policy. This political climate calls on racial equity and diversity advocates and scholars to continue to critically consider new strategies for analysis, legal advocacy, and public policy outreach.

Pending Cases and a Strategy of Legal Intimidation

As the lawsuit against Harvard makes its way through the courts, the legal strategy should continue to introduce findings from research addressing the benefits of race-conscious admissions policies for Asian Americans. As documents filed in the Harvard case demonstrate, these efforts are already underway, with an analysis of Harvard-specific data by highly respected economist and Berkeley professor David Card. This analysis found no anti-Asian racial bias in Harvard's complex holistic review process. There were also numerous *amicus curiae* briefs filed in support of Harvard at the lower court and the court of appeals, including ones filed by hundreds of social scientists and scholars documenting the benefits of race-conscious admissions for Asian American applicants (531 scholars joined the brief filed at the lower court and 678 joined the one at the court of appeals).[89] These efforts have helped establish an important foundation for the legal issues moving forward with two court opinions, the lower court and the court of appeals, concluding that Harvard's race-conscious admissions program is legal. The court of appeals, moreover, considered the empirical evidence and rejected the erroneous claims that undergird SFFA's arguments, based in part on research presented in an amicus brief submitted by social scientists.[90]

The Court's majority opinion in *Fisher II* also points to the importance of continued involvement by a broad coalition of Asian American organizations in filing briefs to support the policy.[91] Justice Kennedy, for example, in his majority opinion, directly cites the Brief for Asian American Legal Defense and Education Fund et al. as *amici curiae* to support the statement that "the contention that the University discriminates against

Asian-Americans is 'entirely unsupported by evidence in the record or empirical data.'"[92] While the majority opinion reflects findings from the evidentiary record in the case, Justice Alito's numerous references in his dissent to Asian Americans reflects the way conservative organizations have shifted framing to focus on discrimination against Asian Americans as the logical outcome of "preferences" for other minorities.[93] Reflecting the argument that conservatives have advanced since the 1980s, Justice Alito asserted that the university's plan "discriminates *against* Asian-American students."[94] This dissenting opinion statement illustrates how the misconstrued narrative around affirmative action and Asian Americans has taken hold among some of the justices in the Court. Addressing this misguided narrative, not only within the legal arena but also in the court of public opinion, will be critical.

Addressing Misinformation and Misperceptions in the Public and Policy Arena

Although litigation in the federal courts is central to the fate of affirmative action, so is the way that race-conscious admissions policies are perceived by the general public and Asian Americans in particular. These perceptions not only influence state policy, but indirectly, legal rulings.[95] For these reasons, it will be important to engage in targeted public information campaigns, and for Asian American ethnic communities more specifically, all of which require an active role on the part of the traditional news media.

With respect to the public, it is possible that the activism among Chinese Americans may lead some—especially those unaware of research documenting how Asian Americans benefit from the policy and the population's consistent support for affirmative action—to believe there is widespread Asian American opposition to the policy and that the policy is harmful to this minority group. A poorly informed public discourse is troubling to healthy public policy debate. Given the important role traditional news media play in shaping the issue for the general public, journalists should provide more comprehensive reporting on Asian American stances on affirmative action and research demonstrating the effects of the policy for Asian Americans.[96]

A targeted public education campaign about affirmative action among Asian Americans is also needed in light of the widespread distortions and misinformation that exist about affirmative action within the community.[97] These misrepresentations are not surprising given that reports about presumed negative effects of affirmative action on Asian Americans have dominated ethnic Chinese social media, while mainstream media have offered little fact-based reporting on the issue as it relates to this diverse population.[98] Given the complexities of holistic review and how this process benefits Asian American applicants, intentional public education should focus on how the process works.[99]

Through such efforts, a strong connection needs to be established between research and policy discourse, particularly around what race-conscious admissions (and relatedly affirmative action) is, how holistic review works in selective admissions, why it is practiced, and who benefits. For example, social media materials could be created to help explain holistic review, question definitions of "merit" that rely solely on standardized test scores, address the myth that Asian American applicants need to score higher on standardized tests to gain admission, discuss the importance of racial diversity to educational environments, including how Asian Americans benefit from affirmative action, and distinguish between affirmative action and racial discrimination.

Emerging research shows that holistic review processes can increase the odds of admission for Asian American applicants and other students of color.[100] In Harvard's robust holistic admissions process, which allows students to demonstrate their diversity of talents and potential for contributing toward the campus educational environment, no one criterion—such as an applicant's test score, high school GPA, athleticism, extracurricular activities, high school attended, race, class, or family background—serves to determine the admission decision for any applicant. Given the great diversity (e.g., educational contexts, achievements, interests, talents, ethnic, economic, and social backgrounds) found among Asian Americans, comprehensive and race-conscious holistic review approaches can greatly benefit Asian American applicants.

News journalists should also produce more in-depth coverage of affirmative action, race-conscious admissions, and Asian Americans. Unfortunately, with few exceptions, media accounts on the current debate over affirmative action are dominated by incomplete analyses on complex matters.[101] The court of public opinion could benefit from concerted, widespread, and culturally relevant efforts to counter the mass distribution of misinformation that form part of the basis in this new wave of attacks in the conservative agenda to dismantle affirmative action.

CONCLUSION

While challenges to affirmative action policies in higher education have played out in the legal and public arena over the last half century, the current wave of attacks against the policy is based on a campaign of misinformation, intimidation, and racial division. These opposition efforts are cynically capitalizing on upstart conservative political activism among a specific segment of Chinese American immigrants and changes under the Trump administration. Despite the efforts of white affirmative action opponents to assert their agenda as one advocating for Asian American rights, the majority of Asian Americans continue to support race-conscious admissions specifically, and affirmative action more generally, as evidenced by voting data, research, and advocacy led by long-established Asian American civil rights organizations. Moving forward, it will be important to address misperceptions and attempts to create racial division on this topic with more comprehensive reporting on Asian American stances on affirmative action, and with targeted outreach to help develop a stronger connection between research and policy discourse around the benefits of race-conscious admissions for Asian American students and the Asian American community at large.

CHAPTER 4

Student Loan Discourses

Understanding How Debt-Contingent Credentials Conceal Whiteness and Capitalism

JALIL B. MUSTAFFA

THE POLITICAL ROOTS of today's federal student loan system are tied directly to the 1965 Higher Education Act (HEA). Many researchers and policy advocates have described the HEA as a product of the 1960s civil rights reforms—a watershed moment in expanding college opportunities for students of color and low-income students.[1] Specifically, it created federal loan programs as a way to expand access to credit lines for middle-income students (who were overwhelmingly white at the time) to pay for college. Low-income students would not be expected to borrow because their tuition and living expenses would be covered via grants and scholarships. Those policy goals did not last long; in fact, within just a few years Congress expanded loan eligibility to more students and fundamentally shifted away from a grant-based aid system to one based on loans.[2] The shift reflected increases in overall college costs as state funding decreased.[3] What was initially designed to be a relatively small lending program narrowly targeted to white middle-class students has become the primary way low-income students now pay for college. At the same time as the shifts in funding, students of color, starting in the 1970s, experienced large increases in enrollment and disproportionately were the low-income, working-class students relying on student loans.[4] This is, at least, how the story goes in research and policy narratives—the story of how student loan policy created a student debt crisis that unequally harms Black people and communities of color. It reads almost as an accident rather than a design.

Yet, HEA was designed in a time when the economic system in the United States worked explicitly to serve white interest, advantage, and accumulation.[5] Scholars of education policy in the civil rights era make clear:[6] policy solutions focused primarily on including marginalized racial groups only to the extent they allowed white supremacy and its capitalist advantages to be preserved. Just as HEA facilitated college enrollment for Black students and students of color, it also left capitalism and its racialized market logics unquestioned. That is to say, HEA did little to redistribute preexisting opportunity and advantages for wealthy white people in wider society; it instead laundered whiteness as not an issue of racial advantage but instead an issue of who worked hard(er) to earn a credential. Ray explains that whiteness represents "institutionalized racial schemas, often laundered through facially-neutral bureaucratic processes."[7] For this chapter, debt-financed college credentials are the bureaucratic process that evades racial and capitalist critiques and conceals power. The result, still playing out today, is that Black people and people of color are included into the discourse of college opportunity while the reality of whiteness and capital remains unchallenged.[8] The decision to finance college on credit, like other credit markets, was always a policy design that would ensure Black people and communities of color lose relative to how much white people already were set to win—either by policymakers' neglect of racial-economic realities or intentional efforts to reproduce them.[9] In this way, the stories of HEA, how the student debt crisis (accidentally) came to be, and college access as racial justice collectively leave a key question unanswered: what about the white and wealth advantage across capitalism from higher education to the labor market?

In this chapter, I provide a new way to view the federal student loan program that is centered around the theory of racial capitalism. By viewing student loan debt through this lens, which centers the role structural racism and racialized market logics play in policymaking—particularly when designing race-neutral programs like loans that have disproportionately extracted capital from communities of color—policymakers will be better able to answer the above question and define racial justice. This chapter disrupts taken-for-granted narratives about higher education and argues that racial justice requires critical attention to the ways whiteness and capitalism are laundered through student debt-contingent credentials. First, I provide a trifecta framework for racial capitalism to understand it as a system and set of logics and center it within education policymaking. Then I apply the theory to the ways student loans were (1) unpayable by design and (2) tools of extraction for Black people and communities of color. The chapter concludes with a call for people-centered policy discourses and solutions, many already emerging, to create a racial justice that is not defined by market logics, but people's needs.

RACIAL CAPITALISM

The politics of education policymaking is always a struggle within and against racial capitalism.[10] Racial capitalism is defined as the structural ways in which capital is extracted and dispossession is inflicted upon groups rendered different through race and other intersecting power dynamics like gender, geography, and sexuality.[11] Struggle refers to fighting within a sociohistorical context where those on the margins—poor communities of color—are legislated as less than. Struggle requires fighting against the ways whiteness and capitalism work together to allocate life chances unequally and without question. Harris explains "the law's construction of whiteness defined and affirmed critical aspects of identity (who is white); of privilege (what benefits accrue to that status); and, of property (what legal entitlements arise from that status). Whiteness at various times signifies and is deployed as identity, status, and property, sometimes singularly, sometimes in tandem."[12] To trace the politics of education policymaking, one must name not just the politics surrounding legislative processes but also the racial capitalist logics at play.

Scholars have used racial capitalism to explain specific power dynamics around slavery, mass incarceration, housing, labor unions, community development, reproductive justice, indigenous land displacement, and the COVID-19 pandemic.[13] This scholarly tradition is often referred to as Black Radical Thought or the Black Radical Tradition.[14] In the field of education, racial capitalism—as in the theory or similar arguments—has been applied to the expansion of charter schools, the closing of public schools, and school-to-prison partnerships.[15] Yet, racial capitalism still holds marginal space in the study of higher education policymaking—and student loan debt in particular. This chapter aims to expand the theory to the field with a focus on one archetype relationship under racial capitalism. The relationship of the debtor to the creditor—in this case, the student loan borrower of color's relationship to higher education actors. Higher education is the institutional system that is legislatively positioned to determine who has access to good jobs and their benefits (living wage, health care, social status, etc.) even if increasingly contingent on student loan debt.[16] The legitimacy of higher education holding this position is explained with such policy frames as earning a degree leads to higher lifetime earnings; higher education is the greatest social equalizer; and for the United States' economy to remain competitive, degree attainment must increase.[17]

Higher education's function and framing situate capitalism as unquestioned and colleges and universities as the engine to increase wages, racial equality, and global competitiveness. A growing body of work argues capitalism, its preservation and growth, underpins how higher education is understood in the twenty-first century although often unnamed.[18] Racial capitalism, as a theory, helps to name capitalism and racism as the purpose of higher education policy and trace how that has violent and unequal consequences for poor communities of color. I summarize racial capitalism through a trifecta schema in figure 4.1; it is not meant to be exhaustive but to help process the interplay of racism, capitalism, and human relations. Capitalism, its contradictions and oppression, is often unnamed in higher education scholarship and policy discussions on equity—particularly in the area of student loan debt.

The trifecta of racial capitalism is based on the mass accumulation of capital, unequal human relations, and logics of (un)deserving. Higher education relies on the trifecta by creating a marketplace of credentials and labor market opportunity that is said to be driven by credentials earned. Unequal human relations exist prior to and emerge from credentialism as those who earn credentials accumulate capital while those without—the uncredentialed—are denied living wage employment and subsequent benefits.[19] Credentials often are not a start but a continuation of the capital accumulation that allows people to successfully attain a credential in the first place. Those white and wealthy are already in a process of accumulation prior to entering the credential and labor marketplaces, and credentialism launders rather than begins the process.[20] The uneven human relations driving accumulation are further exploited across profit-making

FIGURE 4.1 **Framework for understanding racial capitalism**

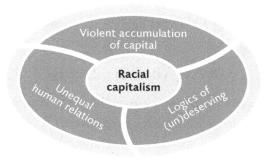

sectors in racial capitalism (e.g., employers paying poverty wages to uncredentialed workers of color) and made normal through the logics of (un)-deserving. Simply, credential logics argue those with credentials should be paid more; those without, paid less. A set of logics racially coded to mask historic racism and discount ongoing oppression as two notions not necessary to understanding racial equity gaps.[21] Put another way, racial capitalism relies on credentials to explain away structural racism. It is either a nonissue or one easily overcome through Black people and communities of color competing better for credentials. Yet, as Ray argues, it is whiteness and wealth that explain in the aggregate who benefits from capitalism and its credential logics.[22]

It is important not to view racial capitalism as only focused on profit—though it is a driving force. The US economy is based on accumulation in one area through the dispossession of people and places in another—the undeserving. Dispossession—excluding working-class groups across races from basic human needs—is not always measured by who profits. Another measure of dispossession is how structures prepare ready-to-be exploited groups and places.[23] For example, an underdeveloped neighborhood now being gentrified or the college student, who is a full-time worker and parent on the margins of traditional higher education, being recruited by a more costly and low-performing for-profit college. The logics of undeserving play out along power; for this chapter, racism is just one lens, which works to normalize the devaluation of Black people and other communities of color to facilitate the accumulation of capital for the already-advantaged and profit-driven.

UNPAYABLE BY DESIGN

Racial disparities in student loans are not happenstance. The line of credit used to finance higher education for Black people is unpayable by design. The design of the higher education system shows capital flows largely away from communities of color.[24] While students of color now comprise 40 percent of college enrollment,[25] only around 40 percent of Black and Indigenous students graduate in six years from four-year institutions, whereas the majority of white students do.[26] Most students of color are not enrolled in four-year institutions but in two-year and technical institutions that are underfunded.[27] They are not in the degree programs often framed as increasing earnings. McMillan Cottom argues the preexisting inequality Black people face across society makes enrolling in higher education an attractive option even when credential attainment may be unlikely, and the loans are unpayable.[28] In addition, discourses based in credential idealism argue away Black people's unequal human relations with the promise that earning a credential, no matter the cost, pays off—the degree-earning premium. Credential + debt = high-paying job is the equation that underlies the idealism around higher education. As I argue elsewhere:

> [T]he main force driving Black student borrowing is the desire for a job that pays a livable wage. The trouble is Black people experience rampant racism in the job market whether we have a degree or not. We are always in danger of being steered toward bad jobs. The whole multibillion-dollar student loan industry—involving colleges and universities, loan servicing companies, Wall Street, the Department of Education, and state governments—relies on Black people's desire for quality employment. This, in turn, means all these entities also rely on Black people's overexposure to bad jobs. Bad jobs versus good jobs epitomize the unequal relations on which racial capitalism thrives (online).[29]

While this analysis focuses on Black borrowers who have the worst outcomes in higher education and student debt repayment, it can be extended to working-class communities of color. For a white bachelor's degree holder, median earnings are $50,000 for women and $62,000 for men; that is 13 percent higher than Latinx women and 18 percent higher than Latinx men. For Black women and men, white earnings for the same degree are 26 percent and 17 percent higher, respectively.[30] Quillian et al.

reviewed hiring discrimination research across thirty years and found, even when controlling for education levels and occupation types, that people of color face consistent employment discrimination.[31] Morgan and Steinbaum, in their study that argues against the degree-earning equation, provide evidence that earning a degree does not increase wages overall.[32] Over the last twenty years, wages overall have been stagnant as educational attainment increases. The premium is simply that those without a college credential are in the bad jobs—paid less to do the same work—and those with degrees (and new debt) are paid the same as the generations prior with less credentials.

For students of color, the disconnect between the labor market and degree attainment means college debt often is not a bridge, but a debt trap.[33] For Indigenous and Black students, 89 and 85 percent, respectively, borrow student loans followed by Latinx students at 67 percent.[34] They carry average loan balances higher than their white counterparts. Scott-Clayton and Li's research shows Black students have an average balance of $53,000 four years after graduating with a bachelor's, whereas white graduates have an average balance of $28,000.[35] Miller found 49 percent of Black students defaulted on their student loans within twelve years of exiting higher education, and those who earned a degree were likely to still owe a median of over 100 percent of their original student loan balance in this same time period.[36] When considering gender, Black women "hold 47% more student debt than White men and 27% more than White women."[37] There are too many contradictions in the degree-earning premium argument to accept the dominant framing of credentials as an unquestioned benefit and social equalizer.

Also, the contradictions are well documented, and simply naming them in research is not the same as analyzing and critiquing the forces that sustain them. In the review of key research in the field of higher education, Rhoades posed the question: "Why in a time of heightened racial tension and class stratification are our analyses of institutional and state policy largely disembodied, devoid of considering racism and class conflict?"[38] The question names how conflict is unfolding across race and class without robust attention to it in the higher education literature. Similarly, it is common practice to name the racial inequities in student loan debt research with no analysis of racism or capitalism; let alone viewing them as joint forces. The analysis is missing partly because capitalism is a defining principle for the extent equity matters in the field of higher education. It has become commonsense to argue that racial equity gaps must be closed to maintain the US economy's competitiveness.[39] The discourse of equity narrows mattering to the extent solutions benefit the economy. Closing racial equity gaps becomes an appeal to capitalists—close equity gaps in order to maintain capital relations and profit. This is not an appeal to be fair or moral to Black people and communities of color.

The equity-economy discourse positions capitalism as the object deserving of protection and investment,[40] whereas Black people and communities of color's degree attainment (the undeserving) is simply the means to that end. The historic pattern is repeated: Black people and communities of color's worth is measured in their productivity to racial capitalism.[41] While many use this discourse because they conclude inequity is wrong, it shows that identifying a problem is not enough. It matters why one thinks racial equity is wrong because the framing of the problem determines one's ability to analyze the interlocked logics and structural forces that sustain it. Here that means naming how the unequal human relations in society and the higher education system function to make student debt unpayable and how explanations of inequity reinscribe racial capitalism as a solution.

STUDENT LOANS AS TOOLS OF EXTRACTION

For student loans to be viewed as extending access and opportunity—a good debt—they have to first be viewed as a solution rather than a tool of extraction. Yet, Black people and communities of color historically and continuously lose in debt-financed education—believed to be a *personal choice* rather than a *structural design*.[42] Also, because the degree-earning equation and higher education obscure whiteness. The ways whiteness credentialed itself across history and systems remain masked to ensure even Black credentialed workers are outcompeted. Ray argues, "[I]ndeed, the organizational reproduction of racial inequality may work best if organizational procedures appear impartial. Organizations help *launder* racial domination [whiteness] by obscuring or legitimating unequal processes."[43] Just finish the degree and the economic returns will follow, so the story goes. This framing protects those who are wealthy and white before and after college more so than Black people and communities of color who are hoping to outcompete their life odds. The problem is that this policy logic is race-neutral: it assumes equal returns for equal education, and that is simply not true for communities of color.[44] Again, these communities are underrepresented in bachelor's degree attainment and underpaid despite education levels.[45] Through making credentialism commonsense, policy logics leave whiteness and wealth unquestioned—student debt is not a race problem, it is a credential problem.

There is a contradiction, however, to the good debt narrative emerging as the public and media discussion increasingly frames student loans not as an opportunity, but a crisis. Appel argues the 2008 recession and policy framing from activist coalitions like Occupy Wall Street made understanding student debt as a crisis a popular frame.[46] The response in the media and the policy arena was to counter that crisis rhetoric as overblown[47]—student debt is still a good debt. The argument shifted the problem from student loans to students who failed to graduate; this group, on average, have loan balances below $10,000 and more issues with default.[48] The counterargument relied on the logics of (un)deserving as those with debt and no degree were framed as the problem; a group disproportionately made up of students of color.[49] Another argument framed the issue around income-based repayment (IBR) plans; reframing student loans as a process problem rather than a one of capitalism.[50] Policymakers responded with reforms like having the federal government directly lend loans and creating new income-based repayment plans to reduce monthly payments.[51] These counterarguments to the existence of the debt crisis have become weaker as the public outcry has grown over student loans and more student debt racial data has become available. For example, recent research has found that default rates are high for Black and Latinx students across loan balances and degree levels even with some of the highest enrollment in IBR plans.[52] As follows, I present evidence to show the accumulation of capital for the government, higher education institutions, and the loan servicing and debt collection industry with limited "good" for students of color.[53]

While student loans were provided to all, it was a racially violent bargain for communities of color. The government has refused to focus on structural equality through redistributive and antiracist policies and now makes the terms of justice and equality (defined as degree attainment) contingent on debt. Communities of color, already disproportionally excluded from wealth-building pathways and nonpredatory credit lines,[54] have no choice but to rely on student loans as college costs increase. These unequal human relations ensure both the borrowing of student loans and continued extraction of payments and fees the more one is unable to pay.

The government still can claim a policy discourse of inclusion as the availability of student loans means higher education technically is accessible and affordable. Seamster and Charron-Chénier refer to these terms of inclusion as predatory inclusion.[55] Simply, student loans allow the government never to account for past centuries of funding a higher education for white upper-middle-class America that was not contingent on debt. Nor account for how it currently has accumulated a student loan portfolio on top of communities of color and working-class communities.

As I argue in other work, it is hard to view higher education student debt policy as violent accumulation due to the idealism around the sector.[56] Higher education, however, is an extension of government policies and mandates. When the US government, across state and federal levels, supported slavery, Jim Crow, tokenism, affirmative action, and race-neutral policies, higher education largely did as well. Further, the system served as a structural and discursive defense for the ways the government has accumulated capital across these eras to the benefit of whiteness and the wealthy. Credentials now are presented as the step necessary for communities of color to gain equality, access good jobs, and have social value in society—if they first borrow student loans. The use of a racialized credit market—student loans—is yet another time higher education enacts a violence already reflected across larger society. Student loans reproduce one of the most predatory human relations in racial capitalism: the creditor's power over the debtor.[57] The creditor-debtor relationship, under racial capitalism, is about extracting and dispossessing capital and human value from communities of color. The government has played this role historically and now again in the student debt crisis.

Similarly, higher education institutions hold responsibility. There are over four thousand institutions with varied relationships to student loans like for-profit colleges, open access public institutions, elite privates, Historically Black Colleges and Universities (HBCUs), Minority-Serving Institutions (MSIs), tribal colleges, and technical schools. Again, some institutions have been limited while others flourished through capitalism. To be clear, many open access institutions have staff that lead multiprong efforts to support the most marginalized students around basic needs like food and housing along with academic support.[58] HBCUs are evidence-based models for what it means to graduate and value Black low-income students.[59] Yet, no institution is exempt from how racial capitalism requires their complicity. While for-profit colleges are the most infamous examples of racial capitalism and using student debt for profit, it is important to explain how traditional higher education institutions fit in.[60]

Mitchell, Leachman, and Saenz found that tuition made up only about 25 percent of public higher education institutions' budget in 1988, but now it is 50 percent.[61] In this same time, student of color enrollment in public higher education grew from 17 to 40 percent. Students of color were enrolling when higher education was no longer a state-funded public good as it was for white generations prior. The reliance on students as a revenue source, from their tuition, room and board, and fees payments, also meant an institutional reliance on students borrowing loans. State and federal funding is still a part of institutional budgets, but not at levels to fill in the overall gaps. Colleges, across the system, utilize various types of marketing and ambiguous recruiting strategies to attract students without providing clear costs of attendance.[62] This disproportionately impacts students of color who are most likely to borrow and least likely to graduate. All colleges are complicit in marketing the promises of a degree, credential idealism, when a structurally racist society means a degree alone cannot be enough. Slaughter and Rhoades have referred to institutions' corporatization, where the focus is on competing for profit over providing a public good, as academic capitalism.[63] While there are various levels of capital accumulation among traditional colleges and universities, they all still benefit from luring students of color into student debt with a credential idealism that is false.

Likewise, the for-profit sector reproduces and intensifies institutional accumulation. They are more expensive, offer less support, and require students to borrow more.[64] They are the institutions that McMillan Cottom's research describes as "Lower Ed" and where Scott-Clayton found that Black and Latinx students who ever attend a for-profit are more likely to default on their student loans.[65] Yet, the institutional sector makes up a small percentage of the higher education system, and even if they were eliminated, racial inequality in student loan outcomes would persist.[66] Researchers and policymakers often rightfully identify for-profits as bottom line-driven, exploitative actors but fail to apply that same analysis to traditional higher education. For-profits' behavior has been parasitic rather than foundational to the racialized student debt crisis; they have preyed on students of color who often were marginalized or already taken advantage of by traditional higher education.[67]

Another parasitic relationship in the student debt crisis is loan servicing and debt collection agencies. Like for-profits, many agencies engage in malpractice or fraud to produce unequal human relations of the creditor over the debtor.[68] As the group already unequally burdened with student debt, communities of color also carry the burden of poor loan servicing. The Consumer Financial Protection Bureau names student lending as a site prime for discriminatory practices.[69] In addition, Scott-Clayton showed that even controlling for traditional variables like family background, education levels, and institution type, the white-Black default gap was still largely unaccounted for, and differences in loan servicing experiences may play a factor.[70] In 2020, the Department of Education failed to restructure loan servicing into a more unified system with more accountability measures despite receiving nearly $500 million to do so since 2015 and having evidence of racial disparities.[71] Loonin highlighted the lack of accountability and transparency around the multimillion dollar loan servicing industry: "The government and its contractors too often create barriers to program usage by failing to inform borrowers about relief programs and about how to access them. In other cases, the government has created eligibility standards that are nearly impossible for borrowers to meet."[72] Similarly, in 2017, the Department of Education awarded contracts to debt collection agencies worth nearly $700 million; for every $1 collected, the agencies make $40.[73] A debt collection industry also built disproportionately through targeting people of color with the worst consequences of nonpayment. For example, one advocacy report found that student borrowers in majority people of color zip codes were most likely to be recommended for debt collection lawsuits, by the Department of Education and Department of Justice, when they were delinquent.[74] Loan servicing and debt collection agencies are proven profit-driven actors. It is a limited analysis, however, when policy discourse highlights them as the engine of the student loan problem. They are taking advantage of credentialism, which ensures there will always be students who borrow without the ability to repay. If repayment struggles are a crisis for students, especially for students of color, they become an opportunity for loan servicing and debt collection agencies. Those who cannot repay are also constant sources of extraction and profit: increased service and collection fees paid from the increasing loan interest and principal. This extraction facilitated by student loan delinquencies by definition is extraction from the most marginalized students. The National Consumer Law Center (NCLC) provided an example of what student loan default means for low-income parents:

> Borrowers in default are often required to pay more per month than similarly situated borrowers in good standing. For example, a single borrower making $25,000 per year with two children would have a $0 payment each month if in good standing on an income-driven repayment plan. That same borrower in default would likely have approximately $250 garnished from her wages. Additionally, that borrower would likely have her tax refund intercepted, losing approximately $4000 in Earned Income Tax credits.[75]

This form of extraction matters for communities of color who are most likely to be low-income parent-students who are reliant on benefits like this credit.[76] Further, the above evidence is mainly on federal student loans, which are meant to be a better option to private student loan lending already riddled with discrimination and profit-first motives.[77] From loan servicing to debt collection, borrowers of color uniquely are subjected to continuous extraction. The dominant narrative of student loans as a good debt and higher education institutions as social equalizers, not driven by debt-financed tuition, obscures racial capitalism. Under the racial-economic status quo, the contradictions of credentialism shown through the racial inequality of student debt policy also are opportunities for profit—a profit facilitated by the government, higher education institutions, and the loan servicing and debt collection industries. Here, racial capitalism first protects preexisting accumulation and advantage by distributing college opportunity through debt rather than a public good, then second by extracting credential-debt payments from communities of color with few alternative options. Student loans, then, are not a crisis on their own, and the crisis does not exist without benefactors. Empirically and experientially, student loan debt fails to be enough to level the playing field in the credential or labor marketplaces; let alone be a social equalizer for Black people and communities of color.

CONCLUSION

The chapter's main goal is to detail what student debt policy discourses need to be named and challenged and show how they uphold a racial-economic hierarchy even when they espouse justice. The chapter first introduces the theory of racial capitalism to challenge the ways the higher education system and underlying credential logics inflict harm. A trifecta schema was provided to understand how racial capitalism functions: mass accumulation of capital, unequal human relations, and logics of (un)deserving. It is as critical to trace how racial capitalism accumulates capital for the already-advantaged people, institutions, and entities as it is to understand the logics employed to explain the corresponding racial inequality. The interplay between structural and discursive forces in higher education policy ensure at worst an antiracist capitalist critique is never at the center of policies and at best the critique is reduced to a degree attainment problem. The master narrative goes if communities of color can earn more credentials, despite the debt costs, they will be able to earn higher-paying jobs. The cited research in this chapter shows the degree-earning equation to be false for communities of color—degrees correlate to increased wages because wages for the uncredentialed (still people of color) have decreased while wages overall have remained stagnant.

Even if the degree-earning premium was true, it still wrongly defines racial justice for communities of color by market logics. The market cannot be the primary answer. The labor market maintains consistent racism within an economy that has never undergone a redistribution of white advantage and wealth to level the playing field. The historic and ongoing racial inequality that policymakers hope degree attainment and student loans will help to address is a problem of racial capitalism and therefore cannot be solved by it. Again, how policy discourse frames the problem determines the solutions put forth.

There is a need for a new discourse on higher education and its value beyond capitalism. A people-centered policy discourse with an antiracist capitalist critique, however, is emerging. There are movements fighting against the defunding of public goods, the reliance on profit-driven actors to meet human needs, and refusals to name racist and capitalist logics. In 2021, those movements largely are led by coalitions like the Movement for Black Lives, Debt Collective, and People's Action, to name a few.[78] A core argument cutting across these coalitions is that people's human needs and racial justice cannot be contingent on meritocracy or debt. This people-centered argument is changing the discourse and policy ideas around health care (Medicare for All), housing (homes-guarantee pledge), environmental regulations (the Green New Deal), and the labor market (a federal job guarantee program).

In addition, the people-centered movements and discourse extend to higher education policy. There is a widespread public stance that a college degree has not paid off and student debt is unpayable—with communities of color carrying the consequences.[79] The new discourse around higher education emerging from movements is generating policy solutions on the national stage. For example, progressive Congress members introduced comprehensive legislation titled The College for All Act of 2019 that cancels all student loan debt and covers all tuition and fees at public higher education institutions and HBCUs. As a start, the legislation recenters higher education as more of a public good and provides relief for communities of color who have found credentials to be a debt trap.[80] Still this type of legislation is a gateway. A network of policies and practices is required for racial justice.[81] Racial capitalism must be challenged in the ways it exists before, during, and after college enrollment. Fortunately, movements already provide a multi-issue, antiracist capitalist critique along with a people-centered model for policymakers and higher education advocates to follow.

CHAPTER 5

In Consideration of Reinstating Pell for Incarcerated Students

Erin S. Corbett, Julie Ajinkya, Cody Meixner, and Haruna Suzuki

THE POLITICAL POLARIZATION of higher education has real and lasting consequences on individuals and their life chances. These politics play out in many domains and, as this chapter outlines, especially at the intersection of criminal justice and education. America's jails and prisons are disproportionately populated by young men—and increasingly women—of color from low-income backgrounds with lower educational attainment than their peers. And this is not by accident. Laws and policies, and the deployment of law enforcement to uphold them, have resulted in Black and Brown communities being disproportionately targeted, policed, and ultimately imprisoned. Not only are these communities disproportionately affected, but legislation has steadily pressed for longer sentences and longer time horizons before individuals can be eligible for parole.[1] Once behind bars, incarcerated individuals could benefit from taking college classes or enrolling in degree programs; however, federal policies have actively prohibited this from happening.

In this chapter, we explain how federal policies have restricted opportunities for incarcerated individuals and what the Higher Education Act (HEA) can do to address the inequalities these policies have upheld. We focus on the federal Pell Grant program as one of the primary policy levers that can change to benefit incarcerated individuals. Although from its beginnings, the US criminal justice system has provided education to incarcerated individuals—including a school at the first state-run prison in Philadelphia—it was not until the latter half of the twentieth century that prisons across the country began offering college-level programming.[2] As the prison population began to increase at record rates in the late twentieth century, higher education programs inside correctional facilities also began to increase to meet the demand of the influx of "college age" persons.[3] From the mid-1970s, incarcerated individuals were allowed to use federal Pell Grants in pursuit of a postsecondary credential, and up until 1994, there were over three hundred higher education programs inside prisons; these programs were jointly run by colleges and universities in partnership with departments of correction(s) across the country.[4] However, the Violent Crime Control and Law Enforcement Act of 1994 (VCA) banned Pell access for individuals incarcerated in federal and state facilities;[5] almost immediately, college in prison programs drastically declined.[6] What remained, however, was an understanding of, and a steadily increasing body of research that touted, the benefits of higher education in prison and linked participation in, and completion of, these programs to higher rates of positive postrelease outcomes.[7]

There is significant bipartisan support among policymakers agreeing that federal financial aid barriers rooted in retributive policies do more harm than good, both fiscally and socially.[8] Programs and policies, at both state and federal levels, that expand access to quality, postsecondary opportunities for incarcerated individuals lead to increased civic engagement, public safety, and social mobility postrelease. Given this idea, the reexamination of the prohibition of Pell Grant access for incarcerated learners is one way to think through strengthening postsecondary pathways to increased societal gains. In 1993, the final year incarcerated students could access Pell funding before the ban, approximately twenty-seven thousand prisoners received $35 million in Pell grants; though this accounted for less than 1 percent of Pell expenditures for that year, it provided tens of thousands of students with opportunities to work toward valuable and life-changing credentials.[9]

Current HEA reauthorization discussions offer the opportunity to thoughtfully explore the impact of federal Pell Grants and answer the question of whether access to this need-based financial aid mechanism has, in fact, increased equitable access to postsecondary opportunities. While the Pell Grant has provided financial relief for many families, educational attainment gaps persist across several identity indicators. Joint work between The Pell Institute and the Penn AHEAD Center examines equity indicators in higher education; the data assert that little has changed since the 1970s.[10] Postsecondary enrollment trends continue to indicate that students from wealthier families enroll in postsecondary education at higher rates, although the differences have decreased over time.[11] Yet, when considering enrollment rates by race and ethnicity, Black and Hispanic students enroll at significantly lower rates than their white counterparts.[12] While it seems that Pell is slowly closing access gaps along some equity indicators such as income, a significant gap in postsecondary access along race and ethnic lines persists. How, then, might Pell dollars be better leveraged to substantively address these gaps? A crucial component of any answer or solution is the reinstatement of Pell Grant access for incarcerated learners by lifting the 1994 ban.

THE HISTORICAL NEED FOR PELL GRANTS

The history of equitable higher education access in the United States is complex, and the need to legislate the inclusion of certain population subgroups is historically rooted. Arguably until 1862—when the first Morrill Act created public land-grant universities—entry to the select few elite postsecondary institutions was primarily limited to upper-income white men; however, this act allowed state legislatures to determine the manner in which postsecondary education was carried out at these institutions.[13] As a result, Black citizens were not allowed to enroll in college if their state restricted access based on race. With the Second Morrill Act—also known as the Agricultural College Act—the federal government provided funds for the expansion of the land-grant universities and, among other pieces, saw the creation of eighteen Black land-grant universities, which would be the precursors to what we now consider Historically Black Colleges and Universities (HBCUs).[14] This act effectively served as the first piece of federal legislation that explicitly addressed inequity in postsecondary access along race/ethnicity lines.

However, this legislation was not enough to address the inequities inherent in the educational system, and cases like *Plessy v. Ferguson* and *Brown v. Board of Education of Topeka*—while not explicitly linked to higher education—set the broader stage for the passing of the Higher Education Act of 1965 (as amended, "HEA"), by addressing racial segregation in access to facilities and education broadly. One primary mechanism that HEA employed to improve equitable postsecondary access focused on decreasing financial barriers for students. For instance, HEA called for the creation of the first ever low-interest student loans; seven years later, in 1972, Senator Claiborne Pell (D-RI) lobbied for what was then called the Basic Educational Opportunity Grant, a program that would provide low-income students with need-based aid that need not be repaid.[15] Renamed the Pell Grant in the senator's honor, this now-well-known financial aid mechanism seeks to address issues of affordability in higher education and provide increased access to those communities most affected by historical marginalization and segregation.

Given the demographic shifts in the student population pursuing higher education since 1965—an increase in women and students of color, in particular—it is fitting that HEA undergo comprehensive reauthorizations to ensure that it continue to deliver on its original intent to improve equitable access for students. The landscape of higher education has changed in ways unimaginable since 1965; for instance, the advent and proliferation of technology in the classroom are responsible for a myriad of innovative content delivery methods available for educators as well as new conversations about affordability.[16] Since its inception, HEA has had eight reauthorizations, and each version has sought to address the evolution of the nation's higher education system and rapidly changing demographics.

PELL GRANTS AND THE RISE OF THE CARCERAL STATE

Until 1994, Pell Grants served not only those students viewed as traditional students but also "nontraditional" students; incarcerated persons, for instance, could access Pell funds to enroll in college courses offered either inside facilities or by correspondence.[17] Indeed, Pell Grants became the primary source of funding for incarcerated students pursuing higher education.[18]

The VCA, however, banned Pell access for all incarcerated persons (and later amendments to the HEA would include those who had completed sentences for a sexual offense conviction but were still under supervision in a mandated civil commitment).[19] The VCA, through the Judiciary Committee, amended the Higher Education Act of 1965, which is under the jurisdiction of the Senate Committee on Health, Education, Labor and Pensions (HELP) and the House Education and Labor Committee. The VCA barred individuals who were incarcerated in federal or state penal institutions from accessing Pell funds.[20] The principal argument for rescinding Pell Grant access for incarcerated learners hinged on the erroneous premise that providing financial assistance to those in prison deprived "needy, nonincarcerated students of educational opportunities."[21] Yet, nothing changed substantially in terms of assisting the country's nonincarcerated undergraduate population; only 0.8 percent to 1.2 percent of all Pell Grants went to incarcerated students.[22]

Contrary to popular belief, the restriction of Pell for confined learners was not a sudden shift but was in fact a process that occurred over the course of two decades and culminated with the 1994 ban.[23] Some of the earliest calls for eliminating Pell Grant access for incarcerated students were based in partisan interpretations of the work of sociologist Robert Martinson. Martinson assessed rehabilitative programs for incarcerated adult men, citing positive outcomes in 48 percent of the programs under evaluation.[24] Yet, critics of correctional education highlighted only those programs that failed to produce positive results, going as far as concluding that rehabilitative programs in general had no appreciable effects on recidivism. Such arguments paved the way for redirecting US correctional philosophy away from rehabilitation toward deterrence and punishment, in turn weakening support for extending Pell Grants to incarcerated students.[25] The late 1980s saw multiple congressional attempts to decrease Pell funding for confined learners through decreases in appropriations.[26] By 1992, concrete federal aid restrictions around student and institutional eligibility were in place, which profoundly impacted confined learners enrolled in postsecondary education. Students sentenced to either life without parole or who were sentenced to death row were deemed ineligible; institutions with more than 25 percent incarcerated students were deemed ineligible; institutions that offered more than 50 percent of their courses through distance methods were deemed ineligible; institutions that enrolled more than 50 percent of their total student body in distance courses were deemed ineligible; and institutions with more than 50 percent of the student body without a secondary credential were deemed ineligible.[27] Despite these regulations' presumed intent to guard against institutional misuse of taxpayer dollars, they in effect constrained postsecondary access for the 1,053,738 persons in carceral custody at the time.[28]

The 1994 ban further impacted program completion rates for the approximately twenty-seven thousand confined learners projected to

access Pell Grant funds for postsecondary coursework in the 1994 academic year.[29] As a direct result of the ban, the number of available programs
plummeted by 40 percent, and enrollment in the remaining programs
decreased by 44 percent due to the prohibitive cost of higher education
for an incarcerated student; seven states (Arkansas, Colorado, Iowa, Kan-
sas, Maryland, Mississippi, and North Carolina) completely eliminated
postsecondary programming in prison.[30] The VCA not only implemented
the Pell ban and decreased the provision of higher education programs in
prison, but also had a disproportionately profound social impact on poor
communities and communities of color. As the country's largest crime bill
in history, it significantly increased policing and invested heavily in prisons, alongside funds for prevention programs.[31] Justice policies enabled
by this legislation, such as community policing (more commonly referred
to as "stop-and-frisk"), arrests, and sentencing (mandatory minimums and
truth-in-sentencing) disproportionately impacted communities of color,
leading to a substantial increase in people of color incarcerated in correctional facilities. In addition, the mid-1990s saw the creation of a generation of "school-to-prison pipeline" policies that brought poor communities
and communities of color into earlier and more frequent contact with law
enforcement and various iterations of confinement and supervision.[32]

Additionally, and closely related to the "school-to-prison-pipeline,"
is the fact that educational attainment of the criminal justice involved
population is much lower than the average United States household.[33] As
school policies in lower-resourced communities continued to suspend,
expel, and arrest young adults before completing high school, the custody population demonstrated less educational attainment. According to
the US Department of Justice, 41 percent of federal and state inmates do
not possess a secondary—high school—credential in comparison to 18
percent of the general population. Data from the Program for the International Assessment of Adult Competencies (PIAAC) Survey of Incarcerated
Adults (2012–14) affirm these equity gaps and indicate that incarcerated
persons consistently demonstrate lower educational attainment than

the overall United States household; incarcerated individuals represent a larger portion of those with less than a high school diploma, yet a smaller portion of those with any postsecondary credential.[34] These data underscore that the nation's incarcerated population more closely resembles the population that the Pell Grant was originally designed to help, those from underserved communities who were systematically denied educational access. Restricting Pell access, and ultimately severely constraining an incarcerated person's access to postsecondary education, exacerbates the inequities that have emerged as by-products of a criminal justice system predicated upon the institutionalization of racism.

The intersection of these criminal justice trends, which also sat at the intersection of social identity indicators like race, gender, and class, created an epidemic of mass incarceration and gave rise to a carceral state that currently sees people of color imprisoned at rates that are on average four times higher than their white counterparts.[35] The Bureau of Justice Statistics estimates that the racial composition of the incarcerated population is 38 percent Black, 21 percent Hispanic, and 39 percent white; this contrasts with the reality that Blacks comprise only 13 percent of the country's overall population, those of Hispanic origin comprise 16 percent, and whites are 64 percent.[36] Incarcerated individuals also report preincarceration income levels far lower than the average household.[37] Given these data, a troubling trend becomes clear: more people were becoming incarcerated at the same time that access to educational opportunities systematically decreased for incarcerated learners, and people of color were disproportionately excluded from postsecondary access because of their incommensurate involvement with the criminal justice system.

None of this information, however, is novel. The fact that access, matriculation, and attainment gaps exist along certain demographic axes is a by-product of the reality that higher education was never designed to comprehensively include and address the needs of students of color.[38] Sincere equity-minded considerations of postsecondary attainment gaps in this country require institutions to interrogate (1) why communities of color report disproportionately low postsecondary attainment rates and (2) the challenges presented by systemic interactions with discrimination that impact access and success for communities of color. This conceptualization of equity encourages institutions to challenge their norms around campus-based instruction and student-body composition, as well as consider what it would mean to offer postsecondary opportunities in correctional facilities and include incarcerated students on their rosters.

In addition to racial, ethnic, and income demographics, we must also consider whether and to what extent women have access to postsecondary opportunities, particularly given the gender breakdown within correctional facilities. What does equitable postsecondary access and attainment along gender lines look like for women who are imprisoned? Rather than a focus on numerical equality in terms of access, it becomes important to also consider the trauma, violence, and exploitation that many incarcerated women experience at extraordinarily high rates.[39] How do their lived experiences, and the trauma embedded in those experiences, impact their ability to participate in, and contribute to, higher education programs and how the content of available programming can address their unique needs.[40]

Implicit in higher education conversations, as well as most equity analyses that continue to advocate for HEA's intent to improve underserved student outcomes, is the assumption that the student populations in question are not incarcerated; these are students who attend school outside of the correctional context. In that regard, incarcerated students have largely been rendered invisible in broader postsecondary equity conversations.[41] The tide is shifting, however, and as the long overdue HEA reauthorization remains a priority for both practitioners and policymakers, the case to improve postsecondary educational access for the incarcerated student, and embed them in conversations about higher education, writ large, continues to gain momentum on both sides of the aisle. The recent economic stimulus package and COVID-19 response illustrate this shift, where the Consolidated Appropriations Act of 2021 ended the ban. This goes a long way in addressing the problems outlined in this chapter, though more work is to be done to fully support educational opportunities for incarcerated individuals.

DEBATING BENEFITS OF POSTSECONDARY EDUCATION FOR INCARCERATED INDIVIDUALS

The debate around the provision of postsecondary education to incarcerated persons has deep historical routes. Data in support of this type of programming date back to the late nineteenth century when Louis Pilsbury, the president of the Board of Managers at the New York State Reformatory at Elmira, noted that inmate behavior was positively impacted by participation in educational programming.[42] Almost a century later, Seashore and Haberfeld penned their seminal work *Prisoner Education: Project NewGate and Other College Programs*, similarly highlighting the benefits of educating incarcerated persons.[43] Following their work, programs continued to increase in states like Texas (Texas Prison College System), Alabama (Ingram State Technical College), and New York (Niagara Consortium at Attica) while research continued to demonstrate the positive impacts of education behind bars.[44]

Research consistently shows formerly incarcerated individuals with a postsecondary credential have a better chance of securing postrelease employment than a formerly incarcerated individual without a credential.[45] But these outcomes are not the same for everybody. Even with the stigma associated with the "ex-offender" label, white ex-offenders are more likely to secure employment postrelease than their similarly credentialed Black counterparts.[46] The research around the importance of higher education programs in prison is clear; on average, returning citizens with education credentials fare better in postrelease employment and other outcomes than those without credentials; however, race and ethnicity still play a significant role.

Despite over a century's worth of research on the benefits of postsecondary access for incarcerated students, the debates were recently reignited by then-President Barack Obama's criminal justice reform agenda. A 2013 RAND study represented the contemporary watershed moment in research examining the impact of educational opportunities on incarcerated students' postrelease outcomes.[47] Commissioned by former Attorney General Eric Holder, the study highlighted the individual and societal postrelease benefits of participating in education programs while behind bars—ex-offenders who completed an education program while incarcerated had 43 percent lower odds of returning to custody than those who did not, translating to a 13 percentage-point reduction in recidivism risk for program participants.[48]

Toward the end of the Obama administration, the Department of Education (ED) used its Experimental Sites Initiative (ESI) authority, permitted by HEA in 1965, to announce a Second Chance Pell pilot program.[49] As a result, sixty-seven colleges and universities were selected to participate and offer credit-bearing postsecondary programs inside correctional facilities, offering a range of credentials that included career and technical certificates, associate's degrees, and bachelor's degrees. The Vera Institute of Justice noted that, by the conclusion of Fall 2017, student enrollment had increased 231 percent since the beginning of the experiment and the number of courses offered had increased 124 percent.[50] In terms of completion metrics, 954 postsecondary credentials have been awarded since the start of the experiment; 701 are certificates, 230 are associate's degrees, and 23 are bachelor's degrees. These data indicate that not only did more students enroll as the program progressed, but institutional capacity increased to accommodate more available courses and, most importantly, incarcerated students were succeeding.

MOVING FORWARD

Ongoing discussions about comprehensive HEA reauthorization have included the possibility of reinstating Pell for incarcerated learners, in no small part due to the attention that the Second Chance Pell pilot program has garnered across the country, and particularly within the beltway. While the Promoting Real Opportunity, Success and Prosperity through Education Reform (PROSPER) Act—introduced in December 2017 by US House Education and Workforce Committee chairwoman, Rep. Virginia Foxx (R-NC) and Rep. Brett Guthrie (R-KY), chairman of the Higher Education and Workforce Development subcommittee—does not propose reinstating Pell access to this population, the Aim Higher Act—introduced in July 2018 by US House Education and Workforce Committee Ranking Member Bobby Scott (D-VA)—repeals the 1994 provision banning Pell access.

In the Senate, however, there has been more bipartisan interest in Pell reinstatement for this population, and members have expressed interest in the ED pilot program as a key opportunity to collect comprehensive data about the impact of higher education programs in prison and effectively inform legislative debate around lifting the ban.[51] For instance, in February 2018, Senate HELP Committee Chairman Lamar Alexander (R-TN) and Ranking Member Patty Murray (D-WA) were individually cited in the media expressing interest in reconsidering Pell Grants for incarcerated students.[52] Both members noted an interest in setting up incarcerated students for success upon release and the need for better data to inform policymakers about the efficacy of such educational opportunities.

Similarly, in the executive branch, ED Secretary Betsy DeVos went on record calling the potential reinstatement of Pell Grants for inmates a "very good and interesting possibility" and her own postsecondary advisors expressed a renewed interest in examining data and learning about best practices in offering postsecondary opportunities to incarcerated individuals.[53] The department's own ESI item inventory, which serves as the basis upon which to evaluate experimental site programs like Second

Chance Pell, highlights the need for practitioners, researchers, and policymakers to collect and analyze data in a way that speaks to program quality, student success, and the nature of education as a transformative endeavor. With political consensus slowly growing—both across party lines and within the branches of federal government—the Consolidated Appropriations Act of 2021 ended the ban and did so without exclusionary carveouts related to sentence or conviction.[54]

The current "education in prison" research paradigm rests squarely on the questions of whether and to what extent education reduces recidivism. While postrelease outcomes are certainly important to note from an accountability perspective, relevant outcomes must be defined beyond public safety. In broader postsecondary education, for instance, outcomes might include employment, civic engagement, leadership roles, and even postgraduation income and earnings data to contemplate return on investment for certain majors and programs.

A narrow focus on recidivism reduction as the ultimate objective of a higher education program in prison ignores the complexity of recidivism as a composite variable. In the same way that socioeconomic status is a combination of a number of variables (i.e., individual income, parent educational level, zip code, individual educational attainment), so, too, is recidivism a combination of variables such as access to housing, the extent of employment discrimination, availability of mental health services, access to public assistance, and other collateral consequences not currently under the prison education research umbrella. To broaden the context within which we think about and define program success, and ultimately how we embed access for this population into HEA reauthorization, we must advocate for rigorous evaluation and nuanced analysis that properly recontextualizes performance indicators for confined learners and embeds their needs in the equity lexicon. This nuanced understanding of the impact of higher education programs in prison has the potential to align itself well within the initial goals of the HEA and the ethos undergirding the existence of Pell Grants.

Senator Pell's passion for access and the removal of barriers to postsecondary education has provided millions of students with the opportunity to realize their college dreams. Given his original advocacy for Pell funds to remain accessible to incarcerated people, it seems that these financial aid mechanisms were in fact designed precisely to increase access to the communities that the 1994 ban excluded from receiving these benefits. While federal action lifted this ban via an appropriations bill, it is noteworthy that any comprehensive HEA reauthorization conversation must continue to advocate for expanding Pell Grants for incarcerated students. We must remind ourselves about the transformative power of postsecondary education in this country and the original intent behind the 1965 legislation that sought to open these opportunities to otherwise marginalized populations. To that end, we recommend a close and critical conversation around the ways in which Pell Grant access for incarcerated students can and should be structured to determine the best tenets of student and institutional eligibility. These conversations must, above all, focus on the humanity of the individuals being served and center the idea that access to education is an essential human right.

CHAPTER 6

How Accountability Can Increase Racial Inequality

The Case of Federal Risk Sharing

NICHOLAS HILLMAN

THE CURRENT ACCOUNTABILITY MOVEMENT in higher education operates on two guiding principles. The first is that better information will help students make well-informed educational decisions. The second is that financial incentives will encourage colleges to focus on—and ultimately improve—educational outcomes. These two principles are complementary since data are at the core of any financial incentive system. However, these two principles can lead policymakers to design accountability systems that reinforce—rather than reverse—inequalities. This chapter uses federal "risk-sharing" proposals to illustrate how efforts based on these principles, even when well intended, can misfire.

Using College Scorecard data, this chapter analyzes loan repayment records for 4,571 US colleges and universities, finding 45 percent of borrowers have reduced their principal balance three years into repayment. There is a wide degree of variation around these rates, but even after controlling for a number of institution-level characteristics (e.g., family income, percent borrowing, graduation rate, etc.), for-profit colleges consistently have the poorest loan repayment outcomes. Low repayment rates are not isolated in the for-profit sector; colleges serving higher shares of low-income students and where high shares of students borrow tend to have the lowest repayment rates. Those serving high-income and white students—the very students who benefit most from racial and economic inequality—have the highest repayment rates. Historically Black Colleges and Universities (HCBUs) and Predominantly Black Institutions (PBIs) have lower repayment rates than other Minority-Serving Institutions (MSIs). The chapter concludes with policy recommendations for improving risk-sharing proposals and alternative accountability strategies designed to promote educational opportunity and equity.

RISK-SHARING PROPOSALS

In 2015, Senator Lamar Alexander, chairman of the Senate Health, Education, Labor and Pensions (HELP) committee, released a white paper outlining the need for a new approach to federal oversight of higher education. It proposed a "market-based" accountability system consistent with the two broad principles outlined above, which would require all colleges participating in federal student aid programs to "share in the risk of lending to student borrowers."[1] Data on student loan default and repayment rates would become primary metrics federal policymakers use to evaluate colleges' performance. Colleges with high default rates or low repayment rates would face financial penalties for these outcomes and in turn would have a financial incentive to improve both. Without these incentives, colleges have little "skin in the game" to deliver the highest-quality education that would guard against these negative outcomes.

The concept initially received bipartisan support, where both Democrats and Republicans introduced stand-alone risk-sharing bills in 2015. That year, Democratic Senators Jack Reed, Dick Durbin, Elizabeth Warren, and Christopher Murphy introduced the Protect Student Borrowers Act, and Senators Jeanne Shaheen and Orrin Hatch introduced the bipartisan Student Protection and Success Act. The former would use the cohort default rate (CDR) to reward and penalize colleges; those with higher default rates would pay larger fines, and these fines would be reinvested into the Pell Grant program and default prevention efforts. The latter proposal would replace the CDR with a cohort-based repayment rate measuring the share of borrowers reducing their outstanding principal balance by at least one dollar within three years of repayment. Colleges with the lowest repayment rates would be required to pay fines into a "College Opportunity Bonus Program" that would go to colleges with high repayment rates but also serving large shares of Pell Grant recipients.

Fast forward to today, when House Republicans and Democrats have each outlined different versions of a comprehensive Higher Education Act (HEA) reauthorization. The stand-alone bills discussed above are not part of the Republican's PROSPER Act or the Democrat's Aim Higher Act. However, the basic idea of releasing more data about loan default and repayment, while tying federal funding to those data points, is very much alive. House Republicans desire to replace the CDR with program-level repayment rates, while House Democrats seek a tiered system rewarding and penalizing colleges based on their default rates.[2] Congress is likely to consider some version of a risk-sharing accountability system, where colleges receiving federal student aid will be required to more closely monitor, improve, and ultimately face penalties for their former students' loan debts.

RELEVANT RESEARCH

With more than 44.7 million people carrying federal student loan debt, there is no simple answer explaining why so many do not repay. And no single answer will sufficiently account for the unique circumstances of each individual borrower. A borrower may have been making on-time payments but then stopped due to unforeseen circumstances, like losing a job, facing health emergencies, or getting behind on other debts.[3] Federal loan programs offer emergency protections that temporarily stop payments for borrowers who fall on hard times. But if borrowers do not know how to navigate this bureaucratic process, or if their loan servicer is not proactively helping them avoid delinquency or default, then they can easily miss payments and get behind on their debts.[4]

The next two tables help contextualize student loan repayment trends. First, table 6.1 shows the current repayment status of all borrowers in the Direct Loan program. Most borrowers are either making on-time repayments (e.g., current) or have payments temporarily paused because they are enrolled in school or recently left and are in their grace period. However, a sizable share of borrowers do not meet these two conditions, suggesting they are either falling behind on debts (at least thirty-one days delinquent) or may face economic hardship or need other temporary stops to their payments (in forbearance or deferment). Approximately 37 percent of borrowers in the federal Direct Loan program are either delinquent (7 percent), in forbearance/deferment (17 percent), or are in default (13 percent). This sums to nearly 14 million borrowers who are not making progress paying down their federal student loan debt.

To avoid these negative outcomes, borrowers may opt into income-driven repayment plans. Similarly, if a student previously defaulted, their servicer may put them into income-driven repayment to help rehabilitate

TABLE 6.1 **Direct Loan portfolio by loan status, number of borrowers (in millions)**

	In repayment		Deferment	Forbearance	In default	In school/ grace period
	Current	Delinquent				
2014	9.1	2.5	3.6	2.2	2.5	10.4
2015	11.1	2.8	3.5	2.6	3.0	9.9
2016	12.5	2.7	3.6	2.8	3.7	9.6
2017	13.9	2.9	3.6	2.6	4.3	9.1
2018	15.3	2.6	3.7	2.7	4.9	8.7

Note: These numbers are from the second quarter of each federal fiscal year, excluding all FFEL loans.

their loans though this does not appear to be standard practice.[5] Federal income-driven repayment plans are designed to help make monthly payments more predictable and manageable, thus promoting *consumption smoothing* where monthly bills are based on the borrower's prior years' earnings.[6] This type of repayment insures against the negative outcomes discussed above, and table 6.2 shows the number of nondefaulted Direct Loan borrowers by repayment plans. Here, we see approximately 6.9 million (or 29 percent of the total) repay through an income-driven plan that ties payments to earnings. Notably, most borrowers do not opt into these programs and instead repay via "level" or "graduated" plans that use fixed monthly payments or payments that grow over time, respectively.

Making on-time payments can be overwhelming when money is tight, and even more so when unforeseen emergencies occur. Compound onto these challenges the administrative burdens and bureaucratic hurdles that vex our current student aid system, and we might also see that *information asymmetry* is behind these repayment problems.[7] In one study, researchers found 43 percent of community college borrowers who defaulted never took any action on their loans prior to default—they did not apply for emergency protections, nor did they opt into an income-driven repayment plan.[8] While we do not know why borrowers fail to take any action on their loans, including making a first payment, it is possible at least some are unaware of their obligations or were poorly informed about

TABLE 6.2 **Direct Loan portfolio by repayment plan, number of borrowers (in millions)**

	Level	Graduated	Income-contingent	Income-based	Pay-as-you-earn	Repay-as-you-earn	Other
2014	12.4	2.0	0.6	1.4	0.2	n/a	0.9
2015	12.9	2.6	0.6	2.3	0.5	n/a	0.9
2016	12.9	3.1	0.6	3.1	1.0	0.2	0.8
2017	12.8	3.1	0.6	3.0	1.1	1.5	0.7
2018	12.8	3.3	0.6	2.9	1.2	2.2	1.0

Note: These numbers are from the second quarter of each federal fiscal year, excluding all FFEL loans.

their repayment options—they may not even know they borrowed a loan in the first place.[9]

Any combination of these three explanations—*unforeseen circumstances, consumption smoothing,* and *information asymmetry*—can provide a plausible reason why borrowers struggle to repay. However, not all borrowers have equal chances of experiencing these adverse events. Wealthier students have family financial resources to fall back on, making them more likely to repay even when facing unforeseen circumstances or low earnings. They may even have family members who have gone through college already and know how to navigate the loan repayment system. But due to racial and economic inequality, Black and Hispanic students are far less likely to have family wealth and income to fall back on, and these same students are more likely to be first in their families to go to college.

DATA AND ANALYSIS

To investigate the relationship between a college-level repayment rate and various institutional characteristics, the following analysis uses the most recent College Scorecard data. The key outcome—student loan repayment rates—measures the proportion of borrowers in a cohort who have paid at least $1 toward their principal balance within three years of entering repayment. This is first modeled via ordinary least squares (OLS) regression to estimate the average relationship between each covariate and the outcome. Next, it extends the OLS analysis by including a quantile regression, which estimates the relationship between each covariate and the outcome but at different points in the distribution. Doing so allows us to see whether variables are more strongly correlated with repayment at the low end of repayment rates (e.g., the tenth percentile) as opposed to the high end (e.g., ninetieth percentile).

To estimate the repayment rate outcome, each regression model controls for the number of undergraduate degree-seeking students (per 1,000); net price; first-time, full-time graduation rate; proportion of students borrowing federal loans; average family income of aid recipients; type of Minority-Serving Institutions; and institutional sector. The analytical sample includes campuses reporting repayment rates and nonmissing covariates, resulting in 4,571 institutions. Results from this analysis are all correlational and designed to answer questions about the distribution of repayment rates; they are not designed to estimate the causal effects of a particular variable on repayment.

FINDINGS

Table 6.3 shows descriptive statistics of all variables used in the analysis. The mean repayment rate for the sample is 45 percent, though there is a wide degree of variation across deciles. The lowest decile repayment rate is 18 percent while the highest is 79 percent. This table also shows the mean income in the lowest repayment decile is around $18,790 but is $87,350 in the highest repayment decile. Similarly, this table shows that 71 percent of institutions in the top repayment decile are nonprofit four-year colleges while 64 percent of the lowest repayment decile consists of for-profit two-year colleges.

Table 6.4 shows the regression results where the first column includes mean OLS estimates and the following five columns report the 10th, 25th, 50th, 75th, and 90th percentiles, respectively. Four main findings emerge from this table. First, colleges with high graduation rates and high income levels tend to have higher repayment rates—this is true on average (OLS) and across the entire repayment distribution. If a college's repayment rate is a function of enrolling high-income students and having high graduation rates (two variables that are already highly correlated), then it may be difficult to know if high repayment rates are due to a college's effort in improving that outcome or simply their ability to enroll wealthy students who are more likely to graduate.

Second, even after controlling for other factors, HBCUs and PBIs have significantly lower repayment rates across the entire distribution.

TABLE 6.3 **Descriptive statistics by repayment decile rank**

					DECILE RANK						
	Mean	Lowest decile	2nd	3rd	4th	5th	6th	7th	8th	9th	Highest decile
Repayment rate (three years)	0.45	0.18	0.25	0.30	0.35	0.40	0.45	0.51	0.58	0.66	0.79
Undergraduates (1,000)	3.25	0.80	2.34	2.75	2.91	2.99	3.01	3.53	3.94	4.78	5.47
Net price	16.68	17.83	16.92	14.37	14.62	13.32	14.24	14.76	16.96	19.78	24.04
FT/FT grad rate (150%)	0.51	0.46	0.44	0.46	0.48	0.47	0.48	0.48	0.53	0.59	0.73
Percent federal loans	0.54	0.69	0.60	0.53	0.51	0.46	0.47	0.49	0.55	0.59	0.52
Percent first-generation	0.45	0.56	0.54	0.52	0.51	0.49	0.47	0.44	0.40	0.34	0.23
Family income ($1,000)	40.18	18.79	22.41	25.40	28.23	30.80	35.75	40.97	49.99	62.14	87.35
MSI type											
HBCU	0.02	0.07	0.05	0.03	0.02	0.01	0.01	0.00	0.00	0.00	0.00
TCU	0.00	0.00	0.00	0.00	0.00	0.00	0.00	0.00	0.00	0.00	0.00
HSI	0.07	0.02	0.03	0.08	0.09	0.10	0.12	0.11	0.06	0.04	0.01
ANNHI	0.00	0.00	0.00	0.00	0.00	0.00	0.00	0.01	0.00	0.00	0.00
PBI	0.02	0.06	0.05	0.03	0.02	0.01	0.01	0.00	0.00	0.00	0.00
AANAPI	0.02	0.00	0.02	0.02	0.01	0.02	0.02	0.05	0.04	0.04	0.02
NANTI	0.00	0.00	0.00	0.00	0.01	0.01	0.02	0.00	0.00	0.00	0.00
Sector											
Public four-year	0.14	0.02	0.04	0.05	0.06	0.08	0.13	0.19	0.26	0.34	0.23
Public two-year	0.20	0.08	0.16	0.28	0.31	0.36	0.32	0.28	0.14	0.05	0.02
Nonprofit four-year	0.23	0.13	0.03	0.05	0.07	0.09	0.13	0.25	0.37	0.47	0.71
Nonprofit two-year	0.03	0.04	0.05	0.05	0.01	0.02	0.03	0.02	0.01	0.04	0.01
For-profit four-year	0.06	0.09	0.20	0.11	0.10	0.03	0.02	0.03	0.03	0.02	0.01
For-profit two-year	0.34	0.64	0.52	0.46	0.45	0.42	0.36	0.23	0.19	0.09	0.02
Observations	4,571	460	455	457	458	456	457	457	457	457	457

On average, HBCUs' repayment rates are 15.8 percent lower than other colleges, though this ranges from a low of 13.8 percent (90th percentile) to a high of 21.6 percent (25th percentile). Similar patterns emerge for PBIs, though with smaller magnitudes. The conclusion here is that even among colleges with the highest repayment rates, HBCUs and PBIs have significantly lower repayment rates.

TABLE 6.4 **OLS and quantile regression estimates of student loan repayment rates (standard errors)**

	OLS	PERCENTILE				
		10th	25th	50th	75th	90th
Undergrad enrollment	−0.001*** (0.000)	0.000 (0.000)	−0.001*** (0.000)	−0.001*** (0.000)	−0.001** (0.000)	−0.001 (0.001)
Net price	−0.002*** (0.000)	−0.001** (0.000)	−0.001*** (0.000)	−0.003*** (0.000)	−0.002*** (0.000)	−0.001* (0.001)
FT/FT grad rate	0.188*** (0.008)	0.113*** (0.010)	0.159*** (0.009)	0.187*** (0.009)	0.233*** (0.011)	0.257*** (0.016)
Percent federal loans	−0.060*** (0.008)	−0.012 (0.010)	−0.032*** (0.009)	−0.044*** (0.009)	−0.068*** (0.011)	−0.098*** (0.016)
Percent first-generation	−0.173*** (0.020)	−0.179*** (0.027)	−0.216*** (0.023)	−0.203*** (0.024)	−0.156*** (0.029)	−0.155*** (0.042)
Family income	0.005*** (0.000)	0.005*** (0.000)	0.005*** (0.000)	0.005*** (0.000)	0.004*** (0.000)	0.004*** (0.000)
HBCU	−0.158*** (0.010)	−0.149*** (0.014)	−0.177*** (0.012)	−0.177*** (0.012)	−0.166*** (0.015)	−0.138*** (0.021)
TCU	−0.064 (0.044)	−0.114 (0.059)	0.014 (0.051)	−0.056 (0.052)	−0.077 (0.063)	−0.061 (0.090)
HSI	0.021*** (0.006)	0.027*** (0.008)	0.023*** (0.007)	0.024*** (0.007)	0.026** (0.008)	0.007 (0.012)
ANNHI	0.052 (0.029)	0.075 (0.039)	0.048 (0.034)	0.039 (0.035)	0.039 (0.042)	0.064 (0.060)
PBI	−0.089*** (0.010)	−0.075*** (0.014)	−0.088*** (0.012)	−0.088*** (0.012)	−0.100*** (0.014)	−0.084*** (0.021)
AANAPI	0.047*** (0.009)	0.035** (0.012)	0.024* (0.010)	0.044*** (0.010)	0.069*** (0.013)	0.055** (0.018)
NANTI	−0.027 (0.019)	0.01 (0.025)	−0.006 (0.022)	−0.031 (0.022)	−0.031 (0.027)	−0.068 (0.039)
Public four-year	0.037*** (0.006)	0.025*** (0.007)	0.041*** (0.006)	0.040*** (0.007)	0.036*** (0.008)	0.029** (0.011)
Nonprofit four-year	0.025*** (0.006)	0.002 (0.008)	0.023*** (0.007)	0.037*** (0.007)	0.033*** (0.009)	0.029* (0.012)
Nonprofit two-year	−0.002 (0.009)	−0.039** (0.012)	−0.045*** (0.011)	−0.031** (0.011)	0.054*** (0.013)	0.090*** (0.019)
For-profit four-year	−0.026*** (0.007)	−0.034*** (0.010)	−0.039*** (0.009)	−0.025** (0.009)	−0.028** (0.011)	−0.030* (0.015)
For-profit two-year	−0.044*** (0.006)	−0.048*** (0.008)	−0.059*** (0.007)	−0.047*** (0.007)	−0.052*** (0.008)	−0.042*** (0.012)
Intercept	0.309*** (0.013)	0.206*** (0.018)	0.273*** (0.015)	0.322*** (0.016)	0.349*** (0.019)	0.414*** (0.027)

Note: * $p<0.05$, ** $p<0.01$, *** $p<0.001$

Third, for-profit four-year and two-year colleges consistently have lower repayment rates than public two-year colleges (the reference group) after controlling for a range of factors expected to correlate with repayment. Across most of the distribution, public and nonprofit four-year colleges have significantly higher repayment rates than community colleges—indicating for-profit colleges systematically differ from public and nonprofit institutions, though they are most similar to nonprofit two-year institutions in the lower end of the repayment distribution.

Fourth, colleges with higher net price and where larger proportions of students borrow tend to have lower repayment rates. A similar pattern emerges with first-generation students, where repayment rates are lower as the share of first-generation students rises. This finding complements the first by suggesting repayment is a function of the college's socioeconomic profile of students. First-generation students may simultaneously be more reliant on loans and enrolled in colleges that do not offer high discount rates (e.g., they have higher net price), making it difficult to disentangle this relationship.

ILLUSTRATIONS

To illustrate these findings a bit further, figure 6.1 shows the relationship between repayment rates and average family income of undergraduates, where there is a clear positive relationship between the two. The richer the school, the better their repayment rates. This graph also highlights schools with the highest percentage of Black and Hispanic students that *also* have the highest percentage of first-generation students to illustrate how repayment rates cut along lines of race and class. Doing so helps show that colleges serving lower-income students also tend to have the highest proportion of Black, Hispanic, and first-generation students, illustrating the tight coupling of race, class, and repayment.

Figure 6.2 takes a closer look at this relationship by differentiating colleges by sector and highlighting Minority-Serving Institutions. As

FIGURE 6.1   Three-year repayment rates by family income, highlighting colleges with highest shares of Black, Hispanic, and first-generation students

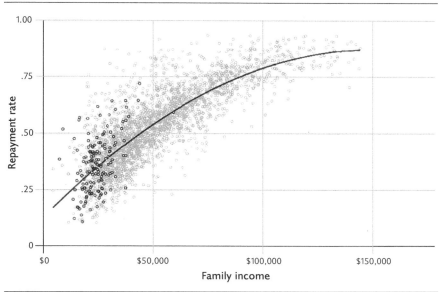

discussed in the regression results, HBCUs and PBIs tend to have the lowest repayment rates among all MSIs, while Hispanic-Serving Institutions (HSIs) tend to have higher rates. This figure further illustrates the tight link between race, income, and repayment where—across all sectors—colleges enrolling high-income students and that are not MSIs tend to have the highest loan repayment rates, while those enrolling students from low-income families and serving minoritized students tend to have the lowest.

The regression results found colleges have higher repayment rates when they also have high graduation rates. Figure 6.3 shows repayment rates for completers (dark circles) and noncompleters (light circles), demonstrating two important patterns. First, students who complete their degrees tend to have higher repayment rates than those who leave college with debt and no degree. Second, we still see the same pattern as

FIGURE 6.2   Three-year repayment rates by family income, highlighting
Minority-Serving Institutions

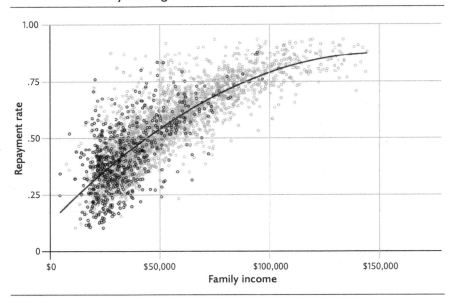

FIGURE 6.3   Three-year repayment rates by degree completion status

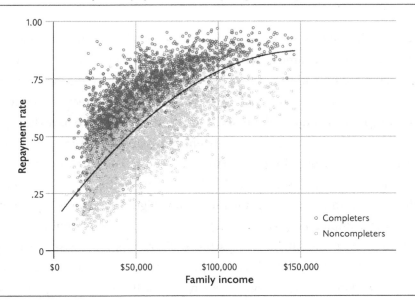

in the previous two figures where income and repayment rates are still highly correlated, but this pattern strongly holds even when comparing completers to noncompleters. In fact, repayment rates at high-income colleges are higher across the board (both among completers and non-completers) than they are for lower-income colleges. Repayment rates for *completers* at low-income colleges are lower than that of *noncompleters* at high-income colleges—a classic example of a poorly designed account-ability metric where rich colleges stand to benefit from inequality while poor ones stand to be harmed the most.

DISCUSSION

Repayment rates do not account for the racial and economic inequali-ties students of color face before, during, and after college. Nevertheless, policymakers are eager to use this new metric to reward or sanction col-leges. It would be fair to do so if colleges have direct and unambiguous control over the repayment outcomes, or if degree attainment somehow erased racial and economic inequality. It would also be fair to hold col-leges accountable for these outcomes if colleges themselves were able to control which repayment plans borrowers elect upon entering repayment (e.g., income-driven repayment rather than the standard mortgage-style plan). But none of these cases apply with respect to the issues raised in this chapter: student loan repayment is complicated by layers of economic and racial injustice. Applying an overly simplistic metric that fails to account for these differences is likely to reinforce existing inequalities.

This problem is not unique to risk-sharing efforts, nor is it simply a function of the repayment rate metric. The repayment rate metric could certainly be improved by distinguishing between repayment plans, disag-gregating by student characteristics (e.g., race/ethnicity, earnings, employ-ment status). But doing so is not going to fix the underlying problems outlined in this chapter—especially when considering the wide degree of variation that exists with respect to the outcome. People struggle in repayment for a number of reasons, and research to date has not fully explained the causal chain of events that drive people into (and out of) these poor repayment outcomes. Even if the causal chain were unambiguous, colleges serving the students struggling the most are likely to have the least resources to improve these outcomes. If, for example, a college-level intervention proved successful in improving student loan repayment, the colleges with the greatest capacity (human, technological, and financial resources) would likely be the ones to initiate the change while those with the least would not.

To paraphrase Campbell's law, the more any quantitative indicator is used for high-stakes accountability, the more likely it is to be corrupted and to distort the very process it seeks to monitor. This is amplified in complex social settings like education, where the process of educating students—or in this case, ensuring students repay their loans—is not a routine or simple task that colleges alone can control. What if we find that a large share of borrowers fail to repay their loans because of medical emergencies that make any other bills unaffordable? In this instance, it is unclear how or why a college would be responsible for nonpayment. Perhaps a college would be more responsible for repayment if borrowers fail to repay because they did not know they had a loan or because they did not know loans had to be repaid. In this instance, the likely solution would be for colleges to adopt more financial literacy interventions; unfortunately, the evidence to date on the efficacy of financial literacy suggests this will unlikely make much impact on the outcome.

These brief examples illustrate the complexity of repayment—in the first case, colleges may have little to no control over the outcome; in the second, colleges may try to improve the outcomes, but their interventions may simply be ineffective. Until we know precisely what a college, or more aptly the professionals working within colleges, should do to improve loan repayment outcomes, it seems premature to hold colleges accountable for those outcomes. This is a common story in performance management literature, where policy actors—in the name of better accountability—rely on overly simplistic performance metrics to measure and ultimately correct complex social problems. Measuring and monitoring complex problems is certainly important and needed in accountability frameworks, but tying high-stakes financial incentives to these indicators—especially when we do not know how to improve them—introduces new risks into the risk-sharing environment.

A college official who now has loan repayment outcomes and financial incentives to improve them would naturally ask, "What do I do and with what resources?" The quickest and easiest answer is to simply limit the amount of loan debt students take on. Wealthy colleges might accomplish this by replacing loans with grants in students' aid packages. But for the majority of colleges that do not have the resources to do so, two options are likely to be on the table: enroll fewer students who have financial need or restrict access to federal loans. On the first option, this is already happening in states that use performance-based funding policies. On the second option, community colleges that opt out of federal loan programs push students into more expensive private loan programs while simultaneously reducing access. There are predictable outcomes that are—at least from a civil rights perspective—undesirable and unfair since they disproportionately harm our nation's most marginalized communities while keeping those with the greatest privileges safe from harm.

ALTERNATIVES TO RISK SHARING

The beginning of this chapter explained how getting "better data" and exposing colleges to more "skin in the game" are core principles in today's accountability conversations. The underlying belief is that more information and greater financial incentives will induce colleges to focus on and ultimately improve key performance indicators. In the case of risk sharing, it assumes professionals working in colleges (1) are not well informed about loan repayment problems; (2) have little incentive to address these problems; (3) know how to improve loan repayment outcomes; (4) have the resources to do so; and (5) would not have done so in the absence of risk sharing. Accountability data can help address (1); and the risk of losing money, along with the potential reward of gaining new money, will address the organizational inertia behind the rest.

An alternative accountability system with equity-based principles and antideficit assumptions may offer a more promising path where federal policymakers and colleges would be more likely to improve student loan repayment problems. Four features of such a system are outlined here:

- *Performance development grants.* At the core of any accountability debate rests a tension between resource capacity and performance. If a college is asked to perform but does not have the resources or capacity to do so, then we might expect to see very little improvement on a particular policy outcome. Alternatively, if a college has ample resources, then why might it not be performing well? To address this tension, federal policymakers could invest in performance development grants—akin to K–12 School Improvement Grants—where the US Department of Education could identify the "poorest-performing" colleges and then assess the extent to which they have the capacity to adopt promising programs and practices that will improve student loan repayment or any other key accountability outcome. Through that review, they may find colleges do not have the financial capacity to hold debt down, or they may not have the technology infrastructure to adequately contact or notify students of various supports that could help in repayment. The grants could then be used to help colleges build and then sustain this capacity; once the college reaches the necessary performance threshold, they would be expected to maintain this success. This equity-based form of accountability would target resources to colleges that have the greatest need while promoting organizational learning and improvement that are unlikely to occur under high-stakes pay-for-performance regimes.

- *Need-based funding for colleges.* Unequal financial resources are behind many of the poor educational outcomes we see in higher education. Colleges receiving the least amount of subsidy tend to produce the poorest outcomes in large part because these same colleges are broad-access and serve students who have faced significant economic, racial, and academic inequalities before college. Now these same colleges are expected to reverse these inequalities with far fewer resources than more selective and wealthier institutions—the same institutions serving the most privileged students. Risk-sharing policies run the risk of penalizing broad-access colleges and Minority-Serving Institutions where students are more likely to borrow—and to borrow more—but are also likely to face labor market inequality after they leave. By investing in these institutions, the federal government may be able to reduce the need for students to borrow in the first place, thus reducing the downstream problems related to loan repayment. Similarly, this investment may be coupled with the previous accountability effort to help colleges adopt and sustain promising interventions that can improve performance outcomes. Such an approach would hold colleges more accountable to taxpayers by helping underresourced colleges prevent adverse downstream outcomes.
- *Comprehensive efforts to improve repayment.* Risk-sharing proposals focus exclusively on one single actor in students' loan experience—their college. But several other actors are involved in repayment outcomes including loan servicers, employers, state policymakers, and even local community-based organizations. Federal policymakers could hold servicers more accountable for ensuring they are moving enough students into good standing on their loans. They could similarly hold employers more accountable for the minimum wages they pay or the health benefits they make available in order for borrowers to have more relief when paying their monthly student loan bill. Similarly, federal policymakers could find ways to hold states

more accountable for maintaining and growing their investment in public higher education as a way to prevent the public sector need for borrowing in the first place. Finally, policymakers could even create innovative programs to help community-based organizations work with struggling borrowers who may be participating in other public benefit programs. These brief examples illustrate that colleges alone cannot and should not be responsible for the repayment outcomes of their former students. By taking proactive and more comprehensive approaches to improving loan repayment, federal policymakers would hold a wider range of stakeholders accountable for addressing and ultimately reversing the very inequalities lurking in these repayment debates.

• *Technical assistance labs.* When social problems are deeply entangled in racial and economic inequality, like the student loan repayment problems outlined here, colleges alone may not have the answers. The previous recommendation encourages policymakers to take a community-based and comprehensive approach to the problem; this recommendation focuses on technical ways to improve repayment. Evaluation, assessment, data sharing, interviews, and a host of other research activities are needed to fully understand the causes and consequences of loan default. To fix a complex social problem, organizations need to know what works—and this can come through technical assistance labs sharing research findings, promising practices, and other lessons—and failures—learned along the way. Student loan repayment is a new frontier in federal higher education policymaking, and very little research exists with respect to how colleges (or other stakeholders) can improve these outcomes. Accordingly, federal policymakers would be more accountable to taxpayers if they carefully analyzed, evaluated, and learned alongside campuses in collective efforts to improve repayment outcomes. This networked approach is also promising since mounting evidence shows organizations improve performance when they use accountability data for internal learning, collaboration, and professional development.

CONCLUSION

A comprehensive reauthorization of the Higher Education Act is due in the coming years, so policymakers interested in improving student loan repayment while holding colleges more accountable may look to "risk sharing" as an answer. However, such an approach is unlikely to improve outcomes and is very likely to worsen inequality. Even using disaggregated data and program-level repayment rates will do little to solve the problem if (1) colleges do not know what works in improving their former students' repayment rates, (2) colleges do not have the resources to improve these outcomes, or (3) these problems are deeply entangled with other social problems that expand far beyond the direct and unambiguous control of colleges. Because of this, risk-sharing policies are likely to do what other high-stakes performance regimes do best: reward the highest performers while doing little to improve the outcomes for those with the least. There is a very good chance the current "carrot-and-sticks" or "market-based" approach to higher education accountability will do little to address or improve the racial and economic inequalities outlined in this chapter.

Accordingly, this chapter offers equity-based accountability efforts that avoid deficit-based assumptions about colleges and their students, professionals, and local communities. To improve student loan repayment, federal policymakers will likely gain the most ground by investing in the very colleges serving students of color and low-income students. By focusing on building the specific capacity needs of particular colleges and pinpointing the repayment problems they face, policymakers will help colleges that need it the most—this form of accountability is radically different from the market-based models that dominate today's federal higher education conversations. Such an approach would include comprehensive efforts involving actors far beyond the walls of colleges in an effort to address the root causes of poor repayment outcomes. A new approach would also prioritize and invest in basic research and technical assistance so colleges and their local networks can share promising lessons with others. Current risk-sharing proposals have none of these design features and, without new ideas on the table, federal policymakers may turn to convenient and technical solutions that fit with today's pay-for-performance mantra. An alternative way forward would pay for equity and, in so doing, promote greater accountability by addressing root causes of complex social problems.

CHAPTER 7

Minority-Serving Institutions

Current Policies and Future Actions

ANDRÉS CASTRO SAMAYOA

MINORITY-SERVING INSTITUTIONS (MSIs) enroll and confer the majority of undergraduate and graduate degrees to students of color in the United States, many of whom enter these institutions from under-resourced and highly unequal K–12 experiences. MSIs play a critical role in promoting opportunity and mobility in America, and politicians give these institutions rhetorical praise. But actions speak louder than words. During the Trump administration, federal appropriations to MSIs were under constant scrutiny while Democrats advocated for greater funding. The political tension, trade-offs, and neglect have serious consequences on these institutions and the students of color they serve. This chapter explores the contours of these federal funding and political debates and emphasizes the need for a serious federal investment strategy that can be achieved through reauthorizing the Higher Education Act (HEA).

This chapter provides an overview of the various legislative decisions that have supported MSIs over generations. It argues that federal policymaking has occurred through incremental change that has galvanized and reinforced unequal federal funding for these institutions. Alongside this legislative history, I offer evidence from an increasingly robust body of educational scholarship that centers MSIs as a unit of analysis. This work is critical in advancing a more nuanced appreciation for both the opportunities and current challenges faced by these institutions. Indeed, what these works suggest is that the importance of MSIs extends beyond the way these institutions can support their own students. Second, I offer evidence showing how—despite a public rhetoric of support for some MSIs—the Republican political strategy has been to curtail appropriations for these institutions without offering compelling evidence to justify these choices. This chapter highlights key actions and inactions by the Trump administration to illustrate these points.

Despite the chronic histories of state and federal underfunding and the pernicious effects of hostile societal environments for youth of color, many MSIs continue to do a promising job of supporting students to degree completion, achieving future gainful employment, and participating in meaningful civic opportunities.[1] As such, MSIs do, indeed, have much to share with all institutions of higher education. Thus, MSIs can serve as the starting point to explore promising practices to better support the very students that decades of scholarship remind us have been least supported by our education system; students whose intersecting racial, ethnic, socioeconomic, migrant, sexual, and gender identities have been consistently minoritized through exclusionary educational practices.[2]

As I explain later in this chapter, both the US House of Representatives and Senate's committees for appropriations categorically dismissed the Trump administration's proposed request to decrease discretionary support for MSIs. Though this rebuff provided a short-term reprieve from an executive leadership's impact on MSIs and their students, it nonetheless underscored the precarious position of MSIs given the potential for executive actions undermining federal support. In turn, I argue for the need to adequately understand why bolstering support for MSIs is not only morally just but also a sound investment toward improving our postsecondary system.

MSIs AS A POLITICAL CONSTITUENCY

Legislators, policy analysts, and educational researchers alike are familiar with categorizing our nation's colleges and universities in particular dyads: public/private, two-year/four-year, rural/urban, open-enrollment/selective, for-profit/nonprofit. All of these descriptors are meaningful ways of understanding a richly complex landscape of postsecondary organizations, though these approaches to clustering institutions of higher education (IHE) may not always tell us what students' experiences are like within IHEs. What, then, might we learn about our current postsecondary system if we encouraged a starting point that centers students of color's presence on these campuses?

This chapter offers one answer to this question by focusing on MSIs as a valuable taxonomy to understand higher education in the United States and to explore how the executive branch under President Donald Trump sought to support (or not) students in the postsecondary system. Centering MSIs enables researchers and policymakers to meaningfully explore how we can work toward systematically improving our postsecondary education system to better support low-income students of color.[3] For one, focusing on MSIs allows us to ask different questions about our nation's colleges and universities by explicitly acknowledging how these institutions were built on de jure racial segregation and emerged within a legal framework that limited people of color's access to just educational opportunities.[4] Indeed, the inequitable foundations of our postsecondary landscape help us to understand how current policies claiming to be invested in every student's success are only truthful to the extent that we also confront these institutions' tarnished histories.

We are (and have been, for some time) in the midst of a political climate where colleges must litigate the value of using an applicant's race as a criterion in holistic admission processes.[5] I argue that it is precisely because of such growing public hostility to race-conscious conversations that we can benefit from better understanding how specific institutions strive to improve learning conditions for students whose experiences have most often been devalued within educational spaces. In effect, an increasing *de facto* resegregation of our K–12 system is well underway, coupled with rife inequities in funding for those in the public sector.[6] Purposeful efforts to amplify postsecondary institutions' work to support diverse student bodies is critical in any attempt to steward consistent progress toward more just educational opportunities in this country.

THE POLITICAL EMERGENCE
AND IMPORTANCE OF MSIs

Though current federal appropriations for Minority-Serving Institutions emerged from amendments introduced across multiple ratifications of the 1965 Higher Education Act, some of these institutions' founding precede the HEA by over a century. Specifically, Historically Black Colleges and Universities (HCBUs) date their origins to the latter part of the nineteenth century (primarily between the late 1860s and early 1900s) during a time when racial segregation prohibited any opportunities for access to (higher) education for Blacks in the United States. The passing of a second Morrill Land-Grant Act in 1890 offered a framework for states to establish land-grant institutions for Blacks in states with segregated education systems. The uncoordinated efforts that followed the second land grant anticipated the "separate but equal" mentality of racial separation upheld by the Supreme Court six years later in *Plessy v. Ferguson* (1896).[7]

Hardly equal in the apportioning of resources for infrastructure development since their inception, colleges with an expressed mission to support the education and development of Black students formally received targeted funding through the 1986 Higher Education Amendments under Title III, Part B. Further support for Historically Black Colleges and Universities has also been established to support particular graduate programs within HBCUs; specifically, Title VII, Part A, Subpart 4, of the HEA. Unlike other MSIs, HBCUs have also received federal support for a Capital Financing Program under the 1992 amendments to the HEA. Passing of this legislation was a congressional attempt to recognize the difficulties for HBCU campuses to support the maintenance of academic and residential facilities because of "their small enrollments, limited endowments, and other financial risk factors."[8]

Given that support for HBCUs is limited to institutions that were founded prior to 1964 with the intent to educate Blacks, Predominantly Black Institutions' (PBIs') programs support IHEs with high enrollments of Black students that may not meet HBCU eligibility criteria. First authorized in 2007 by the College Cost Reduction and Access Act (CCRAA), PBIs are institutions that have low educational and general expenditures and enroll at least 40 percent Black students and financially needy students, with at least one thousand students.[9]

As a response to the shifting demographics within postsecondary educations and in tandem with political lobbying from organizations like the Hispanic Association of Colleges and Universities, Hispanic-Serving Institutions (HSIs) were first recognized in congressional legislation in the 1992 amendments to the HEA. The reauthorization of the HEA six years later, in 1998, offered an opportunity for Congress to recognize "the importance of finding new ways of serving our Nation's rapidly growing Hispanic community, [Congress] has created a new part within Title V dedicated solely to supporting the needs of Hispanic-Serving Institutions."[10] Institutions that enroll at least 25 percent of Hispanic-identifying students within their undergraduate body and meet required enrollment of financially needy students are eligible for these grants. In 2008, through the Higher Education Opportunity Act, Congress also established the Promoting Postbaccalaureate Opportunities for Hispanic Americans

(PPOHA) program expressly for postbaccalaureate certificates within the same IHEs eligible for HSI programs.

An attempt to recognize the specific needs of Asian Americans and Pacific Islanders through the Asian American Native American Pacific Islander-Serving Institution (AANAPISI) designation was first proposed in 2002 by Robert Underwood in H.R. 4825. However, AANAPISIs were not authorized until 2007 under the College Cost Reduction and Access Act. In addition to meeting requirements under HEA Section 312(b), IHEs wishing to receive AANAPISI funds must also enroll at least 10 percent Asian American or Native American Pacific Islander students within their undergraduate student population.

The dispossession of indigenous lands and the specific needs of indigenous people's educational needs were recognized in the 1998 amendments of the HEA through the Strengthening American Indian Tribally Controlled Colleges and Universities Program (TCCU). Notably, though, Tribal Colleges had already been established decades prior, with Diné College first founded in 1968 under the auspices of the Indian Civil Rights Act of 1968.[11] In recognition of institutions that enroll Native American students but are not governed by indigenous leadership, the Strengthening Native American-Serving Nontribal Institutions (NASNTIs) program was first authorized in 2007 under the College Cost Reduction and Access Act.

A CURRENT SNAPSHOT OF MSIs

Given the varied legislative contexts that have supported institutions serving low-income students of color, the number of IHEs receiving federal support under the MSI designation varies every year. The Office of Postsecondary Education (OPE) invites IHEs to submit materials to determine their eligibility for the various competitive grants offered through federal appropriations. The most recent eligibility matrix offers the figures for institutional eligibility under the various grants earmarked for MSIs shown in table 7.1.

TABLE 7.1   **Snapshot of institutions' status for MSI grants for FY 2020**

	Potentially eligible for grant (need a waiver request)	Eligible to apply for program grants	Current program grantees
AANAPISI	161	103	11
AANAPISI-F	171	147	14
ANNH	1	16	12
ANNH-F	31	25	2
HBCU	0	0	96
HBCU Masters	0	0	17
HBGI	0	0	24
HSI Elig	57	266	170
HSI Stem	75	358	88
MSEIP	96	408	38
NASNTI	1	18	6
NASNTI-F	4	22	6
PBI Comp	4	73	24
PBI Mand	5	44	12
PPOHA	17	170	17
SIP	1,117	1,335	218
TCCU	0	0	35

Source: US Office of Postsecondary Education, Program Eligibility Matrix (2020).

Of note, the eligibility matrix is helpful to underscore how TCCUs and HBCUs are fixed in their institutional counts across fiscal years given the specific language used to determine their eligibility.[12] Similarly, some institutions may believe that they are eligible for these grants given that they enroll particular proportion of students of color. However, the language for eligibility also notes that institutions must also demonstrate relatively low educational and general expenditures alongside their enrollment of financially needy students of color.[13] In these cases, institutions are deemed partially eligible and would have to request a waiver to OPE for consideration.

However, only looking toward an institution's eligibility does not account for the challenges that IHEs face in procuring these competitive federal funds. Federal guidelines prevent institutions from securing grants targeted for multiple ethnoracial populations. For example, IHEs are selectively eligible for multiple grants depending on whether they hold concurrent grants disbursed by other MSI programs. The potential MSI "dual-designation" has posed an issue for IHEs as it animates competition between initiatives meant to support different groups of ethnoracial students within a specific campus.[14] As discussed later, the executive branch under President Trump proposed to address this issue by altogether doing away with certain competitive MSI grants for the sake of efficiency. To date, the executive branch has not offered evidence to support how such a proposal would prevent further entrenchment of already inequitable educational outcomes by race and ethnicity.

Given that MSIs receive funds for competitive and mandatory grants through federal appropriations established every fiscal year, examining presidential budgets offers insight into the executive branch's framing and prioritization of MSIs. Indeed, the scholarship on MSIs has demonstrated that securing funds through these various federal appropriations is critical to MSIs' ability to steward academic, administrative, and infrastructure improvements in the service of their students' development.[15] This section details the differences in funding for MSIs from fiscal year (FY) 2017 through the passing of the Coronavirus AID, Relief, and Economic Security (CARES) Act in 2020 as one way of understanding the changing tide of support for MSIs despite the public rhetoric alleging support for them.

In President Barack Obama's last request to support MSIs for the FY 2017 budget, both congressional Committees on Appropriations conferred the funds requested by the executive branch (see table 7.2). Notably, however, both of these committees did not offer support for a new MSI Innovation Fund. In its rejection of this request, the House of Representatives' Committee on Appropriations added that it "continue[d] to support HBCUs and Minority-Serving Institutions through Aid for Institutional Development, and support[ed] efforts to improve college access and completion at these and other institutions through increased funding for TRIO programs."[16]

TABLE 7.2 Overview of appropriations for Minority-Serving Institutions in FY 2017 (in thousands)

Authorizing legislation	Name of grant	FY 2016 enacted ($)	Presidential request ($)	US Senate proposed ($)	US House of Representatives proposed ($)	Final bill ($)
HEA Part III-A	Strengthening Institutions Program	86,534	86,534	86,534	86,534	86,534
HEA Part V-A	Strengthening Hispanic Serving Institutions	107,795	107,795	107,795	107,795	107,795
HEA Part V-B(512)	Promoting Postbaccalaureate Opportunities for Hispanic Americans	9,671	9,671	9,671	9,671	9,671
HEA Part III-B-323	Strengthening Historically Black Colleges and Universities	244,694	244,694	244,694	244,694	244,694
HEA Part III-B-326	Strengthening Historically Black Graduate Institutions	63,281	63,281	63,281	63,281	63,281
HEA Part III-A-318	Strengthening Predominately Black Institutions	9,942	9,942	9,942	9,942	9,942
HEA Part III-A-320	Strengthening Asian American Pacific Islander Serving Institutions	3,348	3,348	3,348	3,348	3,348
HEA Part III-A-317	Strengthening Alaska Native and Native Hawaiian Serving Institutions	13,802	13,802	13,802	13,802	13,802
HEA Part III-A-319	Strengthening Native American Serving Non-Tribal Institutions	3,348	3,348	3,348	3,348	3,348
HEA Part III-A-316	Strengthening Tribally Controlled Colleges and Universities	27,599	27,599	27,599	27,599	27,599
HEA Part VII A-4-723	Strengthening Master's Degree Programs at HBCUs			9,500	—	7,500
	Subtotal, Aid for institutional development	$ 570,014	$ 570,014	$ 579,514	$ 570,014	$ 577,514

Note: HEA = Higher Education Act.

Sources: H. Rep. No. 114-699, at 139 and 256 (2016), S. Rep. No. 114-274, at 189 and 256 (2016), 163 Cong. Rec. H4017 (2017).

In President Trump's budget request during his first year in the White House, every single program for MSIs had a reduced budget, totaling close to $95 million in proposed cuts (see table 7.2). The largest requested reduction for a single program was for the Strengthening Historically Black Colleges and Universities fund ($465,000), despite statements from Trump's prior proclamations that his "administration is committed to investing in HBCUs to help ensure they can educate future generations of American students."[17]

The final congressional appropriations bill, however, increased the funding for the Strengthening Historically Black Colleges and Universities program by almost $35 million, to $279,624,000 in FY 2018 from the preceding FY 2017's $244,694,000. Indeed, every single program for MSIs also received a larger appropriation than what was requested in the proposed presidential budget. Most notably, President Trump's request to altogether undo the Strengthening Institutions Program was not supported by either of the congressional Committees on Appropriations.

In February 2018, the White House released *An American Budget*, with the budget requests for FY 2019. Like its request from the previous year, it also aimed to reduce funds for MSIs, except this time it sought to achieve a substantive change in the existence of MSI grants. In its prose, the White House claimed to

> provide $501 million for Historically Black Colleges and Universities (HBCUs), Minority Serving Institutions (MSIs), and Hispanic-Serving Institutions (HSIs) through the HEA Title III and V programs to help close gaps among racial and socioeconomic groups in college enrollment and degree attainment by improving these institutions' academic programs, institutional capacity and student support services.[18]

The presidential vision aspired to make the "Department [of Education] more efficient while reducing the federal role in education." In particular, this vision for renewed efficiency sought to consolidate a variety of funding sources for Minority-Serving Institutions. The budget overview stated that it could achieve greater efficiencies by "merging six duplicative HEA Title III and V competitive grant authorities into a single institutional formula."[19] The proposal suggested consolidating $30.4 million from the current Aid for Institutional Development (Title III) with $117.5 million from the Aid for Hispanic-Serving Institutions (Title V), claiming that these measures were implemented with the spirit of simplifying "the grant allocation process and redundant activities, improving alignment between Federal resources and need."[20]

Unacknowledged in this change, however, was the fact that the reduction of specific funds for various types of MSIs in favor of a "formula-based allocation" did not provide evidence of the criteria used to implement a formula-based process to disburse appropriations for MSIs.[21] Indeed, these attempts to reduce federal funds to support initiatives geared to low-income students of color were evidenced throughout the budget. Other unfounded claims, for example, criticized the "limited evidence of effectiveness" for programs such as McNair Scholars and thus proclaimed that these initiatives "could be supported with other resources, including through State and institutional funding."[22] On the contrary, peer-reviewed evidence suggests that McNair Scholars and other programs indeed offer opportunities for students to develop valuable competencies and skills.[23] The argument that these programs, which disproportionately serve students of color, are beyond the scope of federal resources belies the articulated commitment to advancing opportunities for students of color as expressed in the rhetoric used by the executive leadership under President Trump. Table 7.3 shows the presidential funding requested for FY 2019. Notably, both the Senate's and House of Representatives' Committees on Appropriations dismissed the presidential request to consolidate grants for MSIs. In fact, the Senate increased support beyond FY 2018's appropriations for all MSI programs, though this level of support was not endorsed within the House of Representatives.

TABLE 7.3 Overview of appropriations for Minority-Serving Institutions in FY 2019 (in thousands)

Authorizing legislation	Name of grant	FY 2018 enacted ($)	Presidential request ($)	US Senate proposed ($)	US House of Representatives proposed ($)	Final bill ($)
HEA Part III-A	Strengthening Institutions Program	98,886	–	101,067	98,886	99,875
HEA Part V-A	Strengthening Hispanic Serving Institutions	123,183	–	125,898	123,183	124,415
HEA Part V-B(512)	Promoting Postbaccalaureate Opportunities for Hispanic Americans	11,052	–	11,296	11,052	11,163
HEA Part III-B-323	Strengthening Historically Black Colleges and Universities	279,624	244,694	285,788	279,624	282,420
HEA Part III-B-326	Strengthening Historically Black Graduate Institutions	72,314	63,281	73,908	72,314	73,037
HEA Part III-A-318	Strengthening Predominately Black Institutions	11,361	–	11,611	11,361	11,475
HEA Part III-A-320	Strengthening Asian American Pacific Islander Serving Institutions	3,826	–	3,910	3,826	3,864
HEA Part III-A-317	Strengthening Alaska Native and Native Hawaiian Serving Institutions	15,772	–	16,120	15,772	15,930
HEA Part III-A-319	Strengthening Native American Serving Non-Tribal Institutions	3,826	–	3,910	3,826	3,864
HEA Part III-A-316	Strengthening Tribally Controlled Colleges and Universities	31,539	27,599	32,234	31,539	31,854
HEA Part VII A-4-723	Strengthening Master's Degree Programs at HBCUs	8,571	7,500	8,760	8,571	8,657
	Subtotal, Aid for institutional development	**$ 659,954**	**$ 343,074**	**$ 674,502**	**$ 659,954**	**$ 666,554**

Note: HEA = Higher Education Act.

Sources: S. Rep 115-289, at 202 (2018); H. Rep. 115-862, at 150 (2018); Presidential FY 2019 Budget Summary and Background Information; Presidential FY 2019 Budget Request for Higher Education.

The discrepancies across both congressional Committees on Appropriations and the presidential requests for FY 2019 point to the inconsistent vision for federal programs seeking to support students of color, not just within MSIs, but also across other programs geared to support low-income students of color throughout their educational trajectories. For example, both the House of Representatives' Committee on Appropriations and the Senate Committee of Appropriations, respectively, caution the US Department of Education's unwarranted changes to programs like TRIO. The presidential request to streamline TRIO programs from a competitive grant into a single state formula program was rejected on grounds that "the Department was unable to provide any information on the details of how the formula grant would be implemented or how accountability for performance would be maintained."[24] Similarly, the Senate's Committee on Appropriations stated it was "concerned with the level of burden TRIO grantees and first-generation students face in documenting their income to meet the definition of 'low-income individual' as required under section 401A(h)(4) of the HEA.'"[25]

Table 7.4 shows the FY 2020 presidential budget that once again repeated the strategy of consolidating MSI grants in the name of efficiency, while the proposed budget from the House of Representatives sought to sustain the support for the various parts of the bill. During early FY 2020 discussions, the 116th Congress introduced the FUTURE Act (H.R. 2486/S. 1279), a bipartisan effort to reauthorize Title III, Part F of the Higher Education Act until the end of FY 2021, though the efforts to reauthorize HEA have largely stalled due to efforts to address federal responsiveness to COVID-19.

ACCOUNTABILITY AND MSIs

Political efforts to eliminate Public Service Loan Forgiveness alongside accountability measures for institutions whose students have difficulty paying loans directly affect the future success of students of color. Others

TABLE 7.4 Overview of proposed appropriations for Minority-Serving Institutions in FY 2020 (in thousands)

Authorizing legislation	Name of grant	FY 2019 enacted ($)	FY 2020 presidential request ($)	Final bill ($)	FY19 v final ($)	Requested v final ($)
HEA** Part III-A	Strengthening Institutions Program	99,875		107,854	7,979	107,854
HEA Part V-A	Strengthening Hispanic Serving Institutions	124,415		143,081	18,666	143,081
HEA Part V-B(512)	Promoting Postbaccalaureate Opportunities for Hispanic Americans	11,163		12,838	1,675	12,838
	Consolidated MSI Grant	—	147,906	—	—	(147,906)
HEA Part III-B-323	Strengthening Historically Black Colleges and Universities	282,420	282,420	324,792	42,372	42,372
HEA Part III-B-326	Strengthening Historically Black Graduate Institutions	73,037	73,037	83,995	10,958	10,958
HEA Part III-A-318	Strengthening Predominantly Black Institutions	11,475		13,197	1,722	13,197
HEA Part III-A-320	Strengthening Asian American Pacific Islander Serving Institutions	3,864		4,444	580	4,444
HEA Part III-A-317	Strengthening Alaska Native and Native Hawaiian Serving Institutions	15,930		18,320	2,390	18,320
HEA Part III-A-319	Strengthening Native American Serving Non-Tribal Institutions	3,864		4,444	580	4,444
HEA Part III-A-316	Strengthening Tribally Controlled Colleges and Universities	31,854	27,599	36,633	4,779	9,034
HEA Part VII A-4-723	Strengthening Master's Degree Programs at HBCUs	8,657	8,657	9,956	1,299	1,299
	Subtotal for institutional aid	$ 666,554	$ 539,619	$ 759,554	$ 93,000	$ 219,935

Note: HEA = Higher Education Act.
Sources: H. Rep. 116-62, at 163 (2019).

have already cautioned that institutions that serve "disadvantaged students may not have sufficient resources to improve repayment outcomes," yet the scant details on how these measures of accountability will be implemented offer little evidence disproving that they will not inequitably affect MSIs.[26] Said simply: the vestiges of inequitable support for MSIs must be addressed if we are to then hold them to the same accountability standards that presume a "traditional" student as those served by other institutions.

In tandem to these concerns, federal oversight to support institutions who are recipients of MSI grants has dwindled. The current hiring freeze compounded by multiple early retirements and staff reallocations has left the federal Office of Postsecondary Education with leaner human capital than what is needed to ensure proper management. OPE's staff is charged with the oversight of IHEs who receive MSI grants. The disconnect between a call for greater accountability is mismatched with the staffing support offered to ensure that current grantees have the necessary support to make the most out of the funding received through allocated appropriations. Notably, this is not an issue that is specific to programs supporting MSIs; rather it is emblematic of broader efforts from former Secretary of Education Betsy DeVos to reduce federal oversight of equitable educational opportunities through staff reductions and rescinding federal guidance language. The prospect of confirming Miguel Cardona, Connecticut's Commissioner of Education with a record of strong support for public schooling and enhanced access to community colleges, presages what might become a new era for MSIs at the Department of Education.[27]

ENVISIONING NEXT STEPS AND AGENDA SETTING

Drawing attention to the divide between political speech and actions offers a fruitful opportunity to recalibrate forthcoming policy discussions. I conclude this chapter by commenting on some of the potential opportunities afforded to MSIs by examining how the transition to a new executive leadership through Joseph R. Biden's election as the forty-sixth president offers possibilities for new forms of federal support for MSIs. In the last months of Donald Trump's presidency, the passage of the CARES Act marked the largest one-year disbursement of funds to colleges since the Great Recession of 2008. Less than 7 percent of the $14 billion secured for postsecondary education through the CARES Act was directed to Minority-Serving Institutions.[28] In the aftermath of the disbursement of CARES, lobbying organizations for Minority-Serving Institutions, like Excelencia in Education, have quickly noted how the implementation of new funding formulas reinforces long-standing inequities. For example, by allocating funds based on the full-time equivalent enrollments of Pell Grant recipients, institutions that enroll part-time students received less funds per student than institutions with a higher number of full-time students.[29] Shortly after President Biden's inauguration, the US Department of Education announced a new plan to disburse the largest pool of funding for students and higher education institutions through the Coronavirus Response and Relief Supplemental Appropriations Act (CRRSAA), which allocated $20.5 billion of support for nonprofit colleges and universities, relying on a similar formula of FTE enrollment as detailed in the December 2020 CARES Act. Despite the lack of details, the stipulations of disbursement of these additional sources of support detailed that, in addition to public institutions, private MSIs would also be eligible for these additional sources of federal support.[30]

As documented in this chapter, the insights from the Trump administration showcased the challenges for MSIs when federal leadership maintains the status quo for MSIs' budgeting and enacts multiple (failed) attempts to decimate the funding for the institutions that serve the majority of students of color in the nation. The challenge ahead for the new Democratic leadership is ensuring that a commitment to enhanced equity minimizing the long-term repercussions of COVID-19 on the higher education landscape purposefully support institutions, like MSIs, that enhance the possibilities of improved equity for all students.

CHAPTER 8

Despite the Evidence

The Mystique of For-Profit Colleges in American Politics

BRIAN PUSSER AND MATT ERICSON

EARLIER IN THIS VOLUME, Rose and Mettler explained the ways in which political polarization makes it difficult for policymakers to conduct comprehensive maintenance and updating of public policies. In this chapter, we extend this argument by turning attention to failed policies that persist—even when research consensus and mounting evidence demonstrate that the policies are ineffective. Nobel Laureate Paul Krugman has labeled these "zombie ideas."[1] As Krugman has argued for nearly twenty years, zombie ideas are the lynchpin of policies "that should have been killed by contrary evidence," but that persist for reasons based on something other than evidence.[2] Krugman documents a wide range of zombie ideas that shape significant policies, including that tax cuts on the wealthy stimulate economic growth and that global warming is a cyclical phenomenon not influenced by human activity. Economist John Quiggin has presented a number of economic concepts, including "market liberalism," and the argument that "any function now undertaken by government could be done better by private firms," as zombie ideas that have moved to the fore of contemporary policy debates.[3] Hochschild and Einstein point to the long, evidence-free challenge to former President Barack Obama's place of birth as one example of political strategies without factual premises, strategies that are used to initiate or preserve comparative advantage in politics and policymaking.[4]

Zombie ideas also drive higher education policies. Familiar examples include the shift from state direct support to higher tuition in public universities, which was promoted as a way to increase competition and affordability by driving down college costs, but has resulted in exceptionally high levels of student debt and increasing socioeconomic inequality within and between public universities.[5] The enforcement of amateurism by the National Collegiate Athletic Association (NCAA) and its member institutions, which has limited the rights of student athletes and contributed to an array of pay-for-play scandals, has long been promoted in legal and legislative struggles as the last defense of the "student" in "student-athlete."[6] This, despite the fact that virtually no other students are required to maintain amateur status, and that the Olympics gave up the pretext of amateurism in athletics some thirty years ago. The concept of "skin in the game," that students perform better when they have invested financially in their own education, was famously put forward without empirical evidence by Milton and Rose Friedman over thirty years ago to argue against free college tuition, yet it persists in arguments over federal subsidies and student debt relief to this day.[7] Other examples include the thin rationales traditionally put forward for the "inter-generational value" underpinning the continuation of legacy admissions and the notions that greater individual wealth accumulation and social mobility inevitably follow college completion.[8]

A credible argument can be made that no aspect of higher education has defied the gravity of evidence more effectively over the past quarter century than for-profit postsecondary education. Despite evidence of lower graduation rates, higher levels of student loan debt and default, institutional failure, and the ineffectiveness of state and federal investments, Congress has not instituted effective regulatory changes, and in many instances, for-profit colleges have succeeded through lobbying and political coalition building in further deregulating the sector.[9] What is demonstrated by the data presented throughout this chapter is that it appears the evidence of the efficacy of the sector and federal rules and legislation governing the sector have long been misaligned, if not disconnected. The data also show that the disjuncture between evidence and policy has had significant consequences for students who enroll in for-profit postsecondary institutions.

We focus attention here on students of color, a diverse group of individuals who have been disproportionately enrolled in for-profit postsecondary institutions and are disproportionately affected by the practices of those institutions. What we argue is that contemporary legislators, primarily Republicans, but including some Democrats as well, who support for-profit universities with funding and deregulatory policies are engaging in what E. E. Schattschneider termed "the mobilization of bias," the process of building and reinforcing a narrowed set of policy options through repeated rhetoric, symbolism, and myth making.[10] In the case of for-profit universities, policymakers claim these institutions play a necessary and even vital role in a competitive marketplace. Despite considerable evidence to the contrary, they accept that for-profit universities—simply by virtue of being market-oriented—improve outcomes for individual students and deliver public benefits. This belief leads to expanding market provision of essential state functions throughout the political economy, and it extends to supporting private for-profit alternatives to public and nonprofit higher education. The endorsement of for-profit universities sends a political message of commitment to the market everywhere and all the time, even when considerable evidence indicates no reasonable basis for believing the public or individual students are better off as a result of congressional or executive branch support of the for-profit education sector.

We begin with the competing proposals advanced in the House of Representatives in late 2017 as part of negotiations over the reauthorization of the Higher Education Act (HEA). Each reauthorization since the mid-1980s had marked an important moment of contest over the effectiveness of for-profit colleges. The hearings begun in 2017 arrived at an auspicious time for the sector, as Republicans controlled the White House, Senate, and the House of Representatives. We turn attention to one highly contested aspect of the reauthorization process, the legislation governing for-profit colleges, and to the data on outcomes for students of color enrolled in for-profit colleges. We do this in service of better understanding the evidence available at the time on for-profit performance and how it shaped the majority's approach to a long-awaited reauthorization of HEA.[11]

THE PROSPER ACT

On December 1, 2017, Congresswoman Virginia Foxx, the Chairwoman of the House Committee on Education and the Workforce, and Representative Brett Guthrie issued a short statement to accompany the introduction of H.R. 4508, the Promoting Real Opportunity, Success and Prosperity through Education Reform (PROSPER) Act. The Representatives' brief statement noted, "With six million unfilled jobs and over a trillion dollars in student debt, simply reauthorizing the Higher Education Act will help no one. A hard truth that students, families, and institutions must face is that the promise of a postsecondary education is broken. We need a higher education system that is designed to meet the needs of today's students and has the flexibility to innovate for tomorrow's workforce opportunities. The PROSPER Act is higher education's long overdue reform."[12]

Proposed changes to existing regulations and policies in the PROSPER Act would have positively impacted America's degree-seeking college students and the institutions that serve them, such as the overhaul of the Free Application for Federal Student Aid (FAFSA). However, taken together, the proposals in the act did not draw upon an array of evidence or strategies, nor did they appear destined to lead to significant reform. Rather, a commitment to deregulation and market competition prevails throughout PROSPER. Despite the endorsement of the Republican House majority and the Department of Education under Secretary of Education Betsy DeVos, history—and contemporary data on for-profit degree-granting colleges—strongly suggested that the PROSPER Act was likely to increase the number of negative outcomes for many students. Beyond the human and financial costs to students, their families, and communities, the provisions in the act would have lowered standards of accountability and transparency, and would likely have further enabled the same practices that had produced a striking level of poor outcomes in the for-profit sector, at considerable cost to students, their families, and taxpayers.

THE PROSPER ACT AND PROPOSED DEREGULATION OF FOR-PROFITS

Policy contests over the eligibility of for-profit colleges to receive federal aid go back to the introduction of the Serviceman's Readjustment Act (G.I. Bill), at which time proprietary schools were included in the omnibus bill.[13] After considerable debate, Title IV of the Higher Education Act of 1965 created the Guaranteed Student Loan (GSL), the first large-scale portable student loan program for higher education in the United States. The reauthorization of 1972 added the Basic Educational Opportunity Grant (BEOG) and proprietary colleges to the set of eligible institutions. Over the past forty years, and through eight reauthorizations, there has been considerable debate over funding for proprietary colleges. One area of contention has concerned the percentage of total institutional revenue that may be generated from federal funds and the type of funding that should be included in that calculation, as, for example, revenue to colleges from veterans receiving benefits from the Post-9/11 G.I. Bill. This was again the case in the PROSPER Act, which proposed to change a number of key standards governing the receipt of federal funding.[14]

The 90/10 Rule

The 90/10 rule is a regulation that requires institutions to garner at least 10 percent of total income from other-than-federal revenue. There are exemptions for federal revenue from certain programs, most notably education funding for servicemen and women, including the Post-9/11 G.I. Bill. An earlier version of the rule was instituted in the 1992 reauthorization with the requirement that for-profit institutions could receive no more than 85 percent of their total revenue from federal grants, loans, or work-study funding. In the 1998 reauthorization, the rule was modified to enable for-profit colleges to receive up to 90 percent of revenue from federal sources.[15] In the PROSPER Act proposal, the 90/10 rule would have been eliminated.

When compared to nonprofit postsecondary institutions, for-profit colleges have for more than a quarter century been producing a lower rate of completion and a higher rate of student debt and default. On that basis, there seems to be little evidence that providing additional access to federal funds for the for-profit sector would be the best policy going forward. It seems more likely that increasing the amount of federal funds available to for-profits would exacerbate the sector's lower levels of completion, greater indebtedness, increased loan delinquency, and higher rates of default for Black students, Hispanic students, American Indian students, those who are low income, and first-generation students, as well as other traditionally underrepresented students in higher education.[16]

Gainful Employment and the Elimination of the Cohort Default Rate Metric

A key aspect of for-profit deregulation in the PROSPER Act was a proposal to eliminate the Gainful Employment (GE) rule. The GE rule was intended to reduce the amount of federal aid dollars available to institutions if their graduates of vocational programs failed to earn an income sufficient to enable them to devote a reasonable percentage of that income to repayment of student loan debt.[17] In the first Department of Education analysis of institutions using the accountability measures of the GE rule, some eight hundred programs did not meet the standards. *Inside Higher Ed* reported that of those eight hundred programs, 98 percent were offered by for-profit institutions.[18]

Research on GE regulations has found not only that students in for-profits find themselves with higher debt and higher rates of default but also that some of those who were enrolled in certificate, associate's, or bachelor's degree programs left for-profit universities earning less in the labor market than when they began their studies.[19]

The cohort default rate (CDR) was designed to limit the funding available to institutions based on the percentage of graduates who subsequently defaulted on student loans. The CDR was slated for elimination in the PROSPER Act in favor of a "programmatic loan repayment rate." The "programmatic rate" would have increased the threshold for sanctions, lengthened the period before delinquencies and defaults were accounted for sanctioning purposes, and effectively counted students in deferment or forbearance as in a repayment program.[20]

Research on the impact of earlier regulations that linked access to federal aid to student success using CDRs suggests that enrollments lost to such sanctions are accompanied by increased enrollments in nonprofit institutions.[21] Thus, linking federal aid to performance may "rebalance" enrollments into less costly and generally more effective institutions.

Loan Repayment, Forgiveness, and Borrower Defenses

The PROSPER Act also included a number of changes to existing loan repayment and forgiveness programs. Of these, the elimination of loan forgiveness through income-contingent payment plans such as the Public

Service forgiveness plan would have increased the challenges faced by those students who are indebted without completing a degree or who had higher levels of indebtedness after completing a degree. This group included significant numbers of students underrepresented in four-year colleges, Black students, Hispanic students, and American Indian students, particularly those who were also low-income students. The National Association of Student Affairs Administrators (NASFAA) noted that the changes to repayment provisions could have had a particularly negative impact on students in graduate and professional programs.[22]

Another essential form of redress for students in for-profit colleges has been rules providing borrowers defense against fraudulent practices. Given previous instances of institutional failure and allegations of fraudulent practices, borrower defense was seen as a significant safeguard for students in for-profit colleges. Under the PROSPER Act, students would have been required to seek redress within three years of a college's misconduct, whether the inappropriate activity had come to light at that point or not. Given the time required to acquire a degree, the historical lack of transparency in the proprietary sector, and the consequences of institutional failure for students, the proposed revision of borrower defense rules was likely to further disadvantage underrepresented students in for-profit colleges.

Incentive Payments to Admissions Recruiters

One of the notable aspects of the for-profit college sector has been the remarkable percentage of institutional revenue devoted to marketing and recruiting campaigns. In 2012, the US Senate Committee on Health, Education, Labor, and Pensions (HELP) reported, "Many for-profit education companies spend less on instruction than public or non-profit institutions, and in some cases even less than the same company spends on marketing and profit."[23] The report also found instances of aggressive recruiting, and noted, "Internal documents, interviews with former employees, and Government Accountability Office (GAO) undercover recordings demonstrate that many companies used tactics that misled prospective students with regard to the cost of the program, the completion rates of other students, the job placement rate of other students, the transferability of the credit, or the reputation and accreditation of the school."[24] More recent studies have shown that some students in for-profits continue to have difficulty garnering accurate and timely information.[25]

Since the 1992 reauthorization, the Department of Education has restricted the process of incentive payments (commissioned sales) to employees of for-profit universities on the basis of enrollments generated. This measure was seen as vital to efforts to stem aggressive recruiting by for-profits and to increase the likelihood that students would be enrolled on the basis of their ability to succeed, without consideration of economic incentives for recruiters to maximize enrollments.[26] A study conducted in 2010 by the GAO found a pattern of "deceptive and questionable practices" in for-profit colleges, including providing a wide range of inaccurate information to encourage students to enroll.[27]

Despite this legacy, the PROSPER Act would have modified the restriction of commissioned sales by enabling colleges to pay third parties on the basis of enrollments generated. There was no evidence suggesting that students would benefit from the change in the regulation of incentive payments, and considerable evidence suggesting that this change could negatively impact students enrolling in for-profit colleges. These elements of the PROSPER Act, in combination with efforts by Secretary of Education Betsy DeVos, would have further deregulated a sector of postsecondary institutions long criticized for exploitation and poor student outcomes at the same time as they reduced the recourse available to students in those institutions.[28]

THE AIM HIGHER ACT

In July of 2018, Democrats on the House Committee on Education and the Workforce introduced H.R. 6543, the Aim Higher Act, a proposal for reauthorization of HEA that embodied a distinctly different approach than that taken in the PROSPER Act. The Aim Higher Act would have directly increased regulations and accountability measures shaping for-profit institutional behavior and indirectly reshaped the landscape in which for-profit universities operate. Among many provisions that would have preserved or increased existing regulations, Aim Higher would have shifted the mandatory level of funding from other-than-federal sources from 10 percent to 15 percent, from 90/10 to 85/15, and it would have redefined funding from G.I. Bill recipients as a federal source in the calculation of institutional revenue. Aim Higher would also have revised the calculation of cohort default rates and provided support for nonprofit institutions with high adjusted cohort default rates. The proposal also provided support for improving the collection and reporting of data on student outcomes by promoting the collection of student-level data and increasing the collection and dissemination of more usefully disaggregated data on postsecondary education. The bill also clarified the definition of nonprofit institutions, provided students additional recourse against failed for-profit institutions, and preserved regulations on gainful employment and student success after college completion. It also offered additional support for *American Indian/Alaska Native* students attending two-year colleges, low-income students, and students in Historically Black Colleges and Universities (HBCUs). Congressman Bobby Scott, the ranking Democrat on the Committee on Education and the Workforce, summed up Aim Higher this way: "The Aim Higher Act is a serious and comprehensive proposal to give every student the opportunity to earn a debt-free degree or credential. It provides immediate and long-term relief to students and parents struggling with the cost of college, it puts a greater focus on helping students graduate on time with a quality degree that leads to a rewarding career, and it cracks down on predatory for-profit colleges that peddle expensive, low-quality degrees at the expense of students and taxpayers."[29]

FOR-PROFIT UNIVERSITIES—
A LEGACY OF CONTROVERSY

While for-profit production of higher education certificates and degrees dates back more than a century, until the emergence of publicly traded for-profit education corporations in the early 1990s, the number of students in degree-granting institutions in the sector was a small percentage of all postsecondary enrollments. It wasn't until the latter portion of the twentieth century that significant numbers of undergraduate and graduate degrees were granted by for-profits. The increased political salience and public awareness of the degree-granting for-profits, driven by the rise of publicly traded for-profits such as the University of Phoenix, began in the 1990s. By 2000, there were approximately 450,000 students in the for-profit sector. By 2010 that number had grown to some 1.6 million students.[30] Annual lobbying on all for-profit education also rapidly increased, from less than $1 million in 2000 to over $5 million in 2019.[31] The pace of growth in for-profit institutions rapidly accelerated the demand for student loans and contributed to a concurrent, remarkable increase in student loan debt.

Given the polarized contemporary political climate, it may come as a surprise that over the past four decades dismay with the sector has been expressed by both Republicans and Democrats. In his review of policies shaping for-profit colleges during the George W. Bush administration, David Whitman notes, "The scandals surrounding for-profit schools in the 1980s were so severe that President Reagan's secretary of education, William Bennett, called them 'an outrage perpetrated not only on the American taxpayer, but, most tragically, upon some of the most disadvantaged, and most vulnerable members of society.'"[32]

Because of the potential risks to students and taxpayers posed by poor performance and institutional failure in the for-profit sector, Congress has frequently considered increasing regulations on recruiting practices, sources of revenue, student lending, and more. While these proposals would have constrained all postsecondary institutions, they would have disparately impacted for-profit colleges. In 1992, Congress added the 85/15 rule, which required that postsecondary institutions receive at least 15 percent of total revenue from sources other than Title IV student aid programs.[33] In 1997, the GAO conducted a study, at the request of Representative Christopher Shays, Chairman of the House Subcommittee on Human Resources, on the relationship between the percentage of institutional revenue received by proprietary institutions from Title IV programs and student outcomes. The fundamental finding of the report was, "Proprietary schools that relied more heavily on Title IV funds tended to have poorer student outcomes. Our analysis showed that, on average, the higher a school's reliance on Title IV, the lower its students' completion and placement rates, and the higher its students' default rates."[34]

Regulations reducing federal funding to institutions with high default rates enacted as part of the 1992 reauthorization of HEA led to more than 1,200 for-profit institutions leaving the field during the Clinton administration.[35] Less than a decade later, under lobbying pressure from proprietary colleges and their allies in Congress, the rule was modified in the reauthorization of the Higher Education Act so that colleges could receive 90 percent of revenue from Title IV program funds, what is now known as the 90/10 rule. By 2009, the fifteen publicly traded for-profit colleges received, on average, 86 percent of their total revenue from Title IV programs. This, despite the fact that revenue from the Post-9/11 G.I. Bill, which provided tuition and other benefits for active-duty service members, was not counted in the 90/10 calculation.[36]

Perhaps the high-water mark of demands for additional oversight and regulation of for-profit college arrived with the majority report released in 2012 from the hearings held by the Senate Health, Education, Labor, and Pensions committee, often referred to as "the Harkin Report," after Senator Tom Harkin, the committee chair. The majority committee staff report found that taxpayers were investing more than $30 billion a year in companies that operated for-profit colleges. That constituted more than 25 percent of the total Department of Education student aid program funds at a time when students in for-profit degree-granting colleges constituted less than 10 percent of total enrollments in four-year colleges. The committee majority also expressed considerable concern over the disproportionate share of Pell Grants going to for-profit colleges. In 2000, students attending all types of for-profit colleges received $1.1 billion in Pell Grant funding. By 2009–10, that number had soared to $7.5 billion. The Senate committee report noted, "Yet, more than half of the students who enrolled in those colleges in 2008–09 left without a degree or a diploma within a median of 4 months."[37]

The Great Recession of 2008 turned national attention to the explosion in student debt that had occurred over the past two decades as tuition rose across America's colleges, and no sector of four-year degree-granting higher education had a more disproportionate share of students with high levels of debt, delinquency, and default than did the for-profits. This was true in all types of for-profit postsecondary institutions, including those offering less than two-year degrees.[38]

The Obama administration implemented a number of rules designed to address the crisis levels of student debt and default, most prominently, the Gainful Employment and Borrower Defense regulations. In addressing these rules, in 2019 the Department of Education introduced far-stricter standards for seeking recourse under borrower defense and also revised the Gainful Employment rule.[39] It is against this backdrop that the House Republicans promoted the PROSPER Act in early 2018. To fully understand the consequences of that effort, we have compiled data on student enrollments in postsecondary institutions, levels of student debt, and rates of default at the time. Those data are presented here and followed by a discussion of the implications for students of color in for-profit institutions and for understanding postsecondary policymaking going forward.

STUDENT DEMOGRAPHICS IN HIGHER EDUCATION IN THE UNITED STATES

As figure 8.1 shows, there were about 13,750,000 students enrolled in four-year colleges and universities in 2016, of which about 980,000 were in four-year, for-profit institutions.

In 2016, 55.6 percent of those undergraduates enrolled in four-year public institutions were white students, 11.2 percent were Black students, 17.2 percent were Hispanic students, 7.1 percent were Asian students, 3.7 percent were multiracial students, and 0.7 percent were American Indian/Alaska Native (AI/AN) students. In four-year, private nonprofit institutions, 61.3 percent of those enrolled were white students, 12.2 percent were Black students, 10.9 percent were Hispanic students, 5.6 percent were Asian students, 3.5 percent were multiracial students, and 0.5 percent were American Indian/Alaska Native students.

FIGURE 8.1   **Total undergraduate enrollments by institutional sector (four-year)**

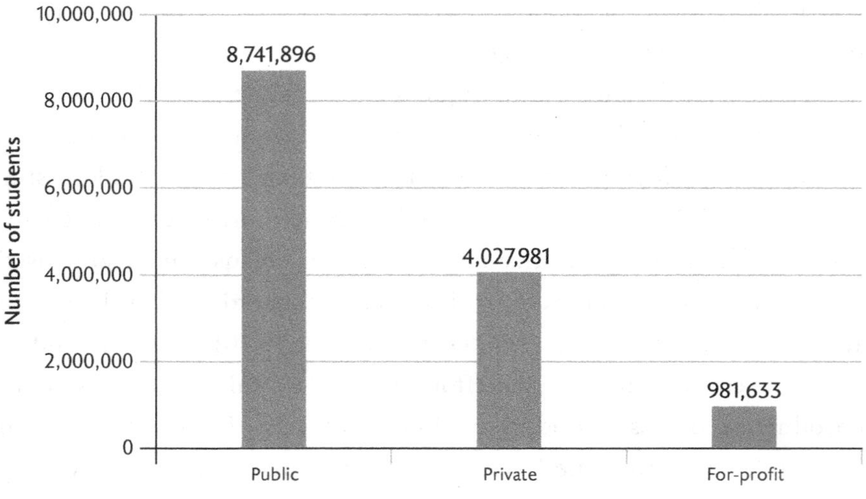

Source: NCES Table 306.50, "Total fall enrollment in degree-granting postsecondary institutions, by control and classification of institution, level of enrollment, and race/ethnicity of student: 2016."

Enrollments in four-year private for-profit institutions were distinctly different: 45.1 percent of those enrolled were white students, 28.1 percent were Black students, 16.7 percent were Hispanic students, 3.3 percent were Asian students, 3.3 percent were multiracial students, and 1 percent were American Indian/Alaska Native students, as shown in figure 8.2.[40]

About 60 percent of those enrolled in postbaccalaureate (graduate and professional) degree programs in public institutions were white students, and approximately the same was true for private nonprofit institutions. Black students constituted 9 percent of enrollments in postbaccalaureate degree programs in nonprofit public and 11.4 percent of private nonprofit institutions. Hispanic students comprised about 9 percent of enrollments in postbaccalaureate degree programs in both the public and private nonprofit sectors. Asian students represented 6.2 percent of enrollments in public postbaccalaureate programs, and 7.7 percent of private nonprofit

FIGURE 8.2 **Student demographics at four-year colleges**

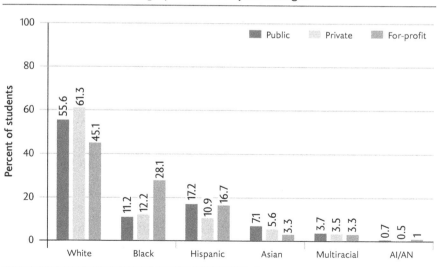

Source: NCES Table 306.50, "Total fall enrollment in degree-granting postsecondary institutions, by control and classification of institution, level of enrollment, and race/ethnicity of student: 2016."

postbaccalaureate programs, 2.4 percent of students in public institutions, and 2.3 percent in private postbaccalaureate programs were multiracial students. American Indian/Alaska Natives made up approximately 1 percent of postbaccalaureate degree granting enrollments in each sector.

Black students comprised almost 34 percent of students in for-profit postbaccalaureate programs, primarily in master's programs. Hispanic students made up 10 percent of the for-profit post-baccalaureate enrollments, with white students constituting 44 percent of students enrolled in the for-profit graduate sector. Asian students constituted just over 5 percent of enrollments in for-profit, postbaccalaureate degree programs; multiracial students represented 2.6 percent of students enrolled in for-profit, postbaccalaureate programs; with American Indian/Alaska Native students comprising less than 1 percent of for-profit, postbaccalaureate enrollments (figure 8.3).[41]

ENROLLMENT BY RACE AND INSTITUTIONAL TYPE

There are some notable disparities in the types of postsecondary institutions chosen by undergraduate students from different racial/ethnic groups who enrolled in 2016. Of white students who were enrolled in a four-year college, 66.8 percent were enrolled in public institutions, 27.8 percent were enrolled in private institutions, and just over 5 percent were enrolled in for-profit colleges. For Hispanic students enrolled in four-year colleges, 74.9 percent were enrolled in public colleges, 17.9 percent were enrolled in private nonprofit colleges, and 7.1 percent enrolled in a for-profit college. Some 65 percent of Asian students were enrolled in public institutions, with 20 percent enrolled in private nonprofits and 15 percent in private for-profit colleges. Of Black students enrolled in four-year colleges, 60.3 percent were enrolled in public colleges, 24.8 percent were enrolled in private, nonprofit colleges, and 14.8 percent were enrolled in for-profit colleges. Of the multiracial students enrolled in

FIGURE 8.3   **Student demographics at post-BA**

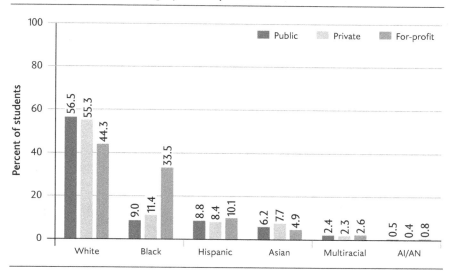

Source: NCES Table 306.50, "Total fall enrollment in degree-granting postsecondary institutions, by control and classification of institution, level of enrollment, and race/ethnicity of student: 2016."

four-year colleges, 73 percent were in public universities, 25 percent in private universities, and 2 percent in for-profit institutions. Of American Indian/Alaska Native students enrolled in four-year colleges, 71 percent were in public colleges, 21 percent in private colleges, and 8 percent in for-profit colleges (figure 8.4). The percentage of Black students who chose a for-profit college was three times that of white students and twice that of Hispanic students.

The enrollment of students in postbaccalaureate degree programs shows a disproportionate percentage of Black students who chose to obtain graduate education in for-profit colleges in comparison with other groups. Almost one-quarter (24.4 percent) of Black students who enrolled in a postbaccalaureate program chose a for-profit college. For Hispanic students who chose to attend a postbaccalaureate program, 10.3 percent chose a for-profit college, while 7.2 percent of white students, 6 percent

FIGURE 8.4 **Percentage of students by race by institution type (four-year)**

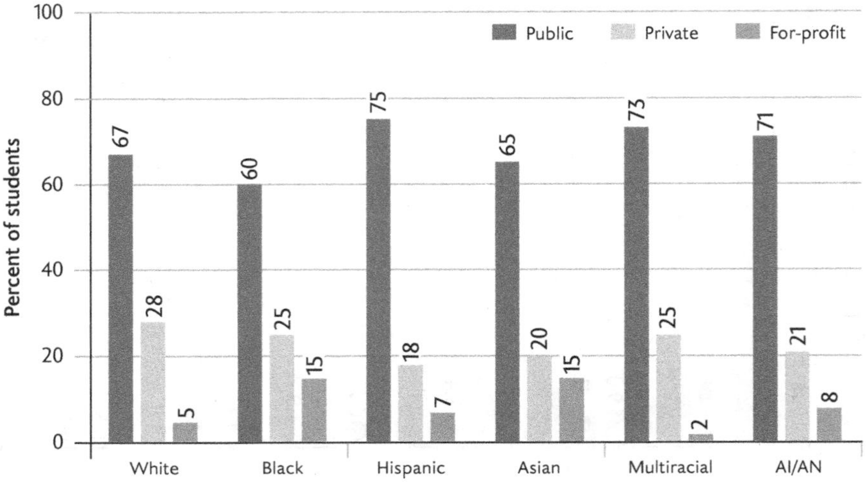

Source: NCES Table 306.50, "Total fall enrollment in degree-granting postsecondary institutions, by control and classification of institution, level of enrollment, and race/ethnicity of student: 2016."

of Asian students, 10 percent of multiracial students, and 15 percent of American Indian/Alaskan Natives who enrolled in postbaccalaureate programs chose a for-profit college (figure 8.5).

UNDERREPRESENTED STUDENTS AND COLLEGE COMPLETION

Fully documenting college completions by race/ethnicity has been a long-standing challenge for researchers. This is due in part to incomplete data on student transitions, including a lack of data on students who complete college at a different institution than the one in which they initially enrolled, and significant challenges in accounting for students who transfer from two-year colleges.[42]

FIGURE 8.5 **Percentage of students by race by institution type (post-BA)**

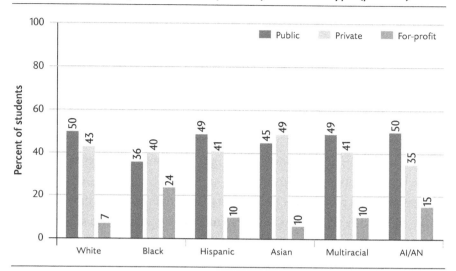

Source: NCES Table 306.50, "Total fall enrollment in degree-granting postsecondary institutions, by control and classification of institution, level of enrollment, and race/ethnicity of student: 2016."

First-Time Enrollees at Four-Year Colleges

For first-time, full-time students enrolled in 2009 in four-year institutions, the overall six-year graduation rate was 59.4 percent. The overall graduation rate for white students was 63.3 percent; for Black students, it was 39.5 percent; for Hispanic students, the graduation rate was 53.6 percent; and for Asian students, it was 73 percent. The completion gap between white students and Black students was over 23 percentage points, the gap between white students and Hispanic students was just under 10 percentage points, the gap between Asian students and white students was just under 10 percentage points, the gap between Asian students and Black students was just over 33 percentage points, and the completion gap between Asian students and Hispanic students was over 19 percentage points. Meanwhile, the overall six-year graduation rate was 59.2 percent for multiracial students and 41.2 percent for American Indian/Alaskan Natives (figure 8.6).

First-Time/Full-Time Enrollees in Four-Year Colleges

The graduation rates for students in different institutional types also varied significantly. In public four-year institutions, the gap in the rate of graduation within six years between first-time, full-time white students and Black students who began in 2009 was 22 percentage points. For white students and Hispanic students, the gap was about 9 percentage points, while the gap between white students and American Indian/Alaska Native students was 24 percentage points. Asian students had the highest graduation rates, with the gap between Asian students and white students at 8 percentage points. In four-year private institutions, the gap in completion

FIGURE 8.6   **Graduation rates by race at all four-year institutions within six years**

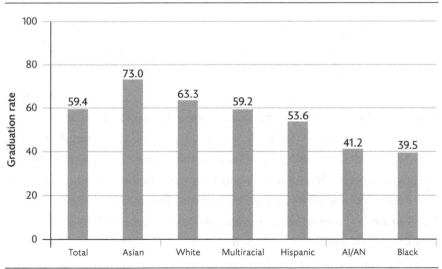

Source: NCES: Table 326.10, "Graduation rate from first institution attended for first-time, full-time bachelor's degree-seeking students at four-year postsecondary institutions, by race/ethnicity: 2016."

between white students and Black students who began in 2009 was 25 percentage points (figure 8.7).

Completion Rates for Attendance at More Than One Institution

A study by the National Student Clearinghouse (NSC) provides data on college completion for those students who began their undergraduate studies in public institutions in 2010 and attended more than one institution.[43] It shows that about 25 percent of graduates who began at a public four-year college when they were twenty years old or younger completed at a different institution than the one in which they initially enrolled. For the age group twenty to twenty-four, that figure was 18.6 percent, and for those who began when over twenty-four years old, 16.2 percent completed

FIGURE 8.7   **Graduation rates by race within six years at four-year institutions by institution type**

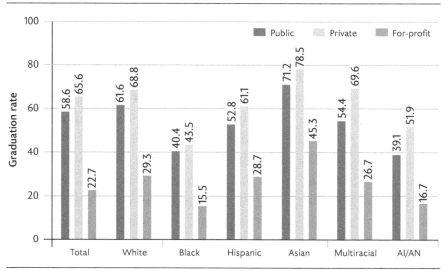

Source: NCES: Table 326.10. "Graduation rate from first institution attended for first-time, full-time bachelor's degree-seeking students at four-year postsecondary institutions, by race/ ethnicity: 2016."

college at a different institution than the one in which they initially enrolled. The NSC does provide statistics on outcomes for the 2010 cohort by race and ethnicity using a purposeful sample designed to address completion rates by different racial and ethnic groups. It found that after six years, 62 percent of white students had completed a degree, with 11.2 percent still enrolled. This number compares to 38 percent of Black students who had completed a degree, with 17.4 percent still enrolled. For Hispanic students, 45.8 percent had completed a degree, with 19.2 percent still enrolled, and for Asian students, 63.2 percent had completed a degree, with 16.8 percent still enrolled. Taken together, 56.2 percent of students in the sample of the 2010 cohort had completed a bachelor's degree, with 13.2 percent still enrolled.

For those students who began in 2010 and attended more than one two-year institution before completion, 29.5 percent had earned an associate's or bachelor's degree (in some cases both). For white students, 31.4 percent had done so; for Black students, 20.6 percent had done so; for Hispanic students, 27.4 percent had completed a degree; and for Asian students, 30.6 percent had done so.

Completion Rates in For-Profit Universities

While the completion rates in public and private nonprofit colleges and universities are cause for concern, the completion rates for students in for-profit colleges have been described as a crisis. Less than one-fourth (22.7 percent) of all first-time, full-time students who began in for-profit institutions in 2009 had earned a degree by 2015. The overall six-year graduation rate for first-time, full-time students in for-profit colleges who began in 2009 (22.7) was barely one-third that of first-time, full-time students in all institutions (59.4 percent). The gap between nonprofit public and for-profit institutions was 35.9 percentage points, and the gap between private nonprofits and private for-profits was 42.9 percentage points. Put another way, first-time, full-time students in the 2009 cohort who entered for-profit institutions were nearly three times as likely not to graduate in six years as those who entered public institutions. They were also almost three times as likely not to graduate as those who entered private nonprofit institutions (figure 8.7).

First-Time, Full-Time Student Completion by Race/Ethnicity in For-Profit Institutions

Just under 30 percent of first-time, full-time white students who began in for-profit colleges completed in six years, a figure which is less than half of the graduation rate for first-time, full-time white students in either public institutions or private nonprofit institutions. Fewer than one in six first-time, full-time Black students (15.5 percent) completed a four-year degree in a for-profit college in six years. While 28.7 percent of first-time, full-time Hispanic students completed a degree in six years; 52.8 percent of first-time, full-time Hispanic students in four-year public institutions graduated in six years; and 61.1 percent of first-time, full-time Hispanic students in nonprofit private institutions graduated in that time frame. Some 45.3 percent of first-time, full-time Asian students, 26.7 percent multiracial students, and 16.7 percent of American Indian/Alaska Native students completed degrees from four-year for-profit colleges within six years (figure 8.7).

STUDENT LOANS, DEBT, DELINQUENCY, AND DEFAULT

Student Loan Debt

Between 2000 and 2014, the outstanding balances on guaranteed student loans in the United States more than tripled, from $310 billion to $1.1 trillion. The number of borrowers more than doubled, to over forty million students, and default rates reached the highest level in two decades.[44] Students in for-profit four-year institutions were considerably more likely to borrow than students in nonprofit institutions. They were also more likely to borrow larger amounts of money to fund college attainment than were students in nonprofit colleges. If they borrowed money, students in for-profit colleges were more likely to become delinquent on their loans and were significantly more likely to default on their loans than were students in nonprofit institutions. This is in part because students in four-year, for-profit colleges who received financial aid paid the highest average net price of attendance for students in any sector.[45] As Smith and Parrish found, "Among those who borrow at four-year institutions, over one-third of for-profit students take out $8,900 or more in a single year, compared with just 10 percent and 14 percent of students attending public and private nonprofit schools respectively." They also found that over 60 percent of graduates of for-profit colleges owed more than $24,000, compared to 45 percent of students in nonprofit private schools, and 29 percent of those who graduated from nonprofit public universities.[46]

Loan Default

Data from the Department of Education present a significant disparity in the three-year loan default rates compiled for the FY 2014 repayment cohort of students in different institutional types. The data show an overall student loan default rate in public colleges of 6.4 percent, a default rate of 6.4 percent for private nonprofit colleges, and for the for-profit sector the default rate was 14.5 percent (figure 8.8).[47]

Students in for-profits also use disproportionate amounts of federal grants and loans. Smith and Parrish found that while 13 percent of students were enrolled in for-profit institutions, they received 20 percent of Pell Grant dollars, 21 percent of federal direct dollars, and 37 percent of the Post-9/11 G.I. Bill funding.[48]

Student Race/Ethnicity and Loan Debt

At the time of the deliberations over the PROSPER Act, Black students were more likely to borrow to finance higher education than any other group enrolled in higher education. A study by Goldrick-Rab, Kelchen, and Houle noted that in 2011–12, over half (52.3 percent) of Black students

FIGURE 8.8 **Federal student loan three-year default rates by sector FY 2014**

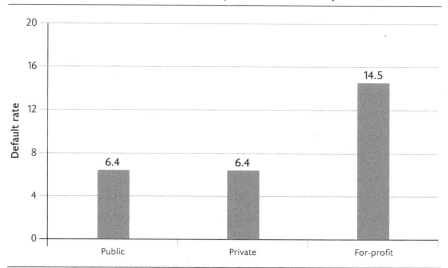

Source: "Comparison of FY 2014 Official National Cohort Default Rates to Prior Two Official Cohort Default Rates." Calculated August 5, 2017. Federal Student Aid–Office of the U.S. Department of Education.

had taken out a student loan, compared to 43.0 percent of American Indian students, 41.9 percent of white students, 35.6 percent of Hispanic students, and 28.4 percent of Asian students.[49]

Based on data from 2012, among those who graduate from college, some 81 percent of Black students held debt from attending public colleges, with 86 percent holding debt from attending private nonprofit colleges. This compares to 63 percent of Hispanic students who graduated holding debt from public colleges and 87 percent who graduated holding debt from private colleges, while 63 percent and 72 percent of white students incurred debt while graduating from public and private colleges, respectively. Both Black students and Hispanic students borrowed more than any other groups in the process of attaining bachelor's degrees from public or private nonprofit colleges and universities, with Black students averaging $35,477 in debt from private nonprofit completion and $29,344 from public nonprofit completion. Hispanic students averaged debt of $36,266 from private nonprofit completion and $23,444 from public non-profit degree attainment.[50]

Among students who do complete college, there are significant dis-parities in total student loan debt four years after completing college and in the percentage of students who default. Using data for students who graduated in 2008, Scott-Clayton and Li found that while Hispanic stu-dents owed slightly more than white students or Asian students, Black students owed nearly twice as much as white students ($52,726 and $28,006, respectively). Black student borrowers were more than three times as likely to default on student loans within four years than were white student borrowers, while Hispanic student borrowers were more than twice as likely to default as were white student borrowers.[51]

The student debt crisis hits hardest on students in for-profit colleges. For borrowers who entered repayment in 2011–12, the rate of default for students in four-year institutions two years after beginning repayment was twice as high in for-profits as in public nonprofits, and more than 2.5 times higher when comparing for-profits to private nonprofits. Eigh-teen percent of students who graduated from four-year for-profits were in default two years after entering repayment, and 28 percent of students in four-year for-profits who did not graduate were in default.[52] A study by Looney and Yannelis found that after five years, a remarkable 47 percent of the 2009 cohort of for-profit student borrowers had defaulted on a fed-eral student loan.[53]

DISCUSSION

The data presented on outcomes for first-time, full-time students in degree-granting for-profit colleges are clear: when compared to first-time, full-time students in public or nonprofit private institutions, students in for-profit colleges have lower rates of completion, higher levels of debt, higher rates of loan delinquency, and higher rates of default. A 2018 analysis of degree-granting for-profit colleges by staff of the Federal Reserve Bank of New York concluded, "Overall, our results indicate that, on average, for-profit enrollment leads to worse outcomes for students than enrolling in a public college or university."[54] In a study comparing students receiving federal aid to attend a range of institutional types offering certificate programs, Cellini and Turner found similarly discouraging results for labor market outcomes, "Across the board, our results show that despite the much higher costs of attending a for-profit institution, the average for-profit certificate student experiences lower earnings relative to public sector students."[55]

For decades, policymakers, institutional leaders, and scholars have debated efforts to increase college success for underrepresented students in America's colleges and universities. Black students and Hispanic students, particularly those who are from families with low incomes, are less likely to enter college than other students and less likely to graduate.[56] Black students are more likely than other students to borrow for college, borrow more money than others in similar degree programs, and are at risk of high rates of loan delinquency and default.[57] In a comprehensive study of the most recent six-year cohort of students who began at either a two-year or four-year college in 2010, Black students were less likely than white students, Asian students, American Indian students, or Hispanic students to have completed a degree and were most likely to no longer be in college.[58] The data on outcomes in for-profit degree-granting institutions for Black students, Hispanic students, and American Indian students is particularly disheartening. They have the lowest average rates of completion, the highest average levels of debt, and the highest rates of default in the postsecondary system.[59] Yet despite the evidence from an array of research studies and policy reports over the years, the regulations and policies proposed in the PROSPER Act fell short of what would be necessary to make a difficult situation for vulnerable students better. The PROSPER Act promised to increase for-profit participation in the higher education arena, proposed fewer constraints on sources of institutional revenue, reduced accountability for students' ability to repay loans through employment, and limited recourse for students who have been poorly served by for-profit institutions. Based on the existing body of research and data on for-profit degree-granting colleges, many of the provisions relating to higher education in the PROSPER Act looked to be another effort to support an underperforming and costly postsecondary sector, without evidence that the legislation would create a path to improving the situation.[60]

THE DEMISE OF THE PROSPER ACT

In November of 2018, Democrats gained control of the House of Representatives. This shift in political power effectively put an end to the PROSPER Act. Efforts to accomplish some of the goals of that legislation were taken up through the Department of Education's rule-making process, led by Secretary DeVos. Representative Bobby Scott became the Chairman of the House Education and Labor Committee, replacing Congresswoman Virginia Foxx. In place of the Aim Higher Act, in October of 2019, Representative Scott introduced H.R. 4674, the College Affordability Act (CAA), as the newest effort to reauthorize the Higher Education Act. In its commitment to greater affordability throughout higher education, it was similar to the Aim Higher Act. It focused on middle-class access and affordability, providing federal support to states that commit to sustained investment in public colleges and universities, increasing the value of Pell Grants; lowering the cost of loans, ease of repayment, and loan forgiveness programs; and providing greater support for Minority-Serving Institutions and institutional accountability. It turned specific attention to for-profit colleges, promising that "The CAA cracks down on predatory for-profit colleges that leave students with exorbitant debt and useless degrees."[61] The bill also set out to revise the 90/10 rule so that Post-9/11 G.I. Bill funding would be included in the calculation, established a debt-to-earnings threshold for programs required to result in gainful employment, added transparency to the emerging process of converting for-profit colleges to nonprofit status, and added bonus funding for certain nonprofit institutions that graduate Pell recipients in a timely manner.[62]

The Widening Divide: Evidence and Neoliberal Policy in Higher Education

Political scientists sometimes refer to a "hurrah vote" on a resolution in Congress. Such a vote is one where 99 percent of members of Congress are likely to vote in favor of the resolution. It is, in effect, a referendum on a proposition that is so widely accepted in the national fabric that virtually no representative would oppose it. As such, it does not require a roll call, only that members shout "hurrah" in unison.[63]

The past four decades have seen the rise of neoliberalism in politics and policy in the US to such an extent that a belief in market ideology drives decision-making for many in the Democratic party in Congress, and has become a concept that warrants a "hurrah vote" from Republicans. As Nobel laureate Amartya Sen put it, "The virtues of the market mechanism are now standardly assumed to be so pervasive that qualifications seem unimportant. Any pointer to the defects of the market mechanism seems to be, in the present mood, strangely old-fashioned and contrary to the contemporary culture, like playing an old 78 RPM record from the 1920s."[64]

The instantiation of neoliberal market policies in higher education is part of a wider political effort that reaches back at least to the Reagan administration, one that seeks to reframe the purposes of the state, and more specifically to reduce state provision of services, and to reduce state regulation, in favor of private markets, civil society institutions, and market competition as its own regulation.[65] This reframing is apparent in Gándara and Jones's presentation of a claim made by a member of Congress in the debate over the PROSPER Act that the Obama administration had shifted the federal student loan process from "private sector competition" to a "government run monopoly at the US Department of Education."[66]

There is some five decades' worth of research challenging the utility of applying market models to higher education institutions. Unlike the ideal competitive markets of economic theory, the provision of postsecondary education is deeply shaped by the dominance of nonprofit institutions, widespread information asymmetries, barriers to entry and exit, and perhaps most important, a structure based on public subsidies that typically result in the "product" being "sold" far below the cost of production.[67]

The potential limitations of markets as providers of public goods and services were also noted by Adam Smith, who raised questions about unfettered individual choice, one of the central tenets of neoliberal policies. Contemporary scholars have also questioned how effectively rational choice describes decision-making behaviors, suggesting that information failures, free riders, and what Smith labeled "animal spirits" may preclude the sum of individual choices aggregating to the greatest good in many instances.[68]

As Krugman notes, zombie policies need not yield to evidence: the benefits that they provide to powerful interests are sufficient for their political legitimacy. What they do need is a strong ideological basis.[69] One aspect of building support for the PROSPER Act, as presented by Gándara and Jones, was the construction by the committee majority of a political discourse that depended on a belief in the efficacy of markets and competition in higher education, to such an extent that the authors noted, "Republicans sought to erase the contrast Democrats constructed between for-profit and nonprofit institutions."[70]

We conclude that, in Congressional negotiations over reauthorization of the Higher Education Act over the past five administrations, for-profit colleges have sustained support less from evidence of their effectiveness than for their role as part of a movement to support a "free-market" alternative to nonprofit provision of higher education.[71] Both parties have supported the imposition of market values and competitive behaviors in all types of higher education institutions, and they have supported consumer choice as a key driver of institutional change.[72] At the same time, the parties have parted company over the degree to which federal funds and regulatory efforts should be devoted to for-profit colleges. The allegiance in Congress to for-profit provision of higher education is based in a broader ideology that, evidence has shown, has proven counterproductive for many students, their families, and the taxpayers of the United States.

There are certainly effective markets. Individuals, organizations, and policymakers do make rational choices with positive outcomes. The PROSPER Act itself called for "evidence-based" research to support postsecondary policymaking.[73] Yet our analysis of the contest over the PROSPER Act suggests that in some cases political leaders and policymakers conflate ideology with evidence to the detriment of postsecondary students and institutions. As long as there are limited consequences for that approach, it is likely that zombie ideas and their attendant policies will continue to flourish. On that point, the evidence seems clear.

CHAPTER 9

Community College Failure

Time for New Policies

GARY ORFIELD

COMMUNITY COLLEGES ARE a vast system, the product of a remarkable movement that put colleges providing the first two years of postsecondary education, as well as a wide array of training in specific job skills and general educational opportunities for the public, all in easy access to virtually all parts of the US. These schools were meant to be open and affordable, enabling a great many students to begin college without moving away from home and at much lower cost to the students and the states. In a society where college is very important for future life and students of color have never achieved equality, these are very important institutions with vast enrollments. Often they are the only chance for students and could produce great gains. But they have typically failed for students of color, and that failure creates a serious civil rights issue. After many years of focusing on the same kinds of remedies—articulation agreements, counseling, academic support, honors programs, and many others—the reality may be that community colleges are simply an inferior method for bachelor's degree education and that the remedy should be found in structural changes in higher education systems designed long ago for different populations in a very different economy. When a set of institutions is not actually designed to accomplish the desired goal and others do it much more efficiently, major changes are in order.

Community colleges are adaptive institutions offering instruction in a dazzling array of fields and often ready to launch almost any new program for which there is a local demand. They serve traditional college-age students but also a great many older students. They often have strong roots in communities. Many college graduates have had at least a passing experience at a community college. These colleges usually get much less aid per student than four-year public colleges and far less than flagship universities and have faculty with less training, and they lack many of the resources of universities; however, they are located nearby and usually enroll almost any student who wants to go. But a great many students, especially students of color, who enroll in local community colleges as the first stage in getting a bachelor's degree get lost along the way.

Community colleges are central institutions for educational mobility in the US. They are very widely distributed, with 942 public community colleges in 2020, many of which have multiple locations, thus producing convenient access for many millions of students. These schools enroll over a third of all US college students but more than 40 percent of Blacks and 50 percent of Latino students. In fall 2019, 5.4 million students were enrolled in public two-year colleges, down 1.4 percent from fall 2018.[1] These colleges are particularly important for students of color who are falling further and further behind white and Asian students whose college completion rates are significantly larger.

According to the National Student Clearinghouse Research Center, among first-time college students who enrolled either part time or full time in a community college in the fall of 2013, 40.8 percent earned a credential from a two- or four-year institution within six years, by 2019. The six-year completion rate for Asian students who started at a community college in the fall of 2013 was 49.8 percent. For white students, it was 49.2 percent; for Hispanic students, it was 37.1 percent; and for Black students, it was 28.8 percent. In other words, half of white and Asian students got bachelor's or associate's degrees or a certificate within six years, but little more than a third of Latinos and a fourth of Blacks did. The statistics for completing a bachelor's degree within six years are sobering: about a fourth of Asians (26.4 percent), a fifth of whites (21.6 percent), but only an eighth of Latinos (13.8 percent), and a tenth of Blacks (9.9 percent).[2] For nine out of ten Blacks entering and five out of six Latinos, there was no BA completion.

Students who did get bachelor's degrees after transferring tended to take significantly more time of study to finish their undergraduate education than those starting in four-year colleges. Though the tuition cost was much lower, the cost in time and income during a longer period of study and time lost in the post-college career were considerable, contributing to the overall gap in completion time. "Nearly 72 percent of white students finish a four-year degree within six years, compared to 56 percent of Hispanic and 46 percent of black students, the National Student Clearinghouse Research Center says."[3]

Community colleges get relatively little attention from serious researchers and research institutions because they are complex, few researchers have worked or taught in them, and they have low budgets and prestige. These colleges offer a low-cost answer to the overwhelming demand for higher education in society,[4] but they are unequal, and, for many, the opportunity is an illusion or even a costly mistake. But for students who have no other choice, which includes a large share of students of color and low-income students, they are critical. These groups that are most dependent on college for economic and social mobility have often experienced unequal public schooling, so this may be the last educational opportunity. These are, of course, also the groups that have, on average, the fewest family educational resources, so they need the most support to succeed in college.

Some states rely primarily on relatively open access four-year schools, but, particularly in areas of major population growth and immigration, community colleges are especially important.

Where there are limited four-year college spaces, inadequate aid, and high college costs, community colleges can sometimes be the only major route for students of color. The cost differential in comparison to four-year public campuses is huge, and since most four-year schools do not provide funding packages, including loans and family contribution, that cover the full cost of attendance, many students and families feel they have no choice. As college credentials become ever more important in the job market and access to the middle class, community college experiences do much to make or break the dreams of students of color. Too often the dreams are broken.

Community college policy has not traditionally focused on racial and ethnic equity within the colleges, though it is often affirmed as a goal, and the efforts of some states to create incentives for stronger success have themselves shown little success. Since community colleges usually have relatively low costs and easy admissions, disadvantaged students can get in. Affirmative admissions policies are unnecessary though affirmative student aid and support are. The question is, can students of color get out with something of lasting value? The great racial question is whether the community colleges are an escalator or a dead end for students of color needing higher education success. Do the colleges offer a real opportunity or an illusion for the great numbers of students who enroll after high school or after they've been out in the labor force or are trying to raise children? Are the nonwhite campuses treated equally, or do they have fewer resources than those serving white and Asian students? Do academically talented students of color who start at a community college when they are eligible for a public university lose badly? Most important, for college access, do the students whose goal is to finish a bachelor's or graduate degree succeed as well as those who start in four-year schools? The answers are very important because, as educational credentials become more and more important in shaping students' future, the gap in college completion for Black, Latino, and Native students has grown and is a fundamental force in perpetuating racial stratification.

Research shows that there have long been very unequal outcomes for Black and Latino students and that reforms have fallen short. Decade after decade we see similar findings and proposals. These facts have been glaring in research on community colleges for many years, and the current statistics show that we are far from resolving the issues.[5] In their massive review of the literature, Pascarella and Terenzini note that "for at least four decades, proponents and critics of community colleges have debated whether these public two-year institutions democratize or divert educational attainment opportunities."[6] Their own research led them to conclude that, controlling for other factors, starting at a two-year campus significantly reduced the likelihood of completing college.

After reviewing many studies, the authors conclude "that students seeking a bachelor's degree who begin their college careers in a two-year public institution continue to be at a disadvantage in reaching their educational goals compared with similar students entering a four-year college or university."[7] Critics of this line of research respond by arguing that, in spite of various statistical controls, the students are different, and point out that the students who start in community colleges who actually succeed in transferring succeed at high rates in many universities. Arthur M. Cohen, longtime director of the Center for the Study of Community Colleges, argued that the colleges were "criticized for their inability to effect miracles with populations that have proved intractable to the ministrations of other schools and social welfare agencies" and says that the critics are outsiders who do not understand the good, hard work that the colleges do and the success of many individual students who have attended them.[8]

Urban community colleges experience very severe problems, and Vincent Tinto, a leading researcher of college attrition, concludes that these colleges, which serve many students of color, have to struggle "to help students come to class and acquire the basic academic skills they need to begin work toward a degree program." The colleges, he says, often face the "monumental task of trying to undo the accumulated damage of many years of inferior schooling and the multiple constraints of poverty," a challenge that "dwarfs the capacity of the institution."[9] He points to the much less focused academic experience for community college students. "Two-year-college students . . . are much more likely to be working while in the college, attending part-time rather than full-time, and/or living at home while in college. . . . They, too, are likely to experience a wide range of competing external pressures on their time and energies and to be unable to spend significant amounts of time on campus interacting with other students and members of the staff."[10] Is it the colleges or the students?

Some see the unequal outcomes as being little more than the natural selection of different groups of students while others see it as an institutional strategy to protect the best opportunities for the privileged students and the well-paid faculty at the prestige institutions where they do relatively little teaching and are much more likely to receive funds and time for their original research. Some see them as a mechanism to perpetuate the stratification of dominant classes or the technical elite, whereas others see them as very important community institutions. Since there are so many institutions serving such different communities, it is possible to find examples of both. The idea that the differences are caused by selection bias, by differences in who enrolls, comes into question, however, when we see that a significant share of very highly qualified students do start in community colleges.

It is important to look at the possible impacts of states deciding to rely more or less on community colleges in terms of student success. A 1992 study comparing the state-by-state differences in the proportion of students enrolling in community colleges found a strong relationship between higher shares in community colleges and lower graduation rates, particularly for students of color.[11] A later and more extensive study found the same relationship but determined that the strongest relationship was between the state's supply of four-year college spaces (which is, of course, related to the share of community college use). A study by Saul Geiser and former University of California President Richard Atkinson found that there was a very strong correlation between the number of four-year college spaces per one thousand college-age students and the completion rate, concluding "there is a strong, positive correlation (0.78) between 4-year enrollment and the number of B.A.s awarded per population 18-to-29 years old."[12] In other words, when a state makes a structural decision to limit access to four-year campuses and, in most cases, covers it with an expansion of community colleges, it is lowering its graduation rate, which, in turn, does disproportionate harm to communities of color.

The basic outcomes for students of color in community colleges have been very bad for many years. The arguments are mainly about the causation and the needed statistical controls for differences in student background.

In his 1979 book, The Dilemma of Access: Minorities in Two Year Colleges, Michael Olivas squarely focused on the racial dimension of reliance on community colleges to educate nonwhite students within highly stratified higher education systems.[13] He pointed out that although students of color were very disproportionately attending two-year colleges, programs to help minority students were not in the mushrooming community colleges but were developed at elite institutions with small minority enrollments.[14] At what turned out to be a high point of equity in access to college in 1976, he noted that 49 percent of the Black enrollment and 59 percent of the Latinos were in community colleges,[15] though data indicated that freshmen were much more likely to remain in college if they began on a four-year campus.[16] Olivas noted that few states had programs that explicitly served students of color in community colleges and that California had by far the largest, which included "financial aid, tutoring, counseling and/or special instruction through EOPS"[17] (California's explicitly race-conscious programs were later cancelled by the passage of Proposition 209 in 1996, which banned what it called "racial preference"). Olivas pointed to the "enormous discrepancies between public subsidies at two and four year levels of statewide higher education systems" with "strikingly smaller" per capita funding for community colleges, raising major civil rights issues.[18] Affirmative action programs were weak, and the affirmative action officers in the colleges were isolated from power. The colleges needed "aggressive affirmative action," particularly for the highly desirable programs that often had admissions criteria working against minority access.[19]

The stratification argument was central in Steven Brint and Jerome Karabel's 1989 book, *The Diverted Dream: Community Colleges and the Promises of Educational Opportunity in America, 1900–1985*.[20] They saw the emergence of the community colleges as a key part of "a hierarchically differentiated educational system closely linked to the labor market." The vastly expanded higher education system of the US by the mid-twentieth century was enrolling more than twice as high a share of its young people in college as any competitor,[21] but Brint and Karabel saw the role of the community college as unfocused, trying to do everything. One major force in its emergence was the universities that saw it as a mechanism to divert an immense demand for higher education that they could not fulfill and did not fit with their priorities.[22] Many of the community colleges' leaders saw more vocational training for specific jobs that did not require a bachelor's degree as their actual central mission, but "no more than 25 to 30 percent of junior college students had ever enrolled in vocational programs."[23]

Some researchers see community colleges as a cheap strategy to protect the elite universities from excessive demand, to give the appearance of going to college without the necessary elements for success, and a process to lower or "cool out" unrealistic aspirations from students who are not really prepared. The first one was created by the University of Chicago with the thought that it would be better to have students trained in the basics elsewhere and come to the university when it was time for serious intellectual work. When the famous California Master Plan for Higher Education was created in 1960, it legitimated a very stratified state system in which the large majority of the state's students would not be eligible for any public four-year campus and only one-eighth for the University of California. Community colleges enable students to go to college with expectations of a bachelor's degree or more, but step by step the students fail and leave or find other goals, preserving the theory of universal access while protecting the status of the elite institutions.[24]

In 2012, a major study in the *Economics of Education Review* concluded that there are "large negative impacts on both educational attainment and labor market outcomes for men and women who begin at two-year colleges, even for those students who expect to complete a bachelor's degree."[25] Bridget Terry Long's 2018 study, *The College Completion Landscape*, reported a six-year completion rate of 26 percent for students enrolling in two-year campuses versus 45 percent for four-year public campuses, 61 percent for public universities, and 77.8 percent for private universities.[26] She notes that all groups of students do better at more selective institutions and that other research shows that although the "preparedness of entering students plays a role, an institution's characteristics and resources are more important in determining graduation rates."[27] Black students have a particularly low completion rate in public two-year schools.[28] She goes on to discuss the life-changing impacts of obtaining a diploma with major impacts on earning, employment, access to benefits and retirement funds, and participation in voting and community activities.[29] One of the reasons the enrollment process is so important is that there is clear evidence that a significant share of students with records that clearly qualify them for admissions to a selective university instead enroll in community colleges. About a third of Black and Latino students with solid high school grades (3.5 or higher) enroll at community colleges, compared to 22 percent of white students with the same grades.[30]

THE DECLINING FEDERAL ASPIRATION

When the federal government first became a major supporter of college access for low-income students from the mid-1960s to the early 1970s, the basic goal was to make four-year public colleges affordable to low-income students through what became the Pell Grant. As college costs multiplied after 1980 and aid fell far behind the rising cost of attendance, the promise of access has increasingly focused on community colleges, which expanded rapidly across the nation in the middle of the twentieth century. They were relatively low-cost options, with low tuitions and located within commuting range for most Americans, unlike the universities, so many students could stay at home. Beginning in the 1980s, there was a massive shift of the cost of public colleges from state governments to families and students, and the maximum federal Pell Grant covered a lower and lower share of the cost of university attendance, which was often well beyond the combined Pell and federally guaranteed student loan. College has always been more accessible for higher-income families, but as incomes became far more unequal during those decades and only upper-income families could readily deal with soaring college costs, the community colleges became a more and more important alternative, often the only alternative.

Since the 1990s, the focus of federal policy has been to make community college attendance affordable through aid. Speaking at a community college during his reelection campaign in 1996, President Bill Clinton said: "Ten years from now many of you will be working in jobs that don't even exist now." He asked, "Why shouldn't we guarantee fourteen years of education so as to keep pace with our rapid technological change?"[31] At the beginning of his second term, President Clinton's central proposal was the creation of the Hope Scholarship, which involved tax credits set at the level to pay the cost of two years of community college tuition. Clinton said this would "open the doors of college education wider than ever before."[32] But he was talking about community college.

President George W. Bush's central domestic policy focus was on education, and he saw community colleges as a key educational resource. Bush asked Congress for $125 million to promote dual-enrollment programs that allow high school students to earn college credit. "Community colleges are available," Bush said, sitting in a gymnasium in front of a sign that said "Jobs and Growth." "They are affordable and they are flexible."[33] President Barack Obama also praised and supported community colleges. Speaking at Pellissippi State Community College in Knoxville, Tennessee, in early 2015, he announced a federal plan to produce free tuition for two years of community college education, much like Bill Clinton had called for two decades earlier. He called it "an ambitious new plan to bring down the cost of community college tuition in America." He said it would help the US "lead the world" and that "A college degree is the surest ticket to the middle class. It ensures you are always employable."[34]

In each case, presidents took a chance to make a bold statement and provide some support for millions of students at a far lower cost than providing major help to support students at bachelor's degree–granting institutions. More recently, several states have enacted "tuition free" plans of various kinds for community colleges (which had often been tuition free when they were founded), and many localities have "promise" programs that promised local support to make college accessible. The civil rights problem is that community colleges do not work well for students of color.

THE CALIFORNIA COMMUNITY COLLEGE STORY

California is critical to any national community college debate. One in every ten community colleges is located in California, where the state accounts for one-fifth of the nation's total community college enrollment.[35] It is a state that made a very conscious decision in its 1960 Master Plan to limit four-year public colleges to the top third of the state's students and the University of California to the top eighth. In a state with only a small sector of private schools and no Historically Black Colleges and Universities, and extremely unequal high schools, that meant the educational fate of nonwhite students depended heavily on the community college system.

Students in California public schools are extremely segregated by race, poverty, and educational quality. Latino students are more segregated from whites than in any other state, and typically, it is double segregation by race and poverty, with the average Latino student in a school with more than two-thirds low-income students. Blacks, for whom California is the nation's second most segregated state, showed a similar pattern of double isolation.[36] The state's Black and Latino students, on average, attended schools that were far more likely to be in the lowest quartile of ranks by the state's Academic Performance Index. Students from those schools were less likely to transfer and tended to transfer to less highly rated colleges and private for-profit schools and were less likely to receive degrees.[37] Preparation is highly unequal. National research in recent years has produced powerful evidence of lifelong damage from this kind of educational segregation.[38]

The reality is that most of California's disadvantaged students enroll in nearby community colleges and have a highly disappointing college experience that does not lead to either a degree or a job-related credential. They lose a chance for a much better future. This experience harms their future families and, in the aggregate, their communities. Most complete few credits and leave as a failure. Some leave with debts from student loans. Only a small group achieve an associate's degree, and fewer successfully transfer and get a bachelor's degree. That should not obscure the fact that the subgroup that does transfer does quite well on their new campus and is about as likely as students who started as freshman at the college or university to graduate.

The success rate of students who come from the segregated concentrated-poverty high schools that most students of color attend is grim. Though community colleges are often thought of as equivalent institutions offering, broadly, the same kind of introductory academic courses needed for the first years of college, they actually differ greatly in their success in transferring students who go on to succeed in four-year campuses. Some are basically back-door entry points into the upper division of good universities while, at the other extreme, there are institutions serving mostly low-income students of color who come from weak high schools; few of them transfer successfully. A few community colleges have become very large, important, and highly regarded institutions, like Miami Dade College in Florida, and some have even been authorized to offer bachelor's degrees in certain fields. Most people are familiar with the vast range of quality in high schools, even in the same district or metro area. Much the same is true of community colleges, which often have feeder patterns from clusters of high schools in an area, even though students often can choose to attend in a less convenient area elsewhere in the same city. Some have highly respected special programs, often with limited enrollment. Community colleges, in their very design and origin, are unequal to four-year colleges, and some are far more unequal than others.

Students of different races attend very different high schools in California. In a 2012 study, researchers looked at the quality of the various schools and then examined where students from different levels of high school went to college and how these patterns were linked related to the race and ethnicity of the students. The study looked at all the high schools of Southern California and the region's fifty-one community colleges. It found 114 "dropout factory" high schools, where 35 to 77 percent of the students dropped out. The students who went to college from those schools went in substantial numbers to highly segregated community colleges, especially in Los Angeles. The strong high schools where at least 85 percent of the students graduated mostly sent significant groups of students who began at community colleges into majority white or majority white and Asian community colleges. The fourth of the community colleges with the lowest transfer rates were segregated nonwhite schools. The highest transfer rate community colleges, whose transfer rate was nearly twice that of the lowest quartile, were largely white and Asian. Even among the schools with the highest transfer rates, however, there were serious racial gaps in successful transfers.[39] So most students of color from poor schools went to community colleges with poor transfer rates.

An analysis by the Institute for Higher Education Leadership and Policy at Sacramento State University found that of the California community college students who said they wanted a degree, just 23 percent transferred to a four-year campus and only 14 percent of the Latino students. Of those who transferred, only half (52 percent) transferred to a public university in the state, and the for-profit sector was a growing destination in spite of the major problems of cost and noncompletion in that sector that led to the collapse of many of those institutions during the Obama administration.[40] In 2018, the Institute found that 70 percent of community college students did not receive an associate's or bachelor's degree or transfer to a four-year college within six years of their enrollment. There were "only 26 percent of African-American students and 22 percent of Latino students earning a degree, certification or transfer to a four-year university within six years."[41]

A 2012 study was able to merge data from the state's high schools with their records in college, following students from California high schools into community colleges and transfers.[42] In California, there is a great sorting at the outset of college. Students of color rarely make it into the most selective public institutions, especially since the state's affirmative action ban was written into the state constitution in 1996. "For example, in 2008, 9 percent of African Americans and 8.8 percent of Latinos who went to college in the state, began at the University of California, while 14 percent of Whites and 36 percent of Asians who went to college in-state enrolled in the University of California, the state's most selective public institution."[43] The students who went to the University of California went to some of the world's best public universities while those who went to the concentrated Black and Latino community colleges received much lower levels of public support.[44]

Students of color attended unequal high schools with poorer resources that led to poorer academic preparation. Classifying high schools by resources, the study found that a third (32.4 percent) of Latinos attended high schools in the lowest category as did a fifth of Black students. But only a tenth of Asians were in those schools and only one in twenty-five (4.1 percent) of whites. Students' high school backgrounds were vastly different by race/ethnicity. White and Asian students were very disproportionately in the highest resource schools.[45] They started college in very different places. For example, in 2008, 9 percent of Black students and 8.8 percent of Latinos who went to college in the state began at the University of California, while 14 percent of whites and 36 percent of Asians who went to college in-state enrolled in the University of California.[46]

The study found that there was only a very narrow path to a bachelor's degree for students from the segregated high poverty high schools that most students of color attended. At that time, there were 112 community colleges in California, but the study found that only five actually enrolled and transferred any significant number of students from the weak high schools into college. Most of the students from those schools left early in their college experience, gaining no community college degree.

When the researchers visited the most successful transfer schools and interviewed their leaders and members of the faculty and counselors, those campuses had serious efforts and dedicated faculty and staff working on helping those students transfer, sometimes in special programs such as Puente. Even then the transfer rates were modest. The study showed that chances for Black or Latino students who attended a weak high school and went to a community college were very limited. From the standpoint of the state, which is now growing at the slowest rate in generations and has an aging and steadily declining white minority, the cost of failing to educate its students of color will be immense if it continues. The state is already short by a million college graduates for what the future labor market is predicted to need and, without significant internal or international migration, will fall further behind, so the only alternatives are decline or educating the students of color.

Community colleges, in spite of their huge enrollments and special importance to disadvantaged students, usually receive little serious substantive attention from federal and state policymakers, who focus much more on the flagships and other public universities and problems of student aid. Federal policy about community colleges has been basically about student aid and about career training. It is mostly about helping students financially, not the institutions themselves. They get their principal funding from state and local taxpayers and from the often relatively modest tuitions and fees. They don't have the multiple funding streams of the major universities. Much state aid is based on per capita enrollment and, typically, the community colleges receive far less per student than four-year schools and do not have the other sources, such as research funding and endowments. Often they are created and located as the result of local pressure to have a college. They try to build local enrollment and local support by effectively responding to the interests of students and the needs of the local employers.

Traditionally, the colleges mostly got state aid on the basis of enrollment statistics, creating an incentive to grow and adapt but not to focus strongly on the eventual graduation and successful transfer of students since they also have so many other functions. Local business often focuses on job-related training, which can work well if there is an active demand from employers and training programs run by faculty connected to the industry itself and who relate well with the employers. Because the schools usually have open enrollment and there are not systematic tests or serious follow-ups on the educational future of students, it is often hard for policymakers to evaluate the outcomes as tides of students flow in and out of the campuses. In assessing graduation and transfer rates, both the denominator and the numerator are often unclear. The colleges can, accurately, say that those students who forget the associate's degree and transfer usually do well in the receiving institutions, but only a small share get the degree and many transfers leave after little time at the college. Should a college be seen as failing if a totally unprepared student who wants a degree quickly leaves or a success if a well-prepared student sails though one or two terms, gets some tuition money, and succeeds after transfer? It is hard to know just how to evaluate the impact of any individual college. Recent efforts to create incentives and sanctions to produce different outcomes, especially high graduation rates, have been highly disappointing.

Rather than get lost in trying to sort all of this out, a more useful approach may be to look at the whole state higher education system of which the community colleges are a major part. Are they, as many students think, "way stations on the road to four-year institutions" or, as universities may view them, an "essential safety valve" and a sorting mechanism that would allow the small minority of qualified students to transfer?[47] From a civil rights perspective, is it better or worse for the system to provide community colleges as the basic option for students of color? Brint and Karabel concluded that in spite of individual successes, the system "accentuated rather than reduced existing patterns of social inequality" as "the bottom tier of a class-linked tracking system in higher education." The reality was that "the very fact of attending a two-year rather than a four-year institution lowers the likelihood that a student will obtain a bachelor's degree."[48] The evidence indicates that students of color relying on community colleges for access to college completion are usually disappointed and have been for many years in spite of isolated successes and many reform efforts.

RECOMMENDATIONS

There are many useful programs at individual colleges and communities designed to help address the problems discussed here—problems from financial aid to counseling, from addressing the excessive numbers of no-credit remedial courses that have discouraged too many students, to improving the transfer of credits and establishing transfer rights with four-year colleges. Properly done, these programs and policies are useful and should be eligible for the use of state and federal funds if they are well implemented and show results. But I chose to focus here on the structural problems that policy needs to address and are lost in the bargaining within higher education politics that tends to subordinate criticism and to divide up gains among the institutions in ways that permit all to continue along the existing paths.

Before that analysis, however, it seems useful to make two basic points. First, there are successes, and they should be supported. Since there are good examples of both programs and campuses that have persisted over time in helping students of color successfully transfer and realize their goals, they should receive resources to expand the programs or the colleges, preferably under the leadership that generated the success, even if those programs have not been successfully replicated elsewhere. Since the basic pattern of inequality has been very persistent, it seems likely that it is not the model but the leadership and institutional commitment that truly matter in these successes. The second general suggestion is to be serious about diversifying faculty and staff. These schools serve many students of color who have not been fairly prepared and are often struggling. There is good evidence that faculty and staff of color (and dedicated white faculty) make a real difference in terms of understanding and supporting the students. Colleges that create and support diversity should be rewarded, and efforts to encourage their own students to aspire to graduate school and eventual faculty positions should be supported.

On a broader scale, however, the effort to extend opportunity to graduate from college to students of color through community colleges has been a long and costly failure. If five of six Black students who enroll don't make it, the considerable cost of their time on campus to the state and local governments that fund the colleges is lost, and the real cost of producing a single graduate is prohibitive compared to the results for similar students starting on four-year campuses. And that is without even counting the loss of income when those students are enrolled, the loss of hope they experience, the debt they may incur, and the dismal future economic prospects that are likely. It is time to look for better alternatives to address a fundamental structural problem.

A new national administration should have a vision and a program to substantially increase college graduation and diminish the severe racial/ethnic gap in attainment. For students, priority should go to a larger Pell Grant and other funding that actually makes four-year colleges possible for students from low-income families with no wealth or savings. Many of the students wishing for college degrees are in community colleges because their families saw no other choice.

We need special college access funds to produce a higher and more equal level of college completion. Such efforts should include a requirement for data, a plan, and evidence of progress. The data should be analyzed with regards to race and ethnicity and to students from areas of concentrated poverty. The data should analyze what happens to each group of students over time. The plans should include the percentage of students of each group expressing a desire to complete a bachelor's degree when they enter, the percentage of them who eventually transfer or attain an associate's degree, and the percentage who ultimately obtain a bachelor's degree within six years.

Addressing the Structural Issue

Reformers attempt to increase preparation, counseling, and other elements in many ways, often producing some gains for students. Those attempts can be positive but have not changed the basic realities in decades' worth of efforts. In terms of the basic structure of a state's higher education system, however, the consistent finding that it is a serious disadvantage to go to a bachelor's degree–granting institution rather than a community college has two logical solutions—greatly increasing the access of the students to four-year campuses or enabling some of the successful community colleges to award bachelor's degrees. Clearly, a graduation goal—and pathway and continuity from the freshman year to graduation—is very helpful for students. Four-year colleges have a clear mission and destination: graduation.

The problem is that it is much more costly to state governments to finance the creation of new universities or major expansions of existing ones than to provide far lower per student cost in community colleges. When it is considered in terms of the public cost per student graduated, the four-year colleges can look far more efficient. If a community college costs one-third less per student enrolled but a four-year college graduates three times as high a share of the students of color seeking a degree, the four-year college is actually far more efficient.

I have been interested in work on college access for more than three decades and have read endless articles, both popular and scholarly, and participated in conferences and research presentations. The discussion is stuck and endlessly repetitive. Yes, the system can and should be improved, but improving it is very hard work, the effort is rarely strongly supported as a top priority at the college, there are intermittent grants or resources that tend to fade away, and there are few real incentives to do them on scale. A few remarkable boutique community colleges do an excellent job, and small programs are run by dedicated staff in many others. They deserve support and praise. But most of the community colleges have too many missions and too little support and do not have strong relationships either with high schools or four-year colleges and universities. If their courses were accepted as truly equivalent and prepared students to flourish in upper-division courses at a university, the whole process would work much better, but often they do not. That most often occurs in affluent communities or in university towns where the college becomes a de facto part of the university and a back-door transfer pathway that really works.

My conclusion, however, is that the problem is not about this program or that program or set of policies. The problem is structural. Four-year colleges are far more effective in producing higher rates of graduation in less time, especially for students of color, controlling for difference in student background. Higher education policy is a "you scratch my back, I'll scratch yours" operation, where the different levels of colleges don't

prey on each other, don't attack each other's claims, and work in a broad
higher education coalition that tries to increase resources for all sectors.
That does nothing about this problem. I think these structural changes
would be important for Congress and state governments to consider:

- A very significant expansion of four-year college capacity and
  enrollment where there is unmet demand
- Financial aid formulas that actually permit families with few or no
  resources to send their children to four-year public campuses
- Expanded dual enrollment in high school, concentrating on
  enrolling more students of color and students from poor families and getting them college experience and credits before their
  freshmen year
- Where there is unmet demand for bachelor's degree enrollment,
  authorizing strong community colleges to give the BA
- Funds to incentivize and develop degree programs in some fields
  under strict state supervision
- Formal merger of community colleges with universities as
  lower-division centers of the universities
- For major changes, planning and implementation grants and independent evaluations

If we are to make community colleges, especially those serving large
populations of students of color, into a strong pathway to higher education success, we need federal policy and state policies that focus on
assuring that a valid transfer system exists in the colleges or that students
seriously committed to college be transferred to another campus that has
these opportunities. This is not in any way to diminish the importance of
the college's other functions. Some community colleges with poor transfer rates have very strong programs in skills that lead to good jobs, and
they are also very important. But if a community college has a long-term
record of very little successful transfer for students of color and the great
majority of those students enter expressing transfer as their goal, the

college should either be required to create a workable transfer path or to advise students wanting to transfer to enroll elsewhere following strong counseling opportunities.

There are, of course, serious civil rights questions about higher education systems that consistently produce dramatically different outcomes for students of color—both the high schools and the colleges—even after controlling for other explanatory factors. If publicly supported schools and colleges perpetuate inequality and widen gaps, it is far from "equal protection under the law." Congress should ask the Government Accountability Office to investigate the issues of racial equality in the state secondary and higher education systems and request the US Commission on Civil Rights, the Department of Education, and the Civil Rights Division of the Department of Justice to analyze and report on possible violations of Title VI and the 1964 Civil Rights Act by those systems. Black and Hispanic caucuses in Congress and state legislatures should ask for hearings and finding on these issues. As part of higher education, legislation funding should be provided for developing and implementing equity plans in colleges and state higher education agencies. There should be regular published reports on progress being made and identification of and rewards to institutions making substantial progress. There are no instant solutions, but a clearly focused and persistent effort to foster institutional adaptation could open a much more powerful pathway to opportunity for students of color. After generations of frustration and promises that have not been fulfilled, these communities deserve no less.

CHAPTER 10

Recentering Civil Rights in Federal Higher Education Policymaking

NICHOLAS HILLMAN AND GARY ORFIELD

THE HIGHER EDUCATION ACT was created in the midst of the civil rights movement of the 1960s and, at least in its initial years, prioritized the welfare of the least advantaged students in America. It created outreach programs, now known as TRIO, designed to expand access for low-income and first-generation students. It created a need-based grant program, eventually named the Pell Grant, which made it possible for low-income students to attend college at low or no cost. It authorized programs and money to strengthen colleges that were "struggling for survival" and even created an emergency fund for colleges in "serious financial distress."[1] The law incorporated some of the innovations of the War on Poverty programs designed to bring and support low-income students into college. The early HEA even required states and colleges to support low-income students in exchange for aid.[2] Many of these benefits and programs supported students of color and what would become Minority-Serving Institutions.

As described in this book, many of the coalitions and policy advocates that were key to the creation of the HEA have lost influence over time as politicians focused on the interests of white middle-class voters. As the states withdrew support for public campuses, they authorized the higher education institutions and systems to cover the costs through tuition increases, helping produce a crushing increase in college costs and demands from all sectors for aid. This resulted in a long series of policy decisions, sometimes intentional and sometimes simply by neglect, that steadily eroded that progress. These steady changes eventually recast the priorities away from expanding opportunity for those with the least resources toward policies that benefited the middle- and upper-income— and largely white—constituencies. The 1980s and 1990s were a key period that created tax credit giveaways to the middle class and wealthy, expanded eligibility low-interest loans to students from middle- and upper-income households, and neglected colleges serving students of color and low-income students. It was also the period in which campuses in the South were forced to begin desegregation, and selective campuses elsewhere adopted voluntary affirmative action plans. Since the last HEA reauthorization, we have come out of the Great Recession only to face the economic shock of COVID-19 and a social reawakening of racial injustice and white America's role in perpetuating racial inequality.

To reverse the decades-long shift toward privileging white middle-class families and their interests, federal higher education policy needs a renewed commitment to students of color and low-income students. That policies drifted so quickly toward white middle-class interests was not an accident—it occurred in large response to more low-income students and students of color gaining access to a college education once held only by the white middle class. White voters saw this as a threat, and politicians played to their interests by extending them benefits while neglecting the institutions serving low-income students and students of color. This policy shift also allowed for-profit colleges to successfully lobby for their own interests, taxpayer alliances to limit social spending, and even the banking industry found ways to influence the loan system to the benefit of their shareholders. The federal government created a great river of largely unsupervised aid and borrowed resources while sectors struggled to channel them to support their institutions, often losing focus on the original intent. Investors and hedge funds found opportunities to rack up massive profits on low-quality for-profit campuses. Federal policy will continue on this path if there are no active or strong coalitions fighting against these forces and in the interests of the most disadvantaged.

THE FUTURE OF CIVIL RIGHTS–BASED REFORM

The civil rights cornerstones of the HEA have eroded, and there has been limited enforcement of the Civil Rights Act, resulting in far too little progress in promoting equal opportunity. Policymakers have not seriously maintained the original intent of the HEA via comprehensive reauthorization, and reauthorizations have not fully addressed racial injustices that exist throughout society and within America's educational systems. The combination of these two forces—political polarization and racial inequality—has resulted in a policy environment that favors those with the most advantage at the expense of the most disadvantaged. In the absence of a countermovement, the federal higher education policy landscape will continue to drift in favor of the interests of white middle-class voters at the expense of communities of color and those with the least financial means.

To help protect against this drift, the following outlines how to recenter civil rights into federal higher education policy debates. First, federal policy needs *race-conscious investment* strategies that build wealth and resources for students of color and the colleges where they enroll. Second, federal policy must vigorously support *civil rights enforcement*. And third, policies must strive for *consumer protections* against debts and severely inadequate programs, particularly among marginalized and minoritized groups. These three strategies, when working to reinforce one another, should promote better opportunities, experiences, and outcomes for people of color and low-income students.

Race-Conscious Investments

At least four key investment strategies would not only enhance civil rights in higher education but would also restore early commitments to supporting students and the institutions where they enroll. Minority-Serving Institutions and Historically Black Colleges and Universities enroll large shares of students of color and play a significant role in promoting upward mobility.[3] Yet, these same institutions often have fewer financial resources to deliver educational opportunities and to help meet students' full financial need. Federal policymakers should expand Title III investments for MSIs and HBCUs with emphasis on colleges that have the least or most volatile financial resources. Second, a comprehensive HEA reform should create a new funding model similar to Title I funding in K–12 schools where colleges serving large shares of low-income students would receive additional financial support to help equalize opportunities among the least-resourced institutions serving students with the greatest financial needs.[4] This combination of investment—one that directly supports colleges serving large shares of students of color and another that focuses on economic inequality—should be the new cornerstone of equity-based funding that supports colleges to ensure they have sufficient resources to help students succeed while also avoiding going into debt. These investments must also support academic advising, outreach efforts, precollege preparation, and efforts to improve campus racial climate for students of color.

In addition to funding colleges directly, a third federal investment strategy would be to greatly enhance need-based grant aid programs like the Pell Grant, where the majority (68 percent) of recipients have family incomes below $30,000.[5] The purchasing power of the Pell Grant has eroded over the course of several decades, so a renewed investment in this aid—by doubling the award amount, as promised by President Joe Biden, and pegging future growth to tuition levels—would be a strong investment in supporting low-income students. This still falls short of what the original Pell Grant covered, yet would go a long way in helping low-income students pay for and persist in college. This investment would likely pay off in the long run by promoting college completion, reducing the need to borrow, and increasing the eventual tax base among recipients.[6] Finally, continued support for precollege programs targeted to elementary and secondary education students from communities of color, low-income neighborhoods, or who are first in their family to go to college would be a strong and race-conscious way to promote opportunity. These programs often take a more holistic approach to supporting students far beyond financial aid, where participants can build community that last throughout their college experience.

Civil Rights Enforcement

As colleges diversify their student body, it is particularly important that historically white universities reckon with the structural racism embedded in many of their administrative, academic, and student life routines.[7] For example, predominantly white institutions are too often hostile to and unsupportive of students of color, where racist and classist behaviors by white students, faculty, and administrators go unchecked.[8] For this reason, the US Department of Education's Office of Civil Rights (OCR) should vigorously enforce civil rights laws to ensure college students' rights are protected.[9] Students should not face discrimination or harassment on the basis of their race, ethnicity, gender, age, national origin, disability, or religion. To ensure the protection of these fundamental rights, and to hold perpetuators accountable, the OCR must have sufficient resources to investigate and help resolve discrimination cases on campuses. Active enforcement of affirmative action employment policies for federal contractors would also support faculty diversity; for example, fellowships for faculty of color with background and research experience in communities of color would support efforts to diversify the professoriate.

A national coalition of civil rights groups has outlined core principles and recommendations for enhancing civil rights in higher education.[10] In addition to supporting the OCR's charge, they also advocate for enhancing Title IX laws and regulations, providing guidance under the Americans with Disabilities Act, and allowing the Secretary of Education to fine colleges for civil rights violations. These actions would go a very long way in promoting equal opportunity and creating a fairer and more humane environment for college students to succeed with proper recourse and protections for any discrimination they experience.

CONSUMER PROTECTIONS AGAINST FRAUD AND LIFETIME INDEBTEDNESS

Similar to the need for robust legal protections, a civil rights–based policy would also focus on protecting individuals from the harms of market forces. For example, when for-profit colleges defraud students—and students of color, military veterans, and students from low-income families in particular—then there must be policies and procedures to remedy these failures. Debt cancellation for defrauded students via the Borrower Defense regulation should be codified into law. Similarly, debt cancellation for borrowers with permanent disability, strong oversight over student loan servicers, and enhanced protections and benefits for student loan borrowers facing economic hardship should all be central to a comprehensive HEA reauthorization and not left to regulatory guidance or administrative procedures. These protections must be enshrined into law to fully protect students from the harms of bad actors.

In addition to enhancing protections for individual students—largely those who borrowed federal loans and are struggling to repay them—the federal government should also undertake an aggressive investigation into identifying which colleges are "bad apples" and restrict them from Title IV aid programs.[11] This cannot be done by passively providing students with information via consumer-facing websites like the College Scorecard; rather, it must be done via proactively holding colleges accountable in meaningful ways. For example, restoring Gainful Employment regulations, enhancing the cohort default rate policy, and tying the loopholes in the "90/10" rule would go a long way in sifting out the poorest performers. But the metrics used in these accountability models are race-neutral, decontextualized from any discussion of racial inequality, and too easily gamed. Inappropriately applied, they could result in sanctions against colleges that serve students from highly disadvantaged communities who have been denied adequate preparation for college. Colleges that educate students from very poor neighborhoods and reservations should be rewarded and supported, not sanctioned. Understanding and judgment and consultation with leaders of color will be necessary to maximize benefits and avoid mistakes in this policy space. Accordingly, future accountability regimes must be centered around civil rights and focused on the disproportionate effects any particular policy is likely to have on students of color, low-income students, and the colleges where they enroll. They should also have an eye toward the practical side of accountability by answering why unequal outcomes exist in the first place, how specific individuals on a college campus might respond, and with what resources.[12] It may very well be that a race-neutral accountability regime will be misaligned with the underlying problem and thus leave it unresolved, so thinking about accountability from a civil rights perspective may help policymakers design and support efforts to address root problems rather than their symptoms.

It is also time for civil rights reviews of state higher education systems through collaboration between the Department of Education's Office for Civil Rights, the Undersecretary of Education, and the Department of Justice to explore policies and procedures related to declining or clearly inadequate access by students of color to various public colleges. The preferred outcome of such investigations would be state civil rights plans for entire higher education systems, including annual reporting, enhanced oversight, and independent monitors to ensure colleges are diligent in confronting and ultimately remedying unequal systems. In so doing, these reports and investigations would be of great use to state policymakers and civil rights groups committed to systemwide improvement.

CONCLUSION

A comprehensive HEA reauthorization is long past due, and this book outlines several causes and consequences of that policy neglect. The politics of higher education have changed considerably since HEA's last comprehensive reauthorization in 2008. There are now several civil rights groups, advocacy coalitions, and think tanks active in the policy debates that were once dominated by the "One DuPont" membership organizations. The next round of HEA reauthorization will need to address racial injustice and economic inequality in ways that it has not done since 1965. In fact, we believe it needs to go even further than it did in 1965 by expressly investing in students of color, low-income students, and the colleges where they enroll, and by taking a race-conscious approach to accountability reforms, including strong consumer protections and civil rights enforcement. Federal higher education policymaking is at a critical moment where the nation is reckoning with racial injustices and a national public health emergency. With civil rights coalitions gaining greater influence in the higher education policy space, the message is clear that federal policy must prioritize action around addressing the racial and economic inequities outlined in this book.

NOTES

CHAPTER 1

1. Erica Frankenberg, Jongyeon Ee, Jennifer B. Ayscue, and Gary Orfield, *Harming Our Common Future: America's Segregated Schools 65 Years After Brown* (Los Angeles: Civil Rights Project, 2019).
2. Brown v. Board of Education, 347 U.S. 483 (1954).
3. Robert Lee and Tristan Ahtone, "Land-Grab Universities," *High Country News*, March 30, 2020, https://www.hcn.org/issues/52.4/indigenous-affairs-education-land-grab-universities.
4. US Census, "Population of the United States in 1860," 1864, https://www2.census.gov/library/publications/decennial/1860/population/1860a-02.pdf.
5. Stephen Provasnik and Linda Shafer, *Historically Black Colleges and Universities, 1976 to 2001* (NCES 2004–062), US Department of Education, National Center for Education Statistics (Washington, DC: Government Printing Office, 2004), 1; Walter R. Allen, Joseph O. Jewell, Kimberly A. Griffin, and De'Sha S. Wolf, "Historically Black Colleges and Universities: Honoring the Past, Engaging the Present, Touching the Future," *Journal of Negro Education* 76, no. 3 (2007): 263–80, http://www.jstor.org/stable/40034570.
6. Second Morrill Act, 51st Cong., Sess. 1 (1890), *Stat.* L-Vol. XXVI-27, Chapter 841, p. 418, August 30, 1890.
7. Second Morrill Act.
8. Second Morrill Act.
9. Second Morrill Act.
10. V. O. Key, Jr., *The Administration of Federal Grants to States* (Chicago: Public Administration Service, 1937), 161–62.
11. William C. Hine, "South Carolina State University," *South Carolina Encyclopedia*, https://www.scencyclopedia.org/sce/entries/south-carolina-state-university/.

12. Hine, "South Carolina State University."
13. Meyer Weinberg, *A Chance to Learn: A History of Race and Education in the United States* (New York: Cambridge University Press, 1977), 272.
14. Hine, "South Carolina State University."
15. Smith-Lever Act, Chapter 79 of the 63rd Congress; Approved on May 8, 1914; 38 Stat. 372, 7 U.S.C. 341 et seq.
16. Carmen V. Harris, "'The Extension Service Is Not an Integration Agency': The Idea of Race in the Cooperative Extension Service," *Agricultural History* 82, no. 2 (Spring 2008), 193–219.
17. E. E. Lewis, "Black Cotton Farmers and the AAA," *Opportunity: A Journal of Negro Life,* 13, no. 3 (March 1935): 72.
18. Suzanne Mettler, *Soldiers to Citizens: The G.I. Bill and the Making of the Greatest Generation* (New York: Oxford University Press, 2005).
19. US Department of Veterans Affairs, Office of Public Affairs, "America's Wars," November 2019.
20. Lorena Oropeza, *Latino Heritage Initiatives Fighting on Two Fronts: Latinos in the Military* (Washington, DC: National Park Service).
21. Sarah Turner and John Bound, "Closing the Gap or Widening the Divide: The Effects of the G.I. Bill and World War II on the Educational Outcomes of Black Americanism" (NBER Working Paper No. 9044, July 2002, JEL No. I2).
22. Mark Fry, "The Impact of Educational Levels on the Development of the U.S. Army in World War II" (unpublished paper, Army Historians Training Symposium, Arlington, VA, July 2015).
23. Fry, "Impact of Educational Levels."
24. Paul B. Sheatsley, "'White' Attitudes Toward the Negro American," *Daedalus* 95, no. 1. See also *The Negro American* 2 (Winter, 1966): 219.
25. Turner and Bound, "Closing the Gap."
26. Turner and Bound.
27. David Onkst, "'First a Negro . . . Incidentally a Veteran': Black World War Two Veterans and the GI Bill or Rights in the Deep South, 1944–1948," *Journal of Social History,* 31, no. 3 (Spring 1998): 517–43.
28. Turner and Bound, "Closing the Gap."
29. Leo Grebler, Joan W. Moore, and Ralph C. Guzman, *The Mexican-American People* (New York: Free Press, 1970).
30. US Department of Commerce, Bureau of the Census, "US Census of Population, 1960," vol. 1, part 1; *Current Population Reports,* Series P-20 and unpublished data; and John K. Folger and Charles B. Nam, *Education of the American Population* (A 1960 Census Monograph (Washington, DC: US Government Printing Office, 1967). From US Department of Education, National Center for Education Statistics, *Digest of Education Statistics, 2007;* U.S. Census Bureau, *Current Population Survey;* U.S. Census Bureau, *Statistical Abstract of the United States.*
31. "Total Fall Enrollment in Degree-Granting Postsecondary Institutions, by

Attendance Status, Sex of Student, and Control of Institution," *Digest of Education Statistics*, 2013. Table 303.10.

32. President's Committee on Civil Rights, *To Secure These Rights: The Report of the President's Committee on Civil Rights* (New York: Simon and Schuster, 1947), 166.

33. Gunnar Myrdal and Associates, *An American Dilemma: The Negro Problem and Modern Democracy* (New York: Harper & Brothers, 1944).

34. Sweatt v. Painter, 339 U.S. 629 (1950).

35. Sweatt v. Painter.

36. Brown v. Board of Education.

37. President John F. Kennedy's address to the nation on radio and television to report on the situation at the University of Mississippi. On September 30, 1962, https://www.jfklibrary.org/archives/other-resources/john-f-kennedy-speeches/university-of-mississippi-19620930; Claude Sitton, "Alabama Admits Negro Students; Wallace Bows to Federal Force; Kennedy Sees 'Moral Crisis' in U.S." *New York Times*, June 12, 1963.

38. See *New York Times*, "Race Relations Tied to South's Economy," March 12, 1956, 19, https://www.nytimes.com/1956/03/12/archives/race-relations-tied-to-souths-economy.html; John Kyle Day, *The Southern Manifesto: Massive Resistance and the Fight to Preserve Segregation* (Jackson: University Press of Mississippi, 2014).

39. Day, *Southern Manifesto*.

40. Day.

41. Gary Orfield, *The Reconstruction of Southern Education: The Schools and the 1964 Civil Rights Act* (New York: John Wiley, 1969).

42. Jo Ann Gibson Robinson, *The Montgomery Bus Boycott and the Women Who Started It* (Knoxville: University of Tennessee Press, 1987).

43. Diane McWhorter, *Carry Me Home: Birmingham, Alabama, the Climactic Battle of the Civil Rights Revolution* (New York: Simon & Schuster, 2001), 237–48.

44. August Meier and Elliot Rudwick, *CORE: A Study in the Civil Rights Movement* (Urbana: University of Illinois Press, 1975), 4–16.

45. Miles Wolff, *Lunch at the 5 & 10* (Chicago: Elephant Paperbacks, 1970).

46. Christopher Wilson, "The Moment When Four Students Sat Down to Take a Stand: One of the Great Monuments to the Greensboro Sit-In Is at the Smithsonian's National Museum of American History," *Smithsonian Magazine*, January 31, 2020, https://www.smithsonianmag.com/smithsonian-institution/lessons-worth-learning-moment-greensboro-four-sat-down-lunch-counter-180974087/.

47. Howard Zinn, SNCC: *The New Abolitionists* (Boston: Beacon Press, 1965), 26–37.

48. W. E. B. DuBois, *Black Reconstruction* (New York: S. A. Russell Co., 1935), 667.

49. Michael Harrington, *The Other America: Poverty in the United States* (New York: MacMillan, 1962).

50. National TRIO Clearinghouse, "The First Summer of Upward Bound–1965,"

www.trioprogrmas.org/clearinghouse/history.html; William H. James, "Upward Bound: Portrait of a Poverty Program," *SAEOPP Journal*, Fall 1986.

51. Office of Postsecondary Education, "History of the Federal TRIO Programs," www2.ed.gov/about/offices/list/ope/trio/triohistory.html.
52. Economic Opportunity Act, Public Law 88-452 August 20, 1964.
53. Economic Opportunity Act, Part C.
54. McWhorter, *Carry Me Home*.
55. McWhorter, 444–50.
56. *President John F. Kennedy's Message to Congress*, June 19, 1963; Committee on the Judiciary, Records of the U.S. Senate, Record Group 46; National Archives Building, Washington, DC.
57. Charles Whalen and Barbara Whalen, *The Longest Debate: A Legislative History of the 1964 Civil Rights Act* (Cabin John, MD: Seven Locks Press, 1985).
58. Orfield, *Reconstruction of Southern Education*.
59. Stephen K. Bailey and Edith K. Mosher, *ESEA: The Office of Education Administers a Law* (Syracuse, NY: Syracuse University Press, 1968).
60. Title IX of the Education Amendments of 1972 (20 U.S.C. 1681 et seq.; Public Law 92–318) [title IX of Pub. L. 92–318.]
61. Regents of the Univ. of California v. Bakke, 438 U.S. 265 (1978).
62. Univ. of California v. Bakke.
63. Arthur O'Sullivan, Terri A. Sexton, and Steven M. Sheffrin, *Property Taxes and Tax Revolts: The Legacy of Proposition 13* (New York: Cambridge University Press, 1995).
64. Adams v. Califano, 430 F. Supp. 118 (D.D.C. 1977)
65. Edward St. John, Britany Affolter-Caine, and Anna S. Chung, "Race-Conscious Student Financial Aid: Constructing an Agenda for Research, Litigation, and Policy Development," in *Charting the Future of College Affirmative Action: Legal Victories, Continuing Attacks, and New Research*, ed. Gary Orfield, Patricia Marin, Stella Flores, and Liliana Garces (Los Angeles: The Civil Rights Project, 2007), 173–204.
66. "Carolina Settles Integration Suit with Universities," *New York Times*, June 21, 1981, 22.
67. Women's Equity Action League v. Lauro F. Cavazos, Secretary of Education, 906 F.2d 742 (D.C. Cir., 1990).
68. San Antonio Independent School District v. Rodriguez, 411 U.S. 1 (1973).
69. Milliken v. Bradley, 418 U.S. 717 (1974).
70. Gary Orfield and Susan Eaton, *Dismantling Desegregation: The Quiet Repeal of Brown v. Board of Education* (New York: The New Press, 1996); Board of Education of Oklahoma City v. Dowell, 498 U.S. 237 (1991).
71. Hopwood v. Texas, 78 F.3d 932 (5th Cir. 1996).
72. Lydia Chavez, *The Color Bind: California's Battle to End Affirmative Action* (San Francisco: University of California Press, 1998).

73. Phillip Oliff, Mark Robyn, and Rebecca Thiess, "Federal Support for Higher Education Comes from Spending Programs and the Tax Code," Pew Research, March 7, 2017, https://www.pewtrusts.org/en/research-and-analysis/articles/2017/03/07/federal-support-for-higher-education-comes-from-spending-programs-and-the-tax-code.

74. College Board, *Trends in Student Aid 2019* (New York: College Board, 2019), 3.

75. Women's Equity Action League v. Cavazos, 906 F.2d 742 (D.C.Cir. 1990).

76. Grutter v. Bollinger, 539 U.S. 306 (Supreme Court, 2003).

77. Schuette v. Coalition to Defend Affirmative Action, 572 U.S. 291 (2014).

78. Michael Avery and Danielle McLaughlin, *The Federalist Society: How Conservatives Took the Law Back from the Liberals* (Nashville, TN: Vanderbilt University Press, 2013).

79. Gary Orfield and Nicholas Hillman, *Accountability and Opportunity in Higher Education* (Cambridge, MA: Harvard Education Press, 2018).

CHAPTER 2

1. Lyndon B. Johnson, remarks at the University of Michigan Online by Gerhard Peters and John T. Woolley, The American Presidency Project, https://www.presidency.ucsb.edu/node/239689.

2. Pew Research Center, "As Economic Concerns Recede, Environmental Protection Rises on the Public's Priority Agenda," February 13, 2020, https://www.pewresearch.org/politics/2020/02/13/as-economic-concerns-recede-environmental-protection-rises-on-the-publics-policy-agenda/.

3. Pew Research Center, "As Economic Concerns Recede"; Anna Brown "Most Americans Say Higher Ed Is Heading in the Wrong Direction but Partisans Disagree on Why," Pew Research Center, July 26, 2018, https://www.pewresearch.org/fact-tank/2018/07/26/most-americans-say-higher-ed-is-heading-in-wrong-direction-but-partisans-disagree-on-why/.

4. Jessica Semega, Melissa Kollar, Emily A. Shrider, and John F. Creamer, "Table B-5. Poverty Status of People by Family Relationship, Race, and Hispanic Origin: 1959 to 2018," *Income and Poverty in the United States: 2019: Current Population Reports*, Current Population Survey, Annual Social and Economic Supplements.

5. Lawrence E. Gladieux and Thomas R. Wolanin, *Congress and the Colleges: The National Politics of Higher Education* (Lexington, MA: Lexington Books, 1976), 17.

6. Gladieux and Wolanin, *Congress*, 11; Deondra Rose, *Citizens by Degree: Higher Education Policy and the Changing Gender Dynamics of American Citizenship* (New York: Oxford University Press, 2018).

7. Gladieux and Wolanin, *Congress*, 18–19.

8. David Carleton, *Student's Guide to Landmark Congressional Laws on Education* (Westport, CT: Greenwood Press, 2002), 147.

9. Gladieux and Wolanin, *Congress*, 12; Suzanne Mettler and Deondra Rose, "Unsustainability of Equal Opportunity: The Development of the Higher

Education Act, 1965–2008" (presented at the annual meeting of the American Political Science Association, 2009); Rose, *Citizens*.

10. Carleton, *Student's Guide*, 148–49.
11. Robert Pernell Huff, *Reengineering College Student Financial Aid* (Palo Alto, CA: Hoover Institution on War, Revolution and Peace, Stanford University, 1998), 8.
12. Huff, *Reengineering*.
13. Suzanne Mettler, *Soldiers to Citizens: The G.I. Bill and the Making of the Greatest Generation* (New York: Oxford University Press, 2005).
14. Gladieux and Wolanin, *Congress*, 18.
15. Gladieux and Wolanin, 18–19.
16. Gladieux and Wolanin, 19.
17. "Higher Education Act of 1965 (H.R. 3220)," *Hearings Before the Subcommittee on Education and Labor* (Washington, DC: U.S. Government Printing Office, 1965), 30.
18. Hugh Davis Graham, *The Uncertain Triumph: Federal Education Policy in the Kennedy and Johnson Years* (Chapel Hill, NC: University of North Carolina Press, 1984), 68.
19. Graham, *Uncertain Triumph*, 81.
20. Gladieux and Wolanin, *Congress*, 12.
21. Graham, *Uncertain Triumph*, xiv.
22. Graham, xiv–xv.
23. The Senate passed the HEA by voice vote, so the totals are not recorded. Suzanne Mettler, *Degrees of Inequality: How Higher Education Politics Sabotaged the American Dream* (New York: Basic Books, 2014), 63.
24. Margot A. Schenet, David A. Powner, James B. Stedman, and Tatiana Shohov, *Pell Grants: Background and Issue* (New York: Novinka Books, 2003).
25. Huff, *Reengineering*, 8–9.
26. Mettler, *Degrees of Inequality*, 63–64.
27. Suzanne Mettler, "The Policyscape and the Challenges of Contemporary Politics to Policy Maintenance," *Perspectives on Politics* 14, no. 2 (June 2016): 369–90.
28. Jacob S. Hacker, "Privatizing Risk Without Privatizing the Welfare State: The Hidden Politics of Social Policy Retrenchment in the United States," *American Political Science Review* 98, no. 2 (2004): 243–60.
29. College Board, "Trends in Higher Education Series: Trends in Student Aid 2019," 2019, 28, https://research.collegeboard.org/pdf/trends-student-aid-2019-full-report.pdf.
30. The average borrower at a public four-year college has accumulated more debt than the average degree recipient, $27,200 in 2017–18. College Board 2019, 21.
31. College Board, "Trends 2019," 16, 20.
32. College Board, "Trends in Higher Education Series: Trends in Student Aid 2018," 2018, Figure 16, https://research.collegeboard.org/pdf/trends-student-aid-2018-full-report.pdf.
33. College Board, "Trends 2019," 23; Ariel Gelrud Shiro and Richard V. Reeves,

"The For-Profit College System Is Broken and the Biden Administration Needs to Fix It," Brookings Institution, January 12, 2021, https://www.brookings.edu/blog/how-we-rise/2021/01/12/the-for-profit-college-system-is-broken-and-the-biden-administration-needs-to-fix-it/.

34. American Council on Education, "Department of Education Repeals Gainful Employment Regulations," July 1, 2019, https://www.acenet.edu/News-Room/Pages/Department-of-Education-Repeals-Gainful-Employment-Regulations.aspx.

35. College Board, "Trends 2019," 28.

36. Frances E. Lee, *Beyond Ideology: Politics, Principle, and Partisanship in the US Senate* (Chicago: University of Chicago Press, 2009).

37. Frances E. Lee, *Insecure Majorities: Congress and the Perpetual Campaign* (Chicago: University of Chicago Press, 2016).

38. Thomas E. Mann and Norman J. Ornstein, *It's Even Worse Than It Looks: How the American Constitutional System Collided with the Politics of Extremism* (New York: Basic Books, 2012).

39. Mettler, "Policyscape," 9–10.

40. Lee Drutman, *The Business of America Is Lobbying* (New York: Oxford University Press, 2015).

CHAPTER 3

1. The authors contributed equally to this chapter and should be considered co-first authors.

2. Fisher v. University of Texas, 579 US (2016). We use the terms *race-conscious admissions* and *affirmative action* interchangeably. However, given the changes to the policy that started in the late 1970s after legal developments, we employ the term *race-conscious admissions* as much as possible to describe the policy as presently endorsed by the US Supreme Court. We recognize the reasons Justice Sonia Sotomayor provided in *Schuette v. Coalition to Defend Affirmative Action*, 134 S. Ct. 1623, p. 1651 n. 2 (2014) (Sotomayor, J., dissenting) explaining why the term *affirmative action* is not accurate to describe the policy in the present. As Justice Sotomayor noted, the Court previously reviewed policies using quotas or point systems that accord an applicant numerical advantage because of race or that admit students solely based on race to address the effects of historical and ongoing discrimination. These policies involved *affirmative action* as historically understood, which opponents frame as granting preferential treatment to individuals. Past Court cases rendered those practices unconstitutional, and the Court has since allowed policies that instead consider race as one factor among many in admissions decisions to promote a diverse student body. These policies, as presently endorsed, are therefore more accurately described as *race-conscious*, or per Justice Sotomayor's preferred terminology, *race-sensitive*.

3. Stanley Augustin, "Justice Department Staffing Up for Its Ill-Conceived Affirmative Action Investigation," Lawyers' Committee for Civil Rights Under Law,

January 25, 2019, https://lawyerscommittee.org/justice-department-staffing-ill-conceived-affirmative-action-investigation/.

4. Nick Anderson and Moriah Balingit, "Trump Administration Moves to Rescind Obama-Era Guidance on Race in Admissions," *Washington Post*, July 3, 2018. The Trump administration moves to rescind Obama-era guidance on race in admissions. In addition, with a second Supreme Court justice appointment to replace recently retired Justice Kennedy, the Trump administration seems poised to entrench conservative ideological control in the Court for years to come, making it more favorable for considering future legal challenges to affirmative action.

5. Florida's ban was implemented by executive order, New Hampshire's by legislative act, and bans in other states via statewide referenda. In November 2020, California voters decided not to repeal California's ban on affirmative action (Proposition 209) with Proposition 16, an initiative that would have amended California's constitution to allow for affirmative action in public employment, contracting, and education.

6. Dana Takagi, *The Retreat from Race: Asian-American Admissions and Racial Politics* (New Brunswick, NJ: Rutgers University Press, 1992).

7. Houston Chinese Alliance, "Edward Blum Speaks About the Legal Battle Against Harvard University" [Video file.]. April 26, 2010, https://www.youtube.com/watch?v=DiBvo-05JRg&t=.

8. Gary Orfield and Dean Whitla, "Diversity and Legal Education: Student Experiences in Leading Law Schools," in *Diversity Challenged: Evidence on the Impact of Affirmative Action*, ed. Gary Orfield (Cambridge, MA: Harvard Educational Review, 2001), 143–74; Julie J. Park, "Taking Race into Account: Charting Student Attitudes Towards Affirmative Action," *Research in Higher Education* 50, no. 7 (2009): 670–90; Karthick Ramakrishnan, "An Agenda for Justice: Contours of Public Opinion Among Asian Americans," AAPI Data, 2014; Karthick Ramakrishnan and Janelle Wong, "Survey Roundup: Asian American Attitudes on Affirmative Action," *Data Bits: A Blog for AAPI Data*, June 18, 2018, http://aapidata.com/blog/asianam-affirmative-action-surveys/.

9. Michele Moses, Daryl Maeda, and Christina Paguyo, "Racial Politics, Resentment, and Affirmative Action: Asian Americans as 'Model' College Applicants," *Journal of Higher Education* 90, no. 1 (April 25, 2018): 1–26, https://doi.org/10.1080/00221546.2018.1441110.

10. OiYan A. Poon, Megan S. Segoshi, Lilianne Tang, Kristen L. Surla, Caressa Nguyen, and Dian D. Squire, "Asian Americans, Affirmative Action, and the Political Economy of Racism: A Multidimensional Model of Raceclass Frames," *Harvard Educational Review* 89, no. 2 (Summer 2019): 201–26.

11. Orfield and Whitla, "Diversity and Legal Education"; OiYan Poon and Megan Segoshi, "The Racial Mascot Speaks: A Critical Race Discourse Analysis of Asian Americans and Fisher v. University of Texas," *Review of Higher Education* 42, no.

1 (2018): 235–67, https://doi.org/10.1353/rhe.2018.0029; Robert Teranishi, "The Attitudes of Asian Americans Toward Affirmative Action," *National Commission on Asian American and Pacific Islander Research in Education*, 2012, https://files.eric .ed.gov/fulltext/ED573712.pdf; Park, "Race into Account"; Ramakrishnan, "An Agenda for Justice."

12. Karen Inkelas, "Diversity's Missing Minority: Asian Pacific American Under-graduates' Attitudes Toward Affirmative Action," *Journal of Higher Education* 74, no. 6 (2003): 601–39; Paul Ong, "The Affirmative Action Divide," in *Asian American Politics: Law, Participation, and Policy*, ed. Don Nakanishi and James Lai (Lanham, MD: Rowman & Littlefield, 2003), 377–406; Ethan Bronner, "Asian-Amer-icans in the Argument," *New York Times*, November 1, 2012, https://www .nytimes.com/2012/11/04/education/edlife/affirmative-action-a-complicated-issue-for-asian-americans.html; Jaweed Kaleem, "Asian Americans Are Divided After the Trump Administration's Move on Affirmative Action," *Los Angeles Times*, August 3, 2017, https://www.latimes.com/nation/la-na-asian-americans-affirmative-action-20170803-story.html.

13. Josie Huang, "SCA 5: A Political Coming-of-Age Story for Chinese-Americans," *Southern California Public Radio*, March 21, 2014, https://www.scpr.org/blogs/ multiamerican/2014/03/21/16152/sca-5-chinese-americans-immigrants-asian-americans/; Ramakrishnan and Wong, "Survey Roundup."

14. Four years later in 1965, President Lyndon B. Johnson referred to the policy in his famous speech at Howard University, describing its intent to achieve "not just equality as a right and a theory but equality as a fact and equality as a result."

15. Ira Katznelson, *When Affirmative Action Was White: An Untold History of Racial Inequality in Twentieth-Century America* (New York: W. W. Norton & Company, 2005).

16. Martha Minow, *In Brown's Wake: Legacies of America's Educational Landmark* (New York: Oxford University Press, 2010).

17. Lisa Stulberg and Anthony Chen, "The Origins of Race-Conscious Affirmative Action in Undergraduate Admissions: A Comparative Analysis of Institutional Change in Higher Education," *Sociology of Education* 87, no. 1 (January 2014): 36–52, https://doi.org/10.1177/0038040713514063.

18. Stulberg and Chen, "Origins."

19. Stulberg and Chen, 42.

20. John Skrentny, *The Ironies of Affirmative Action: Politics, Culture, and Justice in America* (Chicago: Chicago University Press, 1996).

21. The vote in *Bakke* was 4-1-4. Powell agreed with one four-justice block on some aspects of the case and with the other four-justice block on others. Thus, his rationale constituted the controlling opinion, as it resulted in a majority vote (5) on the various legal issues.

22. The Court has not articulated a fixed or singular measure for "narrow tai-loring" but has instead outlined a number of relevant criteria, which are

ultimately context-specific. These criteria include making sure that the policy (a) does not operate as a quota; (b) is adopted after an institution's good faith consideration to workable race-neutral alternatives; (c) involves a flexible, individualized consideration of applicants so that race, while important, is only one of a number of factors being considered; (d) does not unduly burden disfavored groups; and (e) is limited in time or includes a periodic review to assess its continued necessity.

23. Liliana M. Garces, "Aligning Diversity, Quality, and Equity: The Implications of Legal and Public Policy Developments for Promoting Racial Diversity in Graduate Studies," *American Journal of Education* 120, no. 4 (2014): 457–80.

24. Takagi, *Retreat from Race.*

25. According to Takagi (*Retreat from Race*), Brown and Stanford were not subject to federal investigation but did admit to irregularities in their own admissions processes.

26. Takagi, *Retreat from Race.*

27. Jerry Kang, "Negative Action Against Asian Americans: The Internal Instability of Dworkin's Defense of Affirmative Action," *Harvard Civil Rights–Civil Liberties Law Review* 31, no. 1 (1996): 1–47.

28. Takagi, *Retreat from Race*, 9.

29. Don Nakanishi, "A Quota on Excellence? The Asian American Admissions Debate," *Change: The Magazine of Higher Learning* 21, no. 6 (1989): 39–47; Takagi, *Retreat from Race.*

30. Julie J. Park and Amy Liu, "Interest Convergence or Divergence? A Critical Race Analysis of Asian Americans, Meritocracy, and Critical Mass in the Affirmative Action Debate," *Journal of Higher Education* 85, no. 1 (2014): 36–64; Carol Anderson, "The Policies of White Resentment," *New York Times*, August 5, 2017, https://www.nytimes.com/2017/08/05/opinion/sunday/white-resentment-affirmative-action.html; Moses, Maeda, and Paguyo, "Racial Politics."

31. Anderson, "Policies of White Resentment."

32. William C. Kidder, "Negative Action Versus Affirmative Action: Asian Pacific Americans Are Still Caught in the Crossfire," *Michigan Journal of Race and Law* 11, no. 2 (2006): 605–24; Moses, Maeda, and Paguyo, "Racial Politics"; Park and Liu, "Interest Convergence"; Poon and Segoshi, "Racial Mascot."

33. Kevin Kumashiro, *The Seduction of Common Sense: How the Right Has Framed the Debate on America's Schools* (New York: Teachers College Press, 2008); OiYan Poon et al., "A Critical Review of the Model Minority Myth in Selected Literature on Asian Americans and Pacific Islanders in Higher Education," *Review of Educational Research* 86, no. 2 (2016): 469–502; Rowena Robles, *Asian Americans and the Shifting Politics of Race: The Dismantling of Affirmative Action at an Elite Public High School* (New York: Routledge, 2006); Bob H. Suzuki, "Asian Americans as the 'Model Minority': Outdoing Whites? Or Media Hype?," *Change: The Magazine of Higher Learning* (1989): 13–19.

34. William C. Kidder, "Situating Asian Pacific Americans in the Law School Affir-mative Action Debate: Empirical Facts About Thernstrom's Rhetorical Acts," *Asian Law Journal* 7, no. 29 (2000): 29–68; Kidder, "Negative Action Versus Affir-mative Action"; Nancy Leong, "The Misuse of Asian Americans in the Affirma-tive Action Debate," *UCLA Law Review Discourse* 64, no. 89 (2016): 90–98; Poon and Segoshi, "Racial Mascot."

35. Scholars in the interdisciplinary field of Asian American studies have docu-mented and critically examined this history of racism and its contemporary legacies as it relates to various aspects of social life, such as voting, property rights, employment, marriage equality, health-care access, and education in the US.

36. OiYan Poon, "Haunted by Negative Action: Asian Americans, Admissions, and Race in the 'Color-Blind Era,'" *Asian American Policy Review* 18 (2009): 81–90.

37. Moses, Maeda, and Paguyo, "Racial Politics"; Poon and Segoshi, "Racial Mascot."

38. In 2008, a similar initiative was introduced on the ballot in Colorado and rejected only after garnering 49 percent of the vote. Similar initiatives were proposed but failed to reach the ballot—in Florida in 2000, and in Oklahoma and Missouri in 2008, according to Arthur L. Coleman, Katherine E. Lipper, and Jamie Lewis Keith, *Beyond Federal Law: Trends and Principles Associated with State Law Banning the Consideration of Race, Ethnicity, and Sex Among Public Educa-tion Institutions* (Washington, DC: American Association for the Advancement of Science, 2012).

39. The laws also include allowances for bona fide sex-based qualifications, such as separate restrooms for each sex, needed in the operation of employment, education, and contracting, and exemptions for actions necessary to maintain eligibility for federal funds or existing court orders (i.e., enforced desegrega-tion court orders).

40. Schuette v. Coalition to Defend Affirmative Action, 2014.

41. Ben Backes, "Do Affirmative Action Bans Lower Minority College Enrollment and Attainment?: Evidence from Statewide Bans," *Journal of Human Resources* 47, no. 2 (2012): 435–55; Liliana M. Garces, "Understanding the Impact of Affir-mative Action Bans in Different Graduate Fields of Study," *American Educa-tional Research Journal* 50, no. 2 (2013): 251–84; Liliana M. Garces and David Mickey-Pabello, "Racial Diversity in the Medical Profession: The Impact of Affirmative Action Bans on Underrepresented Student of Color Matricula-tion in Medical Schools," *Journal of Higher Education* (Columbus) 86, no. 2 (2015): 264–94; Peter Hinrichs, "The Effects of Affirmative Action Bans on College Enrollment, Educational Attainment, and the Demographic Composition of Universities," *Review of Economics and Statistics* 94, no. 3 (2012): 712–22; Wil-liam C. Kidder and Patricia Gándara, *Two Decades After the Affirmative Action Ban: Evaluating the University of California's Race-Neutral Efforts* (Riverside, CA: UCLA,

The Civil Rights Project/Proyecto Derechos Civiles, October 1, 2016); Linda F. Wightman, "The Threat to Diversity in Legal Education: An Empirical Analysis of the Consequences of Abandoning Race as a Factor in Law School Admission Decisions," *New York University Law Review* 72, no. 1 (April 1, 1997): 1–53.

42. Liliana M. Garces and Courtney D. Cogburn, "Beyond Declines in Student Body Diversity: How Campus-Level Administrators Understand a Prohibition on Race-Conscious Postsecondary Admissions Policies," *American Educational Research Journal* 52, no. 5 (October 1, 2015): 828–60. Recognizing the negative effects of affirmative action bans, some states have tried to restore the policy. For example, in 2014, California State Senator Edward Hernandez sponsored Senate Constitutional Amendment 5 (SCA 5) to overturn Proposition 209. Unfortunately, protests by vocal and well-resourced Chinese Americans stopped the effort (http://aaldef.org/blog/in-california-sca-5-may-be-doa-due-to-asian-americans-against-affirmative-action.html).

43. Thomas Peele, "Unclear Ballot Language, Lack of Time to Connect with Voters Explain Affirmative Action Loss, Backers Say," *EdSource*, November 5, 2020, https://edsource.org/2020/unclear-ballot-language-lack-of-time-to-connect-with-voters-explain-affirmative-action-loss-backers-say/643021

44. Grutter v. Bollinger, 539 U.S. 306 (Supreme Court, 2003); Gratz v. Bollinger, 539 U.S. 244 (Supreme Court, 2003).

45. Greg Stohr, *A Black and White Case: How Affirmative Action Survived Its Greatest Legal Challenge* (Princeton, NJ: Bloomberg Press, 2004).

46. Stohr, *Black and White Case.*

47. Stephanie Mencimer, "Meet the Brains Behind the Effort to Get the Supreme Court to Rethink Civil Rights," *Mother Jones*, March/April, 2016.

48. In addition, four justices—Chief Justice John Roberts and Justices Samuel Alito, Clarence Thomas, and Antonin Scalia—had voted to strike down the use of race in admissions policies under any circumstances, and Justice Anthony Kennedy had dissented in *Grutter*. Only three other current justices at the time—Sonia Sotomayor, Stephen Breyer, and Ruth Bader Ginsburg—had supported race-conscious policies in education. Justice Elena Kagan, who might have sided with the latter group, recused herself in light of her involvement in the case in the early stages of litigation.

49. Hopwood v. Texas, 78 F.3d 932 (5th Cir., 1996).

50. Fisher I; Fisher II.

51. Fisher I, p. 2420; In the legal context, a policy is deemed "race-neutral" when it does not explicitly reference race, even if it indirectly considers race. This legal definition led Justice Ginsburg to state in her dissent in *Fisher I*, "I have said before and reiterate here that only an ostrich could regard the supposedly neutral alternatives [i.e., the Top Ten Percent Plan] as race unconscious" (p. 2433).

52. Fisher II.

53. Houston Chinese Alliance, 2015.

54. SFFA v. Harvard; SFFA v. University of North Carolina et al.

55. Launched in April 2014, these websites specifically sought out Asian American plaintiffs to launch high-profile lawsuits against the University of Wisconsin–Madison, the University of North Carolina–Chapel Hill, and Harvard University, the institution that provided a model for race-conscious admissions that the Court embraced in *Bakke*. Julianne Hing, "Wanted: Disgruntled Asian Americans to Attack Affirmative Action," *Colorlines*, April 25, 2014, https://www.colorlines.com/articles/wanted-disgruntled-asian-americans-attack-affirmative-action. Blum used a similar website in 2007 in search of a plaintiff against the University of Texas at Austin, eventually locating Abigail Fisher as one of the plaintiffs.

56. As a private institution, Harvard is not governed by the Equal Protection Clause (EPC) of the Fourteenth Amendment but is subject to the requirements of Title VI, which apply to private institutions that receive federal funding, as Harvard does.

57. Regents of the University of California v. Bakke, 438 U.S. 265 (Supreme Court, 1978).

58. Fisher II, p. 2213.

59. Mike Hoa Nguyen, Douglas H. Lee, Liliana M. Garces, OiYan A. Poon, Janelle Wong, and Sarah Harrington, "Mobilizing Social Science Research to Inform Judicial Decision-Making: SFFA v. Harvard," *Asian American Law Journal*, forthcoming.

60. Similar complaints were also filed against other institutions, including Brown, Dartmouth, Princeton, Stanford, and Yale, but these cases appear to be closed.

61. Jalin P. Cunningham and Melanie Y. Fu, "Education Department Dismisses Admissions Complaint," *Harvard Crimson*, July 8, 2015.

62. Asian American Coalition for Education, 2018, http://asianamericanforeducation.org/en/home/.

63. Anderson and Balingit, "Trump Administration Moves."

64. Augustin, "Justice Department Staffing."

65. Laura Meckler, "Trump Administration Opens Probe of Yale University," *Washington Post*, September 26, 2018, https://www.washingtonpost.com/local/education/trump-administration-opens-probe-of-yale-university/2018/09/26/9f69b690-c1a9-11e8-b338-a3289f6cb742_story.html.

66. Raga Justin, "UT–Austin Faces a Third Lawsuit Claiming That White Students Were Unfairly Denied Admission Under Affirmative Action," *Texas Tribune*, July 22, 2020, https://www.texastribune.org/2020/07/22/ut-austin-affirmative-action-lawsuit-white/.

67. Scott Jaschik, "Report: College Ending Affirmative Action and Didn't Tell Anyone," Admissions Insider, *Inside Higher Ed*, July 30, 2018, https://www.insidehighered.com/admissions/article/2018/07/30/college-charleston-reportedly-ended-race-based-affirmative-action.

68. Lorelle L. Espinosa, Matthew N. Gaertner, and Gary Orfield, *Race, Class, and College Access: Achieving Diversity in a Shifting Legal Landscape* (Washington, DC: American Council on Education, 2015).

69. Daniel Hirschman and Ellen Berrey, "The Partial Deinstitutionalization of Affirmative Action in US Higher Education, 1988 to 2014," *Sociological Science* 4 (2017): 449–68.

70. "State Propositions: A Snapshot of Voters," *Los Angeles Times*, November 7, 1996, https://www.latimes.com/archives/la-xpm-1996-11-07-mn-62330-story.html.

71. The Nation, "Asian Americans for Affirmative Action," *The Nation*, January 8, 2007, https://www.thenation.com/article/archive/asian-americans-affirmative-action/.

72. Park, "Taking Race into Account."

73. Orfield and Whitla, "Diversity and Legal Education."

74. Ramakrishnan, "Agenda for Justice."

75. Ramakrishnan.

76. Ramakrishnan and Wong, "Survey Roundup."

77. These organizations have included the Asian American Legal Defense and Education Fund (AALDEF), Asian Americans Advancing Justice (formerly the National Asian Pacific American Legal Consortium and Asian Pacific American Legal Center), Chinese for Affirmative Action, and Chinese Progressive Association.

78. Poon and Segoshi, "Racial Mascot."

79. Park and Liu, "Interest Convergence."

80. Michele Moses, *Living with Moral Disagreement: The Enduring Controversy About Affirmative Action* (Chicago: University of Chicago Press, 2016), 30.

81. Thomas J. Espenshade and Alexandria W. Radford, *No Longer Separate, Not Yet Equal: Race and Class in Elite College Admission and Campus Life* (Princeton, NJ: Princeton University Press, 2009).

82. Espenshade and Radford, *No Longer Separate*.

83. Espenshade and Radford.

84. Scott Jaschik, "The Power of Race," *Inside Higher Ed*, November 3, 2009, https://www.insidehighered.com/news/2009/11/03/power-race.

85. Uma Jayakumar, Liliana Garces, and Julie Park, "Reclaiming Diversity: Advancing the Next Generation of Diversity Research Toward Racial Equity," in *Higher Education: Handbook of Theory and Research*, vol 33, ed. M. Paulsen (Dordrecht, The Netherlands: Springer, 2018).

86. Brief for Asian American Legal Foundation and the Asian American Coalition for Education as Amici Curiae Supporting Petitioner, Fisher v. University of Texas, 579 U.S. (2015), p. 23.

87. ⁶ Ramakrishnan and Wong, "Survey Roundup."

88. Poon et al., "Asian Americans, Affirmative Action."

89. Merrit Kennedy, "Justice Department Sides Against Harvard in Racial

Discrimination Lawsuit," Education, *National Public Radio*, August 30, 2018, https://www.npr.org/2018/08/30/643307030/justice-department-sides-against-harvard-in-racial-discrimination-lawsuit.

90. SFFA v. Harvard, F.3d., 2020 WL 6604313 *33 (2020) (noting that "[o]ne of Harvard's amici expands on this point, citing research that Asian American students are more likely than white students to attend public high schools where overloaded teachers and guidance counselors may provide more perfunctory recommendations").

91. Fisher II.

92. Fisher II, p. 2207.

93. Specifically, Justice Alito states: "UT's program is clearly designed to increase the number of African-American and Hispanic students by giving them an admissions boost vis-à-vis other applicants. See, *e.g.*, Supp. App. 25a; App. 445a–446a; cf. 645 F.Supp.2d 587, 606 (W.D.Tex. 2009); see also *ante*, at 2223 (citing increases in the presence of African-Americans and Hispanics at UT as evidence that its race-based program was successful). Given a 'limited number of spaces,' App. 250a, providing a boost to African-Americans and Hispanics inevitably harms students who do not receive the same boost by decreasing their odds of admission" (p. 2227, n. 4).

94. Fisher I, p. 2227 (also citing to the Brief for Asian American Legal Foundation et al. as *Amici Curiae* in support of Fisher).

95. Kevin G. Welner, "Scholars as Policy Actors: Research, Public Discourse, and the Zone of Judicial Constraints," *American Educational Research Journal* 49, no. 1 (2012): 41–63.

96. Michele Moses and Lauren Saenz, "Hijacking Education Policy Decisions: Ballot Initiatives and the Case of Affirmative Action," *Harvard Educational Review* 78, no. 2 (2008): 289–310.

97. Poon et al., "Asian Americans, Affirmative Action."

98. Chi Zhang, *WeChatting American Politics: Misinformation, Polarization, and Immigrant Chinese Media* (New York: Tow Center for Digital Journalism, 2018), https://www.cjr.org/tow_center_reports/wechatting-american-politics-misinformation-polarization-and-immigrant-chinese-media.php.

99. Research on holistic review suggests an alignment between what Asian American affirmative action opponents and supporters describe as their ideal approach to college admissions. Poon et al., "Asian Americans, Affirmative Action."

100. Michael N. Bastedo, D'Wayne Bell, Jessica S. Howell, Michael Hurwitz, and Greg Perfetto, "Information Dashboards and Selective College Admissions: A Field Experiment" (paper presented at Association for the Study of Higher Education Conference, Houston, TX, 2017).

101. For exceptions, see, Alvin Chang, "Asians Are Being Used to Make the Case Against Affirmative Action. Again," *Vox*, August 30, 2018, https://www.vox.com/2018/3/28/17031460/affirmative-action-asian-discrimination-admissions; John

Eligon, "Asian-Americans Face Multiple Fronts in Battle over Affirmative Action," *New York Times*, June 16, 2018, https://www.nytimes.com/2018/06/16/us/affirmative-action-asian-americans.html; Grace Hwang Lynch, "This College Freshman Is Worried About Affirmative Action—But Not That It Will Keep Him Out of Harvard," Education, PRI, August 17, 2017, https://www.pri.org/stories/2017-08-17/college-freshman-worried-about-affirmative-action-not-it-will-keep-him-out; Stacy T. Khadaroo, "Diversity or Discrimination? What's at Stake in the Harvard Admissions Lawsuit?," The Explainer, *Christian Science Monitor*, September 5, 2018, https://www.csmonitor.com/EqualEd/2018/0905/Diversity-or-discrimination-What-s-at-stake-in-the-Harvard-admissions-lawsuit; Khrais, "The Tech Industry vs. The Travel Ban," Marketplace with Kai Ryssdal, *American Public Media*, Los Angeles, CA, June 26, 2018; Moses, Maeda, and Paguyo, "Racial Politics."

CHAPTER 4

1. Sara Goldrick-Rab, *Paying the Price: College Costs, Financial Aid, and the Betrayal of the American Dream* (Chicago: University of Chicago Press, 2016).
2. Angelica Cervantes, Marlena Creusere, Robin McMillion, Carla McQueen, Matt Short, Matt Steiner, and Jeff Webster, *Opening the Doors to Higher Education: Perspectives on the Higher Education Act 40 Years Later* (Round Rock: Texas Guaranteed Student Loan Corporation; 2005).
3. Michael Mitchell, Michael Leachman, and Matt Saenz, *State Higher Education Funding Cuts Have Pushed Costs to Students, Worsened Inequality* (Washington, DC: Center on Budget and Policy Priorities, 2019).
4. Mitchell, Leachman, and Saenz, *State Higher Education*.
5. Manning Marable, *How Capitalism Underdeveloped Black America: Problems in Race, Political Economy, and Society* (Chicago: Haymarket Books, 2015).
6. Gloria Ladson-Billings, "Landing on the Wrong Note: The Price We Paid for Brown," *Educational Researcher* 33, no. 7 (2004): 3–13; Vanessa Siddle Walker, "Second-Class Integration: A Historical Perspective for a Contemporary Agenda," *Harvard Educational Review* 79, no. 2, (2009): 269–84.
7. Victor Ray, "A Theory of Racialized Organizations," *American Sociological Review* 84, no. 1 (2019): 38.
8. Jalil Bishop Mustaffa, "Mapping Violence, Naming Life: A History of Anti-Black Oppression in the Higher Education System," *International Journal of Qualitative Studies in Education* 30, no. 8 (2017): 711–27.
9. Louise Seamster, "Black Debt, White Debt" *Contexts* 18, no. 1 (2019): 30–35.
10. Ebony Rose, "Neocolonial Mind Snatching: Sylvia Wynter and the Curriculum of Man," *Curriculum Inquiry* 49, no. 1 (2019): 25–43.
11. Cedric J. Robinson, *Black Marxism: The Making of the Black Radical Tradition* (Chapel Hill: University of North Carolina Press, 2000); Sarah Haley, *No Mercy Here: Gender, Punishment, and the Making of Jim Crow Modernity* (Chapel Hill:

University of North Carolina Press, 2016).

12. Cheryl I. Harris, "Whiteness as Property," *Harvard Law Review* (1993): 1707–91, 1725.

13. Gaye Theresa Johnson and Alex Lubin, ed. *Futures of Black Radicalism* (New York: Verso Books, 2017); Whitney N. Laster Pirtle, "Racial Capitalism: A Fundamental Cause of Novel Coronavirus (COVID-19) Pandemic Inequities in the United States," *Health Education & Behavior* 47, no. 4 (2020): 504–508.

14. Robinson, *Black Marxism*.

15. Damien M. Sojoyner, *First Strike: Educational Enclosures in Black Los Angeles* (Minneapolis: University of Minnesota Press, 2016); Daniel Morales-Doyle and Eric "Rico" Gutstein, "Racial Capitalism and STEM Education in Chicago Public Schools," *Race Ethnicity and Education* 22, no. 4 (2019): 525–44.

16. Tressie McMillan Cottom, *Lower Ed: The Troubling Rise of For-Profit Colleges in the New Economy* (New York: The New Press, 2017).

17. Jennifer Ma, Matea Pender, and Meredith Welch, *Education Pays 2016: The Benefits of Higher Education for Individuals and Society*, Trends in Higher Education Series (New York: College Board, 2019).

18. Manning Marable, "Race, Class, and Academic Capitalism: The Future of Liberal Education," *Souls* 3, no. 2 (2001): 6–14; Henry Giroux, *Take Back Higher Education: Race, Youth, and the Crisis of Democracy in the Post-Civil Rights Era* (New York: Palgrave Macmillan, 2004); Sheila Slaughter and Gary Rhoades, *Academic Capitalism and the New Economy: Markets, State, and Higher Education* (Baltimore, MD: John Hopkins University Press, 2009); Mark Olssen and Michael Peters, "Neoliberalism, Higher Education and the Knowledge Economy: From the Free Market to Knowledge Capitalism," *Journal of Education Policy* 20, no. 3 (2005): 313–45; Debt Collective and Astra Taylor, *Can't Pay Won't Pay* (Chicago: Haymarket Books, 2020).

19. McMillan Cottom, *Lower Ed*.

20. Sara Goldrick-Rab and Marshall Steinbaum, "What Is the Problem with Student Debt?," *Journal of Policy Analysis and Management* 39, no. 2 (2020): 534–40.

21. Jodi Melamed, *Represent and Destroy: Rationalizing Violence in the New Racial Capitalism* (Minneapolis: University of Minnesota Press, 2011).

22. Ray, "Theory of Racialized Organizations."

23. Melamed, *Represent and Destroy*; Ruth Wilson Gilmore, *Golden Gulag: Prisons, Surplus, Crisis, and Opposition in Globalizing California* (Berkeley: University of California Press, 2007).

24. Anthony P. Carnevale and Jeff Strohl, *Separate & Unequal: How Higher Education Reinforces the Intergenerational Reproduction of White Racial Privilege* (Washington, DC: Georgetown University Center on Education and the Workforce, 2013).

25. Mitchell, Leachman, and Saenz, *State Higher Education*

26. National Center for Education Statistics (NCES), US Department of Education. Table 326.10, "Graduation Rate from First Institution Attended for First-Time,

Full-Time Bachelor's Degree-Seeking Students at 4-Year Postsecondary Institutions," 2017, https://nces.ed.gov/programs/digest/d17/tables/dt17_326.10.asp?referer=raceindicators.

27. Elizabeth Baylor, "Closed Doors: Black and Latino Students Are Excluded from Top Public Universities," Center for American Progress, 2016, https://www.americanprogress.org/issues/education-postsecondary/reports/2016/10/13/145098/closed-doors-black-and-latino-students-are-excluded-from-top-public-universities/.

28. McMillan Cottom, *Lower Ed.*

29. Jalil Bishop, "Student Loans Are a Labor Issue," The Education Trust, 2020, https://edtrust.org/resource/student-loans-are-a-labor-issue/#:~:text=But%20it%20is%20important%20to,%2C%20bail%2C%20and%20private%20loans.

30. Ma, Pender, and Welch, *Education Pays 2016.*

31. Lincoln Quillian, Devah Pager, Ole Hexel, and Arnfinn H. Midtbøen, "Meta-Analysis of Field Experiments Shows No Change in Racial Discrimination in Hiring over Time," *Proceedings of the National Academy of Sciences* 114, no. 41 (2017): 10870–75.

32. Julie M. Morgan and Marshall Steinbaum, *The Student Debt Crisis, Labor Market Credentialization, and Racial Inequality: How the Current Student Debt Debate Gets the Economics Wrong* (New York: Roosevelt Institute, 2018).

33. Tomaz Cajner, Tyler Radler, David Ratner, and Ivan Vidangos, *Racial Gaps in Labor Market Outcomes in the Last Four Decades and Over the Business Cycle* (No. 2017-071) (Washington, DC: Board of Governors of the Federal Reserve System, 2017).

34. National Center for Education Statistics (NCES), US Department of Education, Table 331.95, "Percentage of Undergraduate Degree/Certificate Completers Who Ever Received Loans and Average Cumulative Amount Borrowed," 2016, https://nces.ed.gov/programs/digest/d17/tables/dt17_331.95.asp.

35. Judith Scott-Clayton and Jing Li, "Black-White Disparity in Student Loan Debt More than Triples after Graduation," *Economic Studies* 2, no. 3 (2016).

36. Ben Miller, "New Federal Data Show a Student Loan Crisis for African American Borrowers," Center for American Progress, 2017, https://www.americanprogress.org/issues/education-postsecondary/news/2017/10/16/440711/new-federal-data-show-student-loan-crisis-african-american-borrowers/.

37. Charles H. F. Davis III, Jalil Mustaffa Bishop, Kyah King, and Ayan Jama, *Legislation, Policy, and the Black Student Debt Crisis* (Washington, DC: National Association for the Advancement of Colored People, 2020), 5.

38. Gary Rhoades, "The Higher Education We Choose, Collectively: Reembodying and Repoliticizing Choice," *Journal of Higher Education* 85, no. 6 (2014): 917–30, 921.

39. Michael Nietzel, "The Latest Numbers on Lumina's Big Postsecondary Goal for 2025," *Forbes*, 2020, https://www.forbes.com/sites/michaeltnietzel/2020/02/18/the-latest-numbers-on-luminas-big-postsecondary-goal-for-2025/?sh=7c00dbe3c6a8.

40. Sepehr Vakil and Rick Ayers, "The Racial Politics of STEM Education in the USA: Interrogations and Explorations," *Race, Ethnicity and Education* 22, no. 4 (2019): 449–58.

41. Marable, *How Capitalism Underdeveloped*.

42. Channel McLewis, "The Limits of Choice: A Black Feminist Critique of College 'Choice,'" *Higher Education: Handbook of Theory and Research* (2020): 1–57.

43. Ray, "Theory of Racialized Organizations," 35.

44. Morgan and Steinbaum, *Student Debt Crisis*; Damir Cosic, *College Premium and Its Impact on Racial and Gender Differentials in Earnings and Future Old-Age Income* (Washington, DC: Urban Institute, 2019).

45. Ma, Pender, and Welch, *Education Pays 2016*.

46. Hannah Appel, "There Is Power in a Debtors' Union," *Dissent Magazine*, 2019, https://www.dissentmagazine.org/online_articles/there-is-power-in-a-debtors-union.

47. Beth Akers and Matthew M. Chingos, *Game of Loans: The Rhetoric and Reality of Student Debt* (Princeton, NJ: Princeton University Press, 2018).

48. Adam Looney, David Wessel, and Kadija Yilla, "Who Owes All That Student Debt? And Who'd Benefit if It Were Forgiven?," Brookings Policy, 2020, https://www.brookings.edu/policy2020/votervital/who-owes-all-that-student-debt-and-whod-benefit-if-it-were-forgiven/.

49. Miller, "New Federal Data."

50. Susan Dynarski, *An Economist's Perspective on Student Loans in the United States* (Washington, DC: Economic Studies at Brookings, 2015).

51. Persis Yu, *Relief for Borrowers in Income-Driven Repayment* (Washington, DC: Student Borrower Protection Center, 2020), https://protectborrowers.org/wp-content/uploads/2020/12/Delivering-on-Debt-Relief.pdf#page=74.

52. Miller, "New Federal Data"; Ben Miller, *The Continued Student Loan Crisis for Black Borrowers* (Washington, DC: Center for American Progress, 2019); Tiffany Jones and Andrew H. Nichols, *Hard Truths: Why Only Race-Conscious Policies Can Fix Racism in Higher Education* (Washington, DC: The Education Trust, 2020).

53. Seamster, "Black Debt, White Debt"; Susanne Soederberg, "Student Loans, Debtfare and the Commodification of Debt: The Politics of Securitization and the Displacement of Risk," *Critical Sociology* 40, no. 5 (2014): 689–709.

54. William Darity Jr., Darrick Hamilton, Mark Paul, Alan Aja, Anne Price, Antonio Moore, and Caterina Chiopris, *What We Get Wrong About Closing the Racial Wealth Gap* (Durham, NC: Samuel DuBois Cook Center on Social Equity and Insight Center for Community Economic Development, 2018).

55. Louise Seamster and Raphael Charron-Chénier, "Predatory Inclusion and Education Debt: Rethinking the Racial Wealth Gap," *Social Currents* 4, no. 3 (2017): 199–207.

56. Mustaffa, "Mapping Violence."

57. Robinson, *Black Marxism*.

58. Goldrick-Rab, *Paying the Price.*

59. Andrew H. Nichols and Denzel Evans-Bell, *A Look at Black Student Success: Identifying Top- and Bottom-Performing Institutions* (Washington, DC: The Education Trust, 2017).

60. McMillan Cottom, *Lower Ed.*

61. Mitchell, Leachman, and Saenz, *State Higher Education.*

62. Stephen Burd, Rachel Fishman, Laura Keane, Julie Habbert, Ben Barrett, Kim Dancy, and Brendan Williams, *Decoding the Cost of College: The Case for Transparent Financial Aid Award Letters* (Washington, DC: New America, 2018).

63. Slaughter and Rhoades, *Academic Capitalism.*

64. Mamie Lynch, Jennifer Engle, and Jose Luis Cruz, *Subprime Opportunity: The Unfulfilled Promise of For-Profit Colleges and Universities* (Washington, DC: The Education Trust, 2010).

65. McMillan Cottom, *Lower Ed*; J. E. Scott-Clayton, "What Accounts for Gaps in Student Loan Default, and What Happens After," *Evidence Speaks Reports* 2, no. 57, Center on Children and Families at Brookings.

66. Scott-Clayton, "What Accounts."

67. Lynch, Engle, and Cruz, *Subprime Opportunity.*

68. National Consumer Law Center (NCLC), "Letter to the Honorable John B. King, Secretary of Education," National Consumer Law Center, 2016, https://www.studentloanborrowerassistance.org/wp-content/uploads/2013/05/ltr-sec-king-race-student-debt.pdf.

69. Consumer Financial Protection Bureau (CFPB), *Fair Lending Report of the Consumer Financial Protection Bureau,* 2017, https://files.consumerfinance.gov/f/documents/201704_cfpb_Fair_Lending_Report.pdf.

70. Scott-Clayton, "What Accounts."

71. Ben Miller, *The Looming Student Loan Servicing Crisis* (Washington, DC: Center for American Progress, 2020).

72. Deanne Loonin, "Illusory Due Process: The Broken Student Loan Hearing System," *UC Irvine Law Review* 11 (2020): 173, 198.

73. Colleen Campbell, *Getting Private Collection Agencies Out of Federal Student Loans* (Washington, DC: Center for American Progress, 2018).

74. Margaret Mattes and Persis Yu, *Inequitable Judgments Examining Race and Federal Student Loan Collection Lawsuits* (Boston: National Consumer Law Center, 2019).

75. National Consumer Law Center, "Letter to the Honorable John B. King," 3.

76. Valerie Rawlston-Wilson, Susie Saavedra, and Shree Chauhan, *From Access to Completion: A Seamless Path to College Graduation for African American Students* (New York: National Urban League, 2014).

77. Soederberg, "Student Loans."

78. Debt Collective and Taylor, *Can't Pay.*

79. Debt Collective and Taylor, *Can't Pay*; Davis, Bishop, King, and Jama, *Legislation Policy.*

80. Appel, "There Is Power."

81. William Darity Jr. and Darrick Hamilton, "Bold Policies for Economic Justice," *Review of Black Political Economy* 39, no. 1 (2012): 79–85.

CHAPTER 5

1. Anti-Drug Abuse Act, 99 P.L. 570 (1986).

2. Mary C. Wright, "Pell Grants, Politics, and the Penitentiary: Connections Between the Development of U.S. Higher Education and Prison Post-Secondary Programs," *Journal of Correctional Education* 52, no. 1 (2001): 11–16.

3. The Sentencing Project, *Trends in U.S. Corrections*, 2016, https://sentencing project.org/wp-content/uploads/2016/01/Trends-in-US-Corrections.pdf; Bruce Western and Becky Pettit, *Collateral Costs: Incarceration's Effect on Economic Mobility* (Washington, DC: The Pew Charitable Trusts, 2010).

4. Christopher Zoukis, "Pell Grants for Prisoners: New Bill Restores Hope of Reinstating College Programs," *Prison Legal News*, August, 2015, https://www.prisonlegalnews.org/news/2015/jul/31/pell-grants-prisoners-new-bill-restores-hope-reinstating-college-programs/.

5. "Violent Crime Control and Law Enforcement Act," 103 P.L. 322 (1994).

6. Erin L. Castro et al., "Higher Education in an Era of Mass Incarceration: Possibility Under Constraint," *Journal of Critical Scholarship on Higher Education and Student Affairs* 1, no. 1 (2015): 13–31; Michelle Fine et al., *Changing Minds: The Impact of Change in a Maximum-Security Prison* (New York: The Graduate Center of the City University of New York & Women in Prison at the Bedford Hills Correctional Facility, 2001); Jason Harnish, "Philosophical Implications of Taxpayer Funding for Prison Education," *Critical Education* 10, no. 5 (2019): 1–14, http://ojs.library.ubc.ca/index.php/criticaled/article/view/186298; Wendy Erisman and Jeanne B. Contardo, *Learning to Reduce Recidivism: A 50-State Analysis of Postsecondary Correctional Policy* (Washington, DC: Institute for Higher Education Policy, 2005).

7. Mary Ellen Batiuk et al., "Disentangling the Effects of Correctional Education," *Criminal Justice* 5, no. 1 (2005): 55–74, doi:10.1177/1466802505050979; Cathryn A. Chappell, "Post-Secondary Correctional Education and Recidivism: A Meta-Analysis of Research Conducted 1990–1999," *Journal of Correctional Education* 55 no. 2 (2004): 148–69, http://www.jstor.org/stable/23292162; Ryang Hui Kim and David Clark, "The Effect of Prison-Based College Education Programs on Recidivism: Propensity Score Matching Approach," *Journal of Criminal Justice* 41, no. 3 (2013): 196–204, doi:10.1016/j.jcrimj; Institute for Higher Education Policy, "Pell Grants: Are Prisoners the Program's Biggest Problem?," *Policy Steps* (Spring 1994): 1–8.

8. Andrew Kreighbaum, "New Push to Drop Drug Offenses as Barrier to Student Aid," *Inside Higher Ed*, 2018, https://www.insidehighered.com/news/2018/03/07/higher-ed-groups-want-end-student-aid-restrictions-applicants-drug-convictions.

9. Institute for Higher Education Policy, "Pell Grants."

10. Institute for Higher Education Policy.

11. Sandy Baum, Jennifer Ma, and Kathleen Payea, *Education Pays, 2010: The Benefits of Higher Education for Individuals and Society* (New York: College Board, 2010); Ben L. Castleman and Bridget T. Long, "Looking Beyond Enrollment: The Causal Effect of Need-Based Grants on College Access, Persistence, and Graduation," *Journal of Labor Economics* 34, no. 4 (2016): 1023–73; David T. Ellwood and Thomas J. Kane, "Who Is Getting a College Education? Family Background and the Growing Gaps in Enrollment," quoted in Sheldon Danzinger and Jane Waldfogel, *Securing the Future* (New York: Russell Sage, 2000).

12. Rachel Baker, Daniel Klasik, and Sean F. Reardon, "Race and Stratification in College Enrollment over Time," *AERA Open* 4, no. 1 (2018): 1–28; M. Cahalan, L. W. Perna, M. Yamashita, J. Wright, and S. Santillan, *2018 Indicators of Higher Education Equity in the United States: Historical Trend Report* (Washington, DC: The Pell Institute for the Study of Opportunity in Higher Education, Council for Opportunity in Education [COE], and Alliance for Higher Education and Democracy of the University of Pennsylvania [PennAHEAD], 2018).

13. Elizabeth A. Mack and Kevin Stolarick, "The Gift That Keeps on Giving: Land-Grant Universities and Regional Prosperity," *Environment and Planning C: Government and Policy* 32 (2014): 384–404; George R. McDowell, "Engaged Universities: Lessons from the Land-Grant Universities and Extension," *Annals of the American Academy of Political and Social Science* 585 (2003): 31–50.

14. Marybeth Gasman and Adriel Hilton, "Mixed Motivations, Mixed Results: A History of Law, Legislation, Historically Black Colleges and Universities, and Interest Convergence," *Teachers College Record* 114 (2007): 1–34.

15. Gasman and Hilton, "Mixed Motivations, Mixed Results."

16. David J. Deming et al., "Can Online Learning Bend the Higher Education Cost Curve?," *American Economic Review* 105, no. 5 (2015): 496–501; D. Randy Garrison and Zehra Akyol, "Role of Instructional Technology in the Transformation of Higher Education," *Journal of Computing in Higher Education* 21, no. 1 (2009): 19–30; Jorge Larreamendy-Joerns and Gaea Leinhardt, "Going the Distance with Online Education," *Review of Educational Research* 76, no. 4 (2006): 567–605.

17. Michele F. Welsh, "The Effects of the Elimination of Pell Grant Eligibility for State Prison Inmates," *Journal of Correctional Education* 53, no. 4 (2002): 154–58; 20 U.S.C. § 1070a (1992).

18. John Littlefield and Bruce Wolford, "A Survey of Higher Education in Correctional Institutions," *Journal of Correctional Education* 33, no. 1 (1982): 14–18; Rosemary Sarri, "Educational Programs in State Departments of Corrections: A Survey of the States" (paper presented at the annual meetings of the American Society of Criminology, Phoenix, AZ, 1993); Charles B. Ubah, "Abolition of Pell Grants for Higher Education of Prisoners: Examining Antecedents and Consequences,"

Journal of Offender Rehabilitation 39, no. 2 (2004): 73–85, http://dx.doi.org/10.1300/J076v39n02_05.

19. 20 U.S.C. § 1070a(b)(7), (2008).
20. "Violent Crime Control and Law Enforcement Act," 1828.
21. Jon Taylor, "Should Prisoners Have Access to Collegiate Education? A Policy Issue," *Educational Policy* 83, no. 3 (1994): 319.
22. Erisman and Contardo, *Learning to Reduce Recidivism.*
23. Thom Gehring, "Post-Secondary Education for Inmates: An Historical Inquiry," *Journal of Correctional Education* (1997): 46–55.
24. Robert Martinson, "What Works? Questions and Answers About Prison Reform," *Public Interest* (Spring 1974).
25. Ubah, "Abolition of Pell Grants."
26. Lawrence Gladieux, *Federal Student Aid Policy: A History and an Assessment* (Washington, DC: United States Department of Education, Archived Information on Financing Postsecondary Education), https://www2.ed.gov/offices/OPE/PPI/FinPostSecEd/gladieux.html.
27. 20 U.S.C. § 1070a(b)(8), (1992).
28. Allen J. Beck and Darrell K. Gilliard, *Prisoners in 1994* (Washington, DC: Bulletin from United States Department of Justice, Office of Justice Programs, Bureau of Justice Statistics).
29. Institute for Higher Education Policy, "Pell Grants."
30. Gehring, "Post-Secondary Education."
31. Michael J. Palmiotto, "The 1994 Violent Crime Control and Law Enforcement Act: An Evaluation," *Justice Professional* 10 (1998): 407–14.
32. Aaron Kupchick and Geoff Ward, "Race, Poverty, and Exclusionary School Security: An Empirical Analysis of U.S. Elementary, Middle, and High School," *Youth Violence and Juvenile Justice* 12, no. 4 (2014): 332–54; Jason B. Langberg and Barbara A. Fredders, "How Juvenile Defenders Can Help Dismantle the School-to-Prison Pipeline: A Primer on Educational Advocacy and Incorporating Clients' Education Histories and Records in to Delinquency Representation," *Journal of Law and Education* 42, no. 4 (2013): 653–89; Russell J. Skiba, "The Failure of Zero Tolerance," *Reclaiming Children and Youth* 22, no. 4 (2014): 27–33; Russell J. Skiba et al., "The Color of Discipline: Sources of Racial and Gender Disproportionality in School Punishment," *Urban Review* 34, no. 4 (2002): 317.
33. Michael Teague, "Mass Incarceration: The Juggernaut of American Penal Expansionism," *Prison Service Journal* 227 (2016): 38–44; Western and Pettit, *Collateral Costs.*
34. US Department of Education, "Highlights from the U.S. PIAAC Survey of Incarcerated Adults: Their Skills, Work Experience, Education, and Training," 2016, https://nces.ed.gov/pubs2016/2016040.pdf.

35. Michelle Alexander, *The New Jim Crow: Mass Incarceration in the Age of Colorblind-ness* (New York: The New Press, 2012); Todd R. Clear, *Imprisoning Communi-ties: How Mass Incarceration Makes Disadvantaged Communities Worse* (New York: Oxford University Press, 2007); Marie Gottschalk, *Caught: The Prison State and the Lockdown of American Politics* (Princeton, NJ: Princeton University Press, 2016); Bruce Western, *Punishment and Inequality in America* (New York: Russel Sage Foundation, 2006).

36. Leah Sakala, *Breaking Down Mass Incarceration in the 2010 Census: State-by-State Incarceration Rates by Race/Ethnicity* (Briefing, Prison Policy Initiative, 2014).

37. Bernadette Rabuy and Daniel Kopf, *Prisons of Poverty: Uncovering the Pre-Incarceration Incomes of the Imprisoned* (Briefing, Prison Policy Initiative, 2015).

38. Cahalan et al., *Indicators of Higher Education Equity*; Lori D. Patton, "Disrupting Postsecondary Prose: Toward a Critical Race Theory of Higher Education," *Urban Education* 51, no. 3 (2016): 315–42.

39. Stephanie Covington, "Women and the Criminal Justice System," *Women's Health Issues* 17, (2007): 1–6, doi:10.1016/j.whi.2007.05.004; Bonnie L. Green, "Trauma Exposure, Mental Health Functioning, and Program Needs of Women in Jail," *Crime & Delinquency* 51 (2005): 133–51.

40. Vera Institute of Justice, "Women Behind Bars," 2018, www.vera.org/the-human-toll-of-jail/inmate-turned-advocate/women-behind-bars.

41. Castro et al., "Higher Education in an Era."

42. L. D. Pilsbury, *Report of the Board of Managers: New York State Reformatory at Elmira* (New York, 1877).

43. Marjorie Seashore and Steven Haberfeld, *Prisoner Education: Project NewGate and Other College Programs* (New York: Praeger, 1976).

44. Gehring, "Post-Secondary Education for Inmates."

45. Howard Gordon and Bracie Weldon, "The Impact of Career and Technical Education Programs on Adult Offenders: Learning Behind Bars," *Journal of Correctional Education* 54 (2003): 200–209; Ryang Kim and David Clark, "The Effect of Prison-Based College Education Programs on Recidivism: Propensity Score Matching Approach," *Journal of Criminal Justice* 41 (2013): 196–204.

46. Devah Pager, *Marked: Race, Crime, and Finding Work in an Era of Mass Incarceration* (Chicago: University of Chicago Press, 2007).

47. Lois Davis, Robert Bozick, Jennifer Steele, and Jeremy Miles, *Evaluating the Effec-tiveness of Correctional Education: A Meta-Analysis of Programs That Provide Education to Incarcerated Adults* (Santa Monica, CA: RAND Corporation), https://www.rand.org/pubs/research_reports/RR266.html.

48. Davis, Bozick, Steele, and Miles, *Evaluating the Effectiveness.*

49. US Department of Education, "12,000 Incarcerated Students to Enroll in Post-secondary Educational and Training Programs Through Education Depart-ment's New Second Chance Pell Pilot Program," 2016, https://www.ed.gov/news/press-releases/12000-incarcerated-students-enroll-postsecondary-

educational-and-training-programs-through-education-departments-new-second-chance-pell-pilot-program; Ellen Wexler, "Prisoners to Get 'Second Chance Pell," *Insider Higher Ed*, June 2016.

50. Vera Institute of Justice, "Women Behind Bars."
51. Erica Green, "Senate Leaders Reconsider Ban on Pell Grants for Prisoners," *New York Times*, 2018, https://www.nytimes.com/2018/02/15/us/politics/pell-grants-prisoners.html.
52. Green, "Senate Leaders Reconsider"; Kreighbaum, "New Push."
53. Green, "Senate Leaders Reconsider"; Kreighbaum, "New Push."
54. US Congress, House, *Consolidated Appropriations Act, 2021*. Amendments to HR-133, 116th Congress. Introduced in House December 21, 2020, https://rules.house.gov/sites/democrats.rules.house.gov/files/BILLS-116HR133SA-RCP-116-68.pdf.

CHAPTER 6

1. Lamar Alexander, *Risk-Sharing/Skin-in-the-Game Concepts and Proposals* (Washington, DC: Senate Committee on Health, Education, Labor and Pensions, 2015), 1, https://www.help.senate.gov/imo/media/Risk_Sharing.pdf.
2. Jared Bass and Clare McCann, "Everything You Always Wanted to Know About Higher Education Policy," *Washington Monthly*, August 26, 2018, https://washingtonmonthly.com/magazine/september-october-2018/everything-you-always-wanted-to-know-about-higher-education-policy/.
3. Kristin Blagg, *Underwater on Student Debt* (Washington, DC: Urban Institute, 2018), https://www.urban.org/sites/default/files/publication/98884/underwater_on_student_debt.pdf.
4. Holger M. Mueller and Constantine Yannelis, "The Rise in Student Loan Defaults," *Journal of Financial Economics* 131, no. 1 (2018): 1–19, https://doi.org/10.1016/j.jfineco.2018.07.013.
5. Sandy Baum and Matt Chingos, *Reforming Federal Student Loan Repayment: A Single, Automatic, Income-Driven System* (Washington, DC: Urban Institute, 2017), https://www.urban.org/sites/default/files/publication/93296/2018_01_10_final_baum_chingos_loan_repayment_memo_finalized_0.pdf; Jason Delisle, Preston Cooper, and Cody Christensen, *Federal Student Loan Defaults: What Happens After Borrowers Default and Why* (Washington, DC: American Enterprise Institute, 2018), https://www.aei.org/research-products/report/federal-student-loan-defaults-what-happens-after-borrowers-default-and-why/.
6. Nicholas Barr et al., *Reflections on the US College Loan System: Lessons from Australia and England* (Bonn, Germany: IZA—Institute of Labor Economics, 2018).
7. Susan Dynarski and Judith Scott-Clayton, "Financial Aid Policy: Lessons from Research," *Future of Children* 23, no. 1 (2013): 67–91, https://doi.org/10.1353/foc.2013.0002.
8. Colleen Campbell and Nicholas Hillman, *A Closer Look at the Trillion: Borrowing,*

Repayment, and Default at Iowa's Community Colleges (Washington, DC: Association of Community College Trustees, 2013), http://www.acct.org/files/Publications/2015/ACCT_Borrowing-Repayment-Iowa_CCs_09-28-2015.pdf.

9. Emil Andruska et al., "Do You Know What You Owe? Students' Understanding of Their Student Loans," *Journal of Student Financial Aid* 44, no. 2 (2014), https://ir.library.louisville.edu/jsfa/vol44/iss2/3/.

CHAPTER 7

1. Clifton Conrad and Marybeth Gasman, *Educating a Diverse Nation: Lessons from Minority Serving Institutions* (Cambridge, MA: Harvard University Press, 2015); Lorelle Espinosa, Jonathan Turk, and Morgan Taylor, *Pulling Back the Curtain: Enrollment and Outcomes at Minority Serving Institutions* (Washington, DC: American Council on Education, 2015); Lorelle Espinosa, Robert Kelchen, and Morgan Taylor, *Minority Serving Institutions as Engines of Upward Mobility* (Washington, DC: American Council on Education, 2018); Marybeth Gasman, Dorsey Spencer, and Cecilia Orphan, "'Building Bridges, Not Fences': A History of Civic Engagement at Private Black Colleges and Universities, 1944–1965," *History of Education Quarterly* 55, no. 3 (2015): 346–79.

2. Thai-Huy Nguyen, Andrés Castro Samayoa, Marybeth Gasman, and Steven D. Mobley Jr., "Challenging Respectability: Student Health Directors Providing Services to Lesbian and Gay Students at Historically Black Colleges and Universities," *Teachers College Record* 120, no. 2 (2018): 1–44.

3. Andrés Castro Samayoa and Marybeth Gasman, "The New Urban College Model: A Case Study of Paul Quinn College and Shifting Assessment Standards," *New Directions for Institutional Research* 177 (Spring 2018): 131–40.

4. Craig Steven Wilder, *Ebony and Ivy: Race, Slavery, and the Troubled History of America's Universities* (New York: Bloomsbury Publishing, 2014).

5. Catherine Horn, Patricia Marin, Liliana Garces, Karen Miksch, and John Yun, "Shaping Educational Policy Through the Courts: The Use of Social Science Research in 'Amicus' Briefs in 'Fisher I,'" *Educational Policy* 34, no. 3 (May 2020): 449–76.

6. US Commission on Civil Rights, *Public Education Funding Inequity in an Era of Increasing Concentration of Poverty and Resegregation* (Washington, DC: US Commission on Civil Rights, 2018), https://www.usccr.gov/pubs/2018/2018-01-10-Education-Inequity.pdf.

7. Plessy v. Ferguson (1896).

8. Alexandra Hegji, *Programs for Minority-Serving Institutions Under the Higher Education Act*, CRS Report no. R43237, 2017, https://fas.org/sgp/crs/misc/R43237.pdf.

9. College Cost Reduction and Access Act (CCRAA; P.L. 110-84).

10. Hegji, *Programs for Minority-Serving Institutions*.

11. Marybeth Gasman, Thai-Huy Nguyen, and Clifton Conrad, "Lives Intertwined: A Primer on the History and Emergence of Minority Serving Institutions,"

Journal of Diversity in Higher Education, 8, no. 4 (2015): 120–38.

12. Note that Howard University in Washington, DC, is not included within the HBCU count in the Eligibility Matrix 'HBCU' category, given that it was federally chartered in 1867 (20 U.S.C. 121 et seq.; 20 U.S.C. 128). An endowment for the university was also authorized in FY 1985 under Title II, P.L. 98-480.

13. The Strengthening Institutions Program (SIP) is an exception to this categorization and often not considered within MSI scholarship, given that it supports institutions that serve a high percentage of low-income students alongside relatively low educational and general expenditures regardless of their enrollment of students of color. Support for institutions under SIP has been available through the original Higher Education Act of 1965 (P.L. 89-329, §301).

14. Jennifer Yang and Marietess Masulit, "The Problematic Challenges Faced by Dual Designation at California State Universities," in *Educational Challenges at Minority Serving Institutions*, ed. Marybeth Gasman, Andrés Castro Samayoa, William Boland, and Paola Esmieu (New York: Routledge, 2018), 52–63.

15. Yang and Masulit, "Problematic Challenges."

16. H. Rep. 114-699, at 142, 2016; as noted below, this fund has been incorporated in language within H.R. 6543, Aim Higher Act, a bill to reauthorize the HEA.

17. US Department of Education, "Policy—Executive Order," White House Initiative on Historically Black Colleges & Universities, https://sites.ed.gov/whhbcu/policy/.

18. US Office of Management and Budget (US OMB), "A New Foundation for American Greatness—President's Budget FY 2018," 2017, 2.

19. US Office of Management and Budget (US OMB), "A New Foundation for American Greatness—President's Budget FY 2019," 2018, 11.

20. OMB, 41.

21. OMB, 43.

22. OMB, 43.

23. Julie Renee Posselt and Kim R. Black, "Developing the Research Identities and Aspirations of First-Generation College Students," *International Journal for Researcher Development* 3, no. 1 (2012): 26–48.

24. H. Rep. 115-862, at 153.

25. S. Rep. 115-289, at 205.

26. Tiffany Chou, Adam Looney, and Tara Watson, "A Risk-Sharing Proposal for Student Loans," Brookings Institution, 2017, https://www.brookings.edu/research/a-risk-sharing-proposal-for-student-loans/.

27. Moriah Balingit and Danielle Douglas-Gabriel, "Inside Betsy DeVos's Efforts to Shrink the Education Department," *Washington Post*, November 8, 2017; Kery Murakami, "Biden's Choice for Secretary of Education," *Inside Higher Ed*, January 4, 2021, https://www.insidehighered.com/news/2021/01/04/biden-selects-miguel-cardona-education-secretary.

28. Ben Miller, "A Better Formula for Higher Education's Federal Coronavirus Funding," Center for American Progress, 2020, https://www.american progress.org/issues/education-postsecondary/reports/2020/05/11/484838/ better-formula-higher-educations-federal-coronavirus-funding/.

29. Janette Martinez and Deborah Santiago, "Federal Support for Hispanic-Serving Institutions During COVID-19: Analysis and Recommendations," *Excelencia in Education*, 2020, https://www.edexcelencia.org/research/issue-briefs/ hispanic-serving-institutions-and-cares-act-preliminary-analysis-funding.

30. American Council on Education, "ED Announces Plans for Distribution Emergency Relief; Biden COVID-19 Relief Plan Would Give $35 Billion to Higher Education," American Council on Education, 2021, https://www.acenet.edu/ News-Room/Pages/ED-Announces-Plans-for-Distributing-Emergency-Relief-Biden-COVID-19-Relief-Plan-Would-Give-35-Billion-to-Higher-Education.aspx.

CHAPTER 8

1. Paul Krugman, *Arguing with Zombies: Economics, Politics, and the Fight for a Better Future* (New York and London: W. W. Norton & Company, 2020).

2. Krugman, *Arguing with Zombies*, 3.

3. John Quiggin, *Zombie Economics: How Dead Ideas Still Walk Among Us* (Princeton and Oxford: Princeton University Press, 2010), 2.

4. Jennifer L. Hochschild and Katherine Levine Einstein, *Do Facts Matter? Information and Misinformation in American Politics* (Norman: Oklahoma University Press, 2015).

5. Pamela Burdman, "Colorado's 'Grand Experiment': Voucher Program Could Give the State's Colleges a New Lease on Life," *National CROSSTALK* 11, no. 2 (Spring 2003), http://www.highereducation.org/crosstalk/ct0203/ news0203-colorado.shtml; Brian Prescott, "Is Colorado Worth Vouching For?," *Change* 25 (July/August 2010); Barrett J. Taylor and Brendan Cantwell, *Unequal Higher Education: Wealth, Status, and Student Opportunity* (New Brunswick, NJ: Rutgers University Press, 2019).

6. Charles T. Clotfeter, *Big-Time Sports in American Universities* (New York: Cambridge University Press, 2011); Joe Nocera and Ben Strauss, *Indentured: The Inside Story of the Rebellion Against the NCAA* (New York: Portfolio Press, 2016).

7. Milton Friedman and Rose Friedman, *Free to Choose: A Personal Statement* (New York: Harcourt Brace Jovanovich, 1980).

8. Daniel Golden, *The Price of Admission* (New York: Crown Publishers, 2006); William R. Emmons, Ana H. Kent, and Lowell R. Ricketts, "Is College Still Worth It? The New Calculus of Falling Returns," *Federal Reserve Bank of St. Louis Review*, Fourth Quarter, 101, no. 4 (2019): 297–329; Raj Chetty, John Friedman, Emmanuel Saez, Nicholas Turner, and Danny Yagan, "Mobility Report Cards: The Role of Colleges in Intergenerational Mobility," *The Equality of Opportunity Project*, 2017, http://inequality.stanford.edu/mobile/publications/media/

details/mobility-report-cards-role-colleges-intergenerational-mobility.

9. Suzanne Mettler, *Degrees of Inequality: How the Politics of Higher Education Sabotaged the American Dream* (New York: Basic Books, 2014).

10. Elmer E. Schattschneider, *The Semi-Sovereign People: A Realist's View of Democracy in America* (New York; Holt, Rinehart and Winston, 1960); Peter Bachrach and Morton S. Baratz, *Power & Poverty: Theory and Practice* (New York: Oxford University Press, 2011).

11. The provisions of the Higher Education Act are set to expire every six years, unless reauthorized, amended, or extended temporarily by Congress. The most recent complete reauthorization took place in 2008.

12. Summary: H.R. 4508–115th Congress (2017–2018), https://www.congress.gov/bill/115th-congress/house-bill/4508; Allie Bidwell, "NASFAA Issues Summary of House Republicans' HEA Reauthorization Bill," December 4, 2017, https://www.nasfaa.org/news-item/13822/NASFAA_Issues_Summary_of_House_Republicans_HEA_Reauthorization_Bill.

13. Keith W. Olson, *The G.I. Bill, the Veterans, and the Colleges* (Lexington: University of Kentucky Press, 1974).

14. Brian Pusser and Matt Ericson, "The Impact of the PROSPER Act on Underrepresented Students in For-Profit Colleges," The Civil Rights Project/Proyecto Derechos Civiles, September 2018, https://www.civilrightsproject.ucla.edu/research/college-access/the-impact-of-the-prosper-act-on-underrepresented-students-in-for-profit-colleges/?searchterm=Pusser.

15. Robert Kelchen, "How Much Do For-Profit Colleges Rely on Federal Funds?," *Brown Center Chalkboard*, Brookings Institution, January 11, 2017; A. J. Angulo, *Diploma Mills: How For-Profit Colleges Stiffed Students, Taxpayers, and the American Dream* (Baltimore, MD: Johns Hopkins University Press, 2016).

16. We use the referents *Black, Hispanic, Asian,* and *American Indian/Alaska Native* to match the categorical labels used in the IPEDS data system.

17. Andy Thomason, "DeVos Plans to Ax Gainful-Employment Rule, Which Targeted For-Profit Colleges," *Chronicle of Higher Education*, July 27, 2018.

18. Andrew Kreighbaum, "Overburdened with Debt," *Inside Higher Ed*, January 10, 2017, https://www.insidehighered.com/news/2017/01/10/federal-data-show-hundreds-vocational-programs-fail-meet-new-gainful-employment.

19. Stephanie R. Cellini et al., "Gainful Employment Regulations Will Protect Students and Taxpayers. Don't Change Them," *Brown Center Chalkboard*, Brookings Institution, 2017, https://www.brookings.edu/blog/brown-center-chalkboard/2017/08/04/gainful-employment-regulations-will-protect-students-and-taxpayers-dont-change-them/; David J. Deming, Claudia Goldin, and Lawrence F. Katz, "The For-Profit Postsecondary School Sector: Nimble Critters or Agile Predators?," *Journal of Economic Perspectives* 26, no. 1 (Winter 2012): 139–64; Stephanie R. Cellini and Nicholas Turner, "Gainfully Employed? Assessing the Employment and Earnings of For-Profit College Students Using

Administrative Data," NBER Working Paper No. 22287 (Issued May 2016, Revised January 2018).

20. Michael Itzkowitz, "HEA Replacement for Cohort Default Rate Leaves More Questions Than Answers," *Third Way* (2017), https://www.thirdway.org/memo/hea-replacement-for-cohort-default-rate-leaves-more-questions-than-answers.

21. Stephanie R. Cellini, Rejeev Darolia, and Lesley J. Turner, "The Government Is Sanctioning For-Profit Colleges. What Happens to the Students?," *Brown Center Chalkboard*, Brookings Institution, January 2017.

22. Bidwell, "NASFAA Issues Summary."

23. US Senate Health, Education, Labor, and Pensions (HELP) Committee, *For Profit Higher Education: The Failure to Safeguard the Federal Investment and Ensure Student Success* (Washington, DC: US Senate HELP Committee, July 30, 2012), 112–37, https://www.help.senate.gov/imo/media/for_profit_report/PartI-PartIII-SelectedAppendixes.pdf.

24. US Senate HELP Committee, *For Profit Higher Education*, 4.

25. Constance Iloh, "Exploring the For-Profit Experience: An Ethnography of a For-Profit College," *American Educational Research Journal* 53, no. 3 (June 2016): 427–55; Tressie McMillan Cottom, *Lower Ed: The Troubling Rise of For-Profit Colleges in the New Economy* (New York: The New Press, 2017).

26. The Institute for College Access and Success, "Proposed Education Department Rules Would Curb Financial Aid Fraud and Abuse," Statement of Pauline Abernathy, Vice President, the Institute for College Access & Success, June 16, 2010, https://ticas.org/accountability/proposed-education-department-rules-would-curb-financial-aid-fraud-and-abuse/.

27. Government Accountability Office, Testimony Before the Committee on Health, Education, Labor, and Pensions, US Senate, "For-Profit Colleges: Undercover Testing Finds Colleges Encouraged Fraud and Engaged in Deceptive and Questionable Marketing Practices," Statement of Gregory D. Kutz, Managing Director Forensics Audits and Special Investigations, August 4, 2010.

28. Denisa Gándara and Sosanya Jones, "Who Deserves Benefits in Higher Education? A Policy Discourse Analysis of a Process Surrounding Reauthorization of the Higher Education Act," *Review of Higher Education*, 44, no. 1 (Fall 2020): 121–57.

29. US House of Representatives Education & Labor Committee, "Committee Democrats Unveil Vision for Higher Education," http://democrats-edworkforce.house.gov/media/press-releases/all-17-committee-democrats-unveil-debt-free-college-plan.

30. Luis Armona, Rajashri Chakrabarti, and Michael F. Lovenheim, *How Does For-Profit College Attendance Affect Student Loans, Defaults, and Labor Market Outcomes?* Federal Reserve Bank of New York Staff Reports, Report No. 811, April 2018.

31. "Industry Profile: For-Profit Education: Lobbying 2019," OpenSecrets.org,

Center for Responsive Politics, https://www.opensecrets.org/federal-lobbying/industries/summary?id=H5300&year=2019.

32. David Whitman, "The GOP Reversal on For-Profit Colleges in the George W. Bush Era," The Century Foundation, 2018, https://tcf.org/content/report/gop-reversal-profit-colleges-george-w-bush-era/?session=1.

33. Title IV programs at the time included Pell Grants, Perkins Loans, Federal Family Education loans, Federal Direct Student Loans, and Student Educational Opportunity Grants (Washington, DC: GAO-HEHS 97-103 Proprietary Schools and Student Aid, 1997), 3.

34. Government Accountability Office, *Proprietary Schools: Poorer Student Outcomes at Schools That Rely More on Federal Student Aid* (Washington, DC: Government Accountability Office, 2018). https://www.gao.gov/assets/230/224202.pdf.

35. Government Accountability Office, *Proprietary Schools*.

36. US Senate HELP Committee, *For Profit Higher Education*.

37. US Senate HELP Committee.

38. Deming, Goldin, and Katz, "The For-Profit Postsecondary School Sector," 143.

39. American Council on Education, "Department of Education Repeals Gainful Employment Regulations," ACE Newsroom, July 1, 2019, https://www.acenet.edu/News-Room/Pages/Department-of-Education-Repeals-Gainful-Employment-Regulations.aspx.

40. US Department of Education, Fall Enrollment component. See *Digest of Education Statistics 2017*, table 306.50.

41. US Department of Education, Fall Enrollment component.

42. Doug Shapiro et al., "A National View of Student Attainment Rates by Race and Ethnicity—Fall 2010 Cohort," Signature Report No. 12b (Herndon, VA: National Student Clearinghouse Research Center, April 2017).

43. Doug Shapiro et al., "Completing College: A National View of Student Attainment Rates—Fall 2010 Cohort," Signature Report No. 12 (Herndon, VA: National Student Clearinghouse Research Center, November 2016).

44. Adam Looney and Constantine Yannelis, "The Crisis in Student Loans? How Changes in the Characteristics of Borrowers and in the Institutions They Attended Contributed to Rising Loan Defaults," Abstract, and Comment by Karen Pence (Brookings Paper on Economic Activity, Fall 2015).

45. Alisa F. Cunningham and Gregory S. Kienzle, "Delinquency: The Untold Story of Student Loan Borrowing," Institute for Higher Education Policy Reports, March 2011; Judith Scott-Clayton and Jing Li, "Black-White Disparity in Student Loan Debt," *Evidence Speaks Reports* 2, no. 3, Economic Studies at Brookings, 2016; Peter Smith and Leslie Parrish, *Do Students of Color Profit from For-Profit Colleges? Poor Outcomes and High Debt Hamper Attendees' Futures* (Durham, NC: Center for Responsible Lending, 2014).

46. Smith and Parrish, *Do Students of Color Profit?*, 11.

47. The three-year default rate is calculated as "the percentage of borrowers in

each repayment cohort who default on a federally-held loan within three years of entering re-payment." College Board, *Trends in College Pricing and Student Aid*, Figure SA 13-B (2020, 41).

48. Smith and Parrish, *Do Students of Color Profit?*

49. Sara Goldrick-Rab, Robert Kelchen, and Jason Houle, "The Color of Student Debt," Table 1: Federal Loan Takeup Rates and Amounts Borrowed by Institutional Type and Race/Ethnicity, 1995–96 to 2011–12. Panel A: Any federal loan.

50. Mark Huelsman, *The Debt Divide: The Racial and Class Bias Behind the "New Normal" of Student Borrowing* (New York: Demos.org, 2015).

51. Scott-Clayton and Li, "Black-White Disparity."

52. College Board, "Figure 2016_12A: Two-Year Federal Student Loan Default Rate Among Borrowers Entering Repayment in 2011–12"; Wesley Whistle, Tamara Hiler, and Michael Itzkowitz, "Giving Students a Better Shot at Graduating than Defaulting: Policy Ideas for Delivering Value to Students and Taxpayers," Third Way, June 6, 2018, https://www.thirdway.org/report/giving-students-a-better-shot-at-graduating-than-defaulting.

53. Looney and Yannelis, "Crisis in Student Loans?"

54. Armona, Chakrabarti, and Lovenheim, *How Does For-Profit College Attendance Affect*.

55. Cellini and Turner, "Gainfully Employed?," 26.

56. Stella M. Flores, Toby J. Park, and Dominique J. Baker, "The Racial College Completion Gap: Evidence from Texas," *Journal of Higher Education* 88, no. 6 (2017): 894–921, https://doi.org/10.1080/00221546.2017.1291259; Shapiro et al., "Completing College."

57. Cunningham and Kienzle, "Delinquency"; Scott-Clayton and Li, "Black-White Disparity"; Goldrick-Rab, Kelchen, and Houle, "Color of Student Debt"; Smith and Parrish, *Do Students of Color Profit?*

58. Scott A. Ginder, Janice E. Kelly-Reid, and Farrah B. Mann, "Graduation Rates for Selected Cohorts, 2007–12; Outcome Measures for Cohort Year 2007; Student Financial Aid, Academic Year 2014–15; and Admissions in Postsecondary Institutions, Fall 2015: First Look (Provisional Data)," First Look, National Center for Education Statistics, February 2017, https://nces.ed.gov/pubsearch/pubsinfo.asp?pubid=2017084; Shapiro et al., "A National View."

59. Smith and Parrish, *Do Students of Color Profit?*; Scott-Clayton and Li, "Black-White Disparity."

60. Over the past decade there have been significant changes in the number of students enrolled in degree-granting four-year institutions. From a high of approximately 1.6 million students in 2010, enrollments of first-time, first-year students declined to approximately 830,000 in 2018.

61. US House of Representatives Committee on Education and Labor, *College Affordability Fact Sheet* (Washington, DC: US House of Representatives Committee on Education and Labor, October 15, 2019).

62. US House, *Fact Sheet*.

63. Stephen Ansolabehere, James M. Snyder Jr., and Charles Stewart III, "The Effects of Party and Preferences on Congressional Roll-Call Voting," *Legislative Studies Quarterly* 26, no. 4 (November 2001): 533–72.

64. Amartya Sen, *Development as Freedom* (New York: Basic Books, 2000), 111.

65. Jeffrey. R. Henig, *Rethinking School Choice: Limits of the Market Metaphor* (Princeton, NJ: Princeton University Press, 1994); David Harvey, *A Brief History of Neoliberalism* (London: Oxford University Press, 2005); Brian Pusser, "The State and the Civil Society in the Scholarship of Higher Education," in *Handbook on the Politics of Higher Education*, ed. Brendan Cantwell et al. (Cheltenham, UK: Edward Elgar Publishing, 2018), 11–29.

66. Gándara and Jones, "Who Deserves Benefits?," 141.

67. Larry L. Leslie and Gary P. Johnson, "The Market Model and Higher Education," *Journal of Higher Education* 45 (1974): 1–20; Simon Marginson, *Markets in Education* (Melbourne: Allen & Unwin, 1997).

68. Quiggin, *Zombie Economics*; George A. Akerlof and Robert J. Shiller, *Animal Spirits: How Human Psychology Drives the Economy, and Why It Matters for Global Capitalism* (Princeton, NJ: Princeton University Press, 2009); Deborah Stone, *Policy Paradox: The Art of Political Decision Making*, 3rd ed. (New York and London: W. W. Norton & Company, 2012), 234–36.

69. Krugman, *Arguing with Zombies*.

70. Gándara and Jones, "Who Deserves Benefits?," 139.

71. Pusser, "State and the Civil Society."

72. Sheila Slaughter and Larry Leslie, *Academic Capitalism* (Baltimore, MD: John Hopkins University Press, 1997); Sheila Slaughter and Gary Rhoades, *Academic Capitalism and the New Economy* (Baltimore, MD: Johns Hopkins University Press, 2004); Simon Marginson, *Markets in Education* (Melbourne: Allen & Unwin, 1997).

73. H.R. 4508, 115th Congress, 2017/18 Text of the PROSPER Act. Library of Congress. Washington, DC.

CHAPTER 9

1. Community College Research Center, https://ccrc.tc.columbia.edu.

2. Community College Research Center, "Community College FAQs," https://ccrc.tc.columbia.edu/Community-College-FAQs.html.

3. Jon Marcus, "Facts About Race and College Admission: Political Winds May Shift, but Racial Factors in College Success Statistics Don't," *Hechinger Report*, July 6, 2018.

4. Their total expenditure per student in 2016–17 was $10,700 compared to $19,900 for students attending universities awarding doctorates. College Board, *Trends in College Pricing 2019* (New York: College Board, 2019), 27.

5. Ernest T. Pascarella and Patrick T. Terenzini, *How College Affects Students, A Third Decade of Research*, vol. 2 (San Francisco: Jossey-Bass, 2005), 375.

6. Pascarella and Terenzini, *How College Affects Students*, 376.

7. Pascarella and Terenzini, 381.

8. Arthur M. Cohen and Florence B. Brawer, *The American Community College*, 2nd ed. (San Francisco: Jossey-Bass, 1989), 385.

9. Vincent Tinto, *Leaving College: Rethinking the Causes and Cures of Student Attrition*, 2nd ed. (Chicago: University of Chicago Press, 1993), 198.

10. Tinto, *Leaving College*, 78.

11. Gary Orfield and Faith Paul, *State Higher Education Systems and College Completion: Final Report to the Ford Foundation* (Northbrook, IL: Public Policy Research Consortium, 1992).

12. Saul Geiser and Richard C. Atkinson, *Beyond the Master Plan: The Case for Restructuring Baccalaureate Education in California* (Berkeley, CA: Berkeley Research and Occasional Papers, 2010), 9–10, https://escholarship.org/uc/item/19d0t1gn.

13. Michael A. Olivas, *The Dilemma of Access: Minorities in Two Year Colleges* (Washington, DC: Howard University Press, 1979).

14. Olivas, *Dilemma of Access*, 3.

15. Olivas, 26.

16. Olivas, 41–44.

17. Olivas, 153–54.

18. Olivas, 175.

19. Olivas, 178.

20. Steven Brint and Jerome Karabel, *The Diverted Dream: Community Colleges and the Promise of Educational Opportunity in America, 1900–1985* (New York: Oxford University Press, 1989), 5.

21. Brint and Karabel, *Diverted Dream*, 8.

22. Brint and Karabel, 10.

23. Brint and Karabel, 12.

24. Burton R. Clark, "The 'Cooling-Out' Function in Higher Education," *American Journal of Sociology* 65 (1965): 569–76.

25. C. Lockwood Reynolds, "Where to Attend? Estimating the Effects of Beginning College at a Two-Year Institution," ~~~I~~~Economics of Education Review %%%I%%%31, no. 4 (August 2012): 345–62.

26. Bridget Terry Long, *The College Completion Landscape: Trends, Challenges and Why It Matters* (Washington, DC: American Enterprise Institute, 2018), 5.

27. Long, *College Completion Landscape*, 10–11.

28. Long, 11.

29. Long, 12–15.

30. Marcus, "Facts About Race and College Admission."

31. Glendale Community College, "President Bill Clinton at GCC," June 1996, https://www.glendale.edu/about-gcc/gcc-overview/gcc-history/president-bill-clinton-at-gcc.

32. Rene Sanchez and Clay Chandler, "Education Aid at What Cost? Clinton's $50

Billion Plan Has Skeptics Even on Campus," *Washington Post*, February 3, 1997, A01.

33. Associated Press, "Bush Boosts Nation's Community Colleges," May 2, 2005, https://www.nbcnews.com/id/wbna7067604.

34. Greg Jaffe, "Obama Announces Free Community College Plan," *Washington Post*, January 9, 2015.

35. US Department of Education, "Table 308.10. Total 12-Month Enrollment in Degree-Granting Postsecondary Institutions, by Control and Level of Institution and State or Jurisdiction: 2015–16 and 2016–17," 2019, https://nces.ed.gov/programs/digest/d18/tables/dt18_308.10.asp?current=yes; US Department of Education, "Table 317.20. Degree-Granting Postsecondary Institutions, by Control and Classification of Institution and State or Jurisdiction: 2018–19," 2019, https://nces.ed.gov/programs/digest/d19/tables/dt19_317.20.asp?current=yes.

36. Erica Frankenberg, Jongyeon Ee, Jennifer B. Ayscue, and Gary Orfield, *Harming Our Common Future: America's Segregated Schools 65 Years After Brown* (Los Angeles: Civil Rights Project/Proyecto Derechos Civiles), 27–30; Gary Orfield and Jongyeon Ee, *Segregating California's Future: Inequality and Its Alternative* (Los Angeles: Civil Rights Project/Proyecto Derechos Civiles, May 2014).

37. Patricia Gándara, Elizabeth Alvarado, Anne Driscoll, and Gary Orfield, *Building Pathways to Transfer: Community Colleges That Break the Chain of Failure for Students of Color* (Los Angeles: Civil Rights Project/Proyecto Derechos Civiles, 2012).

38. Rucker C. Johnson, "The Impact of Parental Wealth on College Degree Attainment: Evidence from the Housing Boom and Bust," *American Economic Review: Papers & Proceedings* 110 (2020): 405–10.

39. Mary Martinez-Wenzl and Rigoberto Marquez, *Unrealized Promises: Unequal Access, Affordability and Excellence at Community Colleges in Southern California* (Los Angeles: Civil Rights Project/Proyecto Derechos Civiles, 2012).

40. Colleen Moore and Nancy Shlock, *Divided We Fail: Improving Completion and Closing Racial Gaps in California's Community Colleges* (Sacramento, CA: Institute for Higher Education Leadership and Policy, October 2010).

41. Grace Chen, "New Study: 70% of California Community College Students Fail," *Community College Review*, April 5, 2018.

42. Gándara, Alvarado, Driscoll, and Orfield, *Building Pathways to Transfer*, 4.

43. Gándara, Alvarado, Driscoll, and Orfield, 20.

44. Donald E. Heller, "Public Subsidies for Higher Education in California: An Exploratory Analysis of Who Pays and Who Benefits," *Educational Policy* 19, no. 2 (May 2005): 349–70.

45. Gándara, Alvarado, Driscoll, and Orfield, *Building Pathways to Transfer*, 4.

46. Gándara, Alvarado, Driscoll, and Orfield, 4.

47. Brint and Karabel, *Diverted Dream*, 208.

48. Brint and Karabel, 226.

CHAPTER 10

1. Public Law 89-329, Sec. 301(a). Higher Education Act of 1965: Statement of Purpose and Appropriations Authorized (November 1965), https://www .govinfo.gov/content/pkg/STATUTE-79/pdf/STATUTE-79-Pg1219.pdf; and Public Law 92-318, Sec. 122(a)(2)(A). Education Amendments to the Higher Education Act of 1965: Emergency Assistance for Institutions of Higher Education (June 1972), https://www.govinfo.gov/content/pkg/STATUTE-86/pdf/STATUTE-86-Pg235.pdf.

2. PL 89-329 and PL 92-318.

3. Lorelle Espinosa, Robert Kelchen, and Morgan Taylor, Minority Serving Institutions as Engines of Upward Mobility (Washington, DC: American Council on Education, 2018), https://www.acenet.edu/Documents/MSIs-as-Engines-of-Upward-Mobility.pdf .

4. Tamara Hiler and Wesley Whistle, "Creating a 'Title I' for Higher Ed," Third Way, December 2018, https://www.thirdway.org/memo/creating-a-title-i-for-higher-ed.

5. US Department of Education, "Pell Grant End of Year Report, Table 3," 2020, https://www2.ed.gov/finaid/prof/resources/data/pell-data.html.

6. Tuan Nguyen, Jenna Kramer, and Brent Evans, "The Effects of Grant Aid on Student Persistence and Degree Attainment: A Systematic Review and Meta-Analysis of the Causal Effects," Review of Educational Research 89, no. 6 (2019): 831–74.

7. Victor Ray, "A Theory of Racialized Organizations," American Sociological Review 84, no. 1 (2019): 28–53.

8. Nolan Cabrera, White Guys on Campus: Racism, White Immunity, and the Myth of "Post-Racial" Higher Education (Brunswick, NJ: Rutgers University Press, 2019).

9. The Leadership Conference Education Fund, Civil Rights Principles for Higher Education (Washington, DC: Leadership Conference Education Fund, July 2019), http://civilrightsdocs.info/pdf/reports/Higher-Ed-Civil-Rights-Principles.pdf.

10. Leadership Conference Education Fund, Civil Rights Principles.

11. Daniel Klasik and Ethan Hutt, "Bobbing for Bad Apples: Accreditation, Quantitative Performance Measures, and the Identification of Low-Performing Colleges," Journal of Higher Education 90, no. 3 (2019): 427–61.

12. See, for example, Nicholas Hillman, "The Practical Side of Higher Education Accountability," National Student Financial Aid Administrators, Student Aid Perspectives, March 2020, https://www.nasfaa.org/news-item/21293/The_Practical_Side_of_Higher_Education_Accountability.

ACKNOWLEDGMENTS

SEVERAL OF THE PAPERS written for this volume were first presented at a Capitol Hill briefing in Washington, DC, in September 2018. This briefing was coordinated by the Civil Rights Project/*Proyecto Derechos Civiles* at UCLA, so we are grateful for their administrative support in making the event possible and for the valuable feedback we received from event participants. Additionally, we thank Joshua Bach-Hanson, Ellie Bruecker, Kim Dancy, Nate Kelty, Laurie Russman, and Kate Westaby for their exceptional editorial support throughout this process. We would also like to thank the team at Harvard Education Publishing Group for their commitment to this project. And finally, we are forever grateful for our families, who accommodated and supported us through this process.

ABOUT THE EDITORS

NICHOLAS HILLMAN is a professor in the Department of Educational Leadership and Policy Analysis at the University of Wisconsin–Madison, where he also is a faculty affiliate with the Institute for Research on Poverty and the La Follette School of Public Affairs. His research focuses on postsecondary finance and financial aid policy, primarily as they relate to college access and equity. Hillman has testified to the US House of Representatives and the Wisconsin State Assembly on issues related to higher education accountability and finance. He teaches courses in politics of higher education, higher education finance, educational policy, and research methods. He also directs the Student Success Through Applied Research Lab, a research-practice partnership with the University of Wisconsin–Madison Division of Enrollment Management.

GARY ORFIELD is Distinguished Research Professor of Education, Law, Political Science and Urban Planning at the University of California, Los Angeles, where he is also codirector of the Civil Rights Project he cofounded at Harvard University in 1996. He is a political scientist whose work includes more than a dozen authored or edited books, one of which was cited by the Supreme Court in upholding affirmative action. Orfield's work focuses on equal opportunity and civil rights and has been included in testimony in more than twenty major class action civil rights lawsuits on school segregation, housing discrimination, and other civil rights violations. He has taught at six universities, including Harvard University and the University of Chicago, and is a member of the National Academy of Education.

ABOUT THE CONTRIBUTORS

JULIE AJINKYA is Senior Vice President at APIA Scholars, a nonprofit organization that works to improve college access and success for low-income, first-generation Asian American and Pacific Islander students. Prior to APIA Scholars, Ajinkya was Vice President of Applied Research at the Institute for Higher Education Policy. Ajinkya is a visiting professor of government at Cornell University's campus in Washington, DC, and in 2019, *Diverse: Issues in Higher Education* named her one of the "Top 35 Women in Higher Education."

ANDRÉS CASTRO SAMAYOA is an assistant professor of Educational Leadership and Higher Education at the Boston College School of Education and Human Development. His expertise includes the social history of large-scale datasets in postsecondary education; educational researchers' use of data to explore issues of diversity; and the institutionalization of services for lesbian, gay, bisexual, queer, and transgender students. He is currently a member of the Association of Higher Education as well as the American Educational Research Association.

ERIN S. CORBETT is the CEO of Second Chance Educational Alliance, Inc., a nonprofit organization offering bachelor's degrees to confined learners in Connecticut. Prior to running Second Chance Educational Alliance full time, she was the Director of Policy at the Katal Center for Health, Equity, and Justice, an organization dedicated to building power in communities, ending mass incarceration, and educating people about the importance of health and harm reduction.

LILIANA M. GARCES is an associate professor at the University of Texas at Austin and affiliate faculty at the University of Texas School of Law. Her research centers on the intersection of law and educational policy on access, diversity, and equity in higher education. Her projects to date have examined affirmative action policies in postsecondary admissions and the use and influence of research in law. Combining her expertise in law and education, Garces has represented the education community in the filing of legal briefs in US Supreme Court cases that have played consequential roles in interpreting law around race-conscious policies in education.

MATT ERICSON completed his work as a doctoral candidate at the University of Virginia, where his research focused on the economics and sociology of higher education. He is now a data scientist at Google.

CODY MEIXNER is Assistant General Counsel for The Pennsylvania State University, where he addresses a broad range of higher education legal matters including the First Amendment and free speech, civil rights, Title VI and Title IX, copyright, and academic and student affairs. Meixner is licensed to practice law in the District of Columbia and the Commonwealth of Pennsylvania (Limited In-House License).

SUZANNE METTLER is the John L. Senior Professor of American Institutions in the Department of Government at Cornell University. Her research and teaching interests include American political development, inequality, public policy, political behavior, and democracy. She is the author of several books, including *The Government-Citizen Disconnect* (Russell Sage, 2018); *Degrees of Inequality: How the Politics of Higher Education Sabotaged the American Dream* (Basic Books, 2014), *The Submerged State: How Invisible Government Programs Undermine American Democracy* (University of Chicago, 2011), and *Soldiers to Citizens: The G.I. Bill and the Making of the Greatest Generation* (Oxford University Press, 2005). She was elected to the American Academy of Arts and Sciences in 2017 and awarded Guggenheim and Radcliffe Fellowships in 2019.

JALIL B. MUSTAFFA is the Vice-Provost Postdoctoral Scholar and Lecturer at the University of Pennsylvania's Graduate School of Education. He completed his doctoral studies at the University of California, Los Angeles, in Higher Education and Organizational Change. His critical policy research agenda focuses on the geography of college opportunity, Black student loan debt and credentialism, and student activists' role in institutional policymaking. He utilizes qualitative, historical, and policy-oriented methods coupled with critical theory—often in collaboration with community coalitions and organizations.

OIYAN POON is a program officer at the Spencer Foundation and an associate professor affiliate in the Department of Educational Policy Studies at the University of Illinois at Chicago. Previously, she was an associate professor of Higher Education Leadership at the Colorado State University. Her research interests focus on the racial politics and discourses of college access, higher education organization and policy, affirmative action, and Asian Americans.

BRIAN PUSSER is an associate professor in the Department of Leadership, Foundations, and Policy at the University of Virginia Curry School of Education and Human Development. His research addresses the political economy of higher education organizations and governance. He is the author of *Burning Down the House: Politics, Governance, and Affirmative Action at* the University of California (SUNY, 2004) and coedited Earnings from Learning: The Rise of For-Profit Universities (SUNY, 2006).

DEONDRA ROSE is an assistant professor at the Duke University Sanford School of Public Policy while also serving as Director of Research in the Center for Political Leadership, Innovation, and Service. Her research focuses on the feedback effects of landmark social policies on the American political landscape. She is the author of Citizens by Degree: Higher Education Policy and the Changing Gender Dynamics of American Citizenship (Oxford University Press, 2018). In addition to US public/social policy, Rose's research and teaching interests include higher education policy, American political development (APD), political behavior, identity politics (e.g., gender, race, and socioeconomic status), and inequality.

HARUNA SUZUKI is director of Adult, Family, and Community Empowerment programs at Helps Education Fund, a nonprofit organization dedicated to advancing educational equity through free dissemination of evidence-based educational programs. In this role, she directs a family literacy program in the North Carolina Correctional Institution for Women, home- and school-based literacy programs, and a variety of adult empowerment programs. Haruna is also completing her doctorate in the Educational Leadership, Policy, and Human Development department at North Carolina State University, with a concentration in Higher Education. Her research focuses on examining the nature and quality of postsecondary educational opportunities available in state and federal prisons.

INDEX